Also by Tom Peters

*In Search of Excellence
(with Robert H. Waterman, Jr.)*

*A Passion for Excellence
(with Nancy Austin)*

Thriving on Chaos

Liberation Management

The Tom Peters Seminar

The Pursuit of Wow!

THE
CIRCLE
OF
INNOVATION

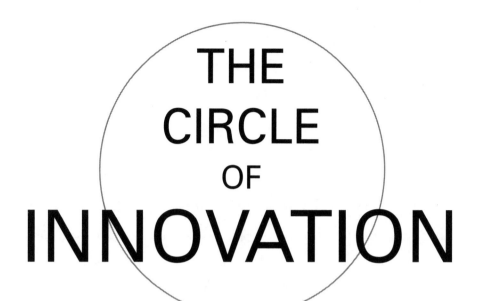

THE
CIRCLE
OF
INNOVATION

You Can't

Shrink

Your

Way

to

Greatness

BY TOM PETERS

ALFRED A. KNOPF
NEW YORK 1997

Book Design by Ken Silvia Design Group

For
*Susan * Donna * Ken*
*Sonny * Herb * Larry * Ian*
Whose integrity and appetite for life
epitomize the message of this book.

Whatever made you
successful in the past
won't
in the future.

— Lew Platt, chairman and CEO,
Hewlett-Packard

It's the **end** of
the world
as we know it.

— Peter Georgescu, chairman and CEO,
Young & Rubicam

FOREWORD . . . DEAN LEBARON

Business—successful business—is more visceral than cerebral. If we study what others do, we may find ways to read markets, but we will never discover ways to lead them.

Tom Peters is more visceral than cerebral. He feels business in his gut. I don't mean to ignore his doctorate from Stanford, his years in McKinsey's ivory tower, or his enormous contributions to management theory and practice, beginning with the publication of *In Search of Excellence.*

But what distinguishes Tom is this: passion and passionate energy. He moves when he sees opportunity. He hurts when he sees mediocrity. He exults when he sees innovation.

Tom is a friend. A few months ago, he invited me to one of his trademark seminars in Detroit. I had read his books, worked with him on business problems, dined with him, bantered with him as friends often do. In our case, given the global nature of our travel schedules, the banter is frequently electronic. While I watched him in Detroit, I was reminded of evangelists. Like them, Tom is transforming peoples' lives. Like them, he conveys profound and passionate beliefs. And, like them, he heals. While evangelists use the power of the spirit to heal the body, Tom uses the power of ideas to transform business.

Tom moves globally (he's comfortable anywhere), pillories the guilty (including himself), never sleeps (I can tell by the time stamp on his e-mails), and reads and retains everything (his reading list would credit a good college library). He processes ideas from everywhere and puts his own spin on them.

No one is a harsher critic of Tom than Tom. The decay rate of ideas in his head is faster than a child's attention span. Tom is always testing himself. He thrives in the soup of change. He is always, if you will forgive the pun, in search of something better, something "WOW!" His intellectual bar is rising all the time. So he experiments, usually in public. Once in a while, he falls flat, but most of the time he soars. You have to make mistakes, he says. You need to have a quota of mistakes, and Tom has his. Tom is sometimes accused of inconsistency, and he is guilty—thank goodness. He believes that any idea worth having is worth changing, and I, and many others, agree.

Creative thinkers like Tom are different from the rest of us. They see what we overlook.

Tom takes an idea and turns it into what others can't. He turns learning organizations into forgetting organizations. He turns change management into an exercise in destruction. He turns hotel housekeepers into Michelangelos.

Like all explorers, Tom leads us on a path of discovery. Like all true innovators, he is both a maverick and a champion of mavericks. We meet people he admires, such as Percy Barnevik of ABB Asea Brown Boveri, Bill Gates of Microsoft, and Alfred Sloan of General Motors. You don't have to be alive to be admired by Tom, but you do have to really have lived.

His many stories of success and failure illuminate our own situations. Lakeland hospital shows us that no job description is sacrosanct. It illustrates the limits of reengineering as well as opportunities for entirely new structures. It demonstrates that technology we can't understand, can't anticipate, and can't control may be life or death for us and our businesses.

We can appreciate the originality of Tom's books and seminars, but we really should do more. What Tom writes is important, but what you do with it is what really counts. His exhortations are nothing if not applied.

I suspect Tom places more value in how we read his book than how he writes it. It is easy to follow him—just go with the flow. It's tempting to read quickly, not pausing to ponder nuances. Personally, I imagine Tom would approve of that approach. But I suggest a second read with a pencil or highlighter. Take notes. They are the first step in what I'm sure will be an unfolding conversation with Tom. I know from experience it's a conversation like no other.

Tom ends his book with a chapter entitled, "We're Here to Live Life Out Loud." It's a paraphrase of a quote from French novelist Émile Zola, and one I've heard him repeat often, and, I might add, loudly. Tom has turned up the volume for me. I think *The Circle of Innovation* will do the same for you.

Dean LeBaron
Weesen, Switzerland
August 11, 1997

Dean LeBaron, founder of investment innovator Batterymarch Financial Management and trustee of the Santa Fe Institute, is known for his relentless aversion to conventional thinking. His citation for Distinguished Alumni Achievement by the Harvard Business School reads: "Stellar student of securities, institutional investor extraordinaire, your storied successes as a contrarian are legion and legendary."

CONTENTS

KLM 0807 . . .

explosion. EXPLOSION. E-X-P-L-O-S-I-O-N. Not the heat that smacks me in the face as I enter the jetway, at the end of 11 cramped hours on KLM 0807, May 31, 1997.

Hot? Yes!

But . . .

It was insane when I was last here, in June 1993. And now? Sheer madness!

Saturday 2 p.m. Another busy work day. Bumper-to-bumper-to-bumper traffic.

Saturday 8 p.m. Full crew on the construction job (high rise, of course) that I see from my 27th-floor hotel room window.

Look up . . . AND UP . . . and I see the newly completed Petronas Tower. Tallest building in the world. (Tops the Sears/Chicago Tower by 33 feet.)

Kuala Lumpur.

Malaysia.

Asia.

I read . . . AND READ . . . and read. I'm well prepared for my seminar the day after tomorrow here in Kuala Lumpur . . . and the day after the day after that in Hong Kong . . . 26 days before its turnover to China.

But I am not prepared—even by a visit to India just 60 days ago—for the latest reminder of the physical and mental intensity of the . . . ECONOMIC-EXPLOSION-CALLED-ASIA-WHICH-IS-ALTERING-THE-WORLD-BY-THE-HOUR, 7-DAYS-A-WEEK, 24-HOURS-A-DAY.

Back home—A-M-E-R-I-C-A—we devote column foot after column foot of media babble to Bill's house. (Gates.) Bill's hemorrhoids. (Gates.) And . . . of course . . . Bill's software. I know HE is "changing the world." But HE seems such small change here. Global village . . . yeah, yeah, yeah. Telecom's revolution . . . yeah, yeah, yeah. But THIS (Kuala Lumpur, construction, economic breakout) is far more PRIMAL.

And the world, tilting at enormous speed (second derivative: i.e., acceleration) toward A-S-I-A, will N-E-V-E-R be the same again. NOT EVEN CLOSE.

What's going on beneath my window on the 27th floor (of my relative low rise)? Not much: Just planetary economic, social, and political upheaval on a scale—and at a pace—unprecedented in human history. My temples are literally throbbing.

* * *

News item: In the next 20 years . . . 1.7 billion new, literate Asian workers will enter the world's work force. (Yup . . . B-I-L-L-I-O-N.) And . . . Asia's share of world economic output is set to double . . . to 50 percent+ . . . during the same period.

Ho-hum? or Ho-ly . . . .

* * *

2:30 a.m. Sunday, June 1, 1997. Insomnia keeps me awake. Or was it . . . yes(!) . . . the harsh, unmistakable sound of a pile driver. ANOTHER FOUNDATION IN PROGRESS. Traffic? Still heavy, not all that diminished from mid-afternoon. And so it goes . . . and goes . . . AND GOES.

T-H-O-W-A-A-K. T-H-O-W-A-A-K. T-H-O-W-A-A-K . . . (a.k.a. pile driver-on-the-brain.) . . . T-H-O-W-A-A-K . . . A-S-I-A . . . T-H-O-W-A-A-K . . . A-S-I-A . . . T-H-O-W-A-A-K. . . .

It is the end of the world as we know it. And whatever made you successful in the past won't in the future.

And the answer is . . .

IT'S I-N-N-O-V-A-T-I-O-N . . . STUPID!

This book is five years . . . and roughly 400 seminars . . . in the making.* The circle per se (as in Circle of Innovation) is on about its seventieth draft. I'm comfortable . . . for now. Hence . . . finally . . . this book.

It's about one B-I-G idea: innovation/a "top-line" obsession.

And it's about 15 discrete/b-i-g-g-i-s-h ideas . . . each of which is a stop on our Circle of Innovation. Each of the 15 biggish ideas stands on its own . . . and all 15 logically *and* systemically *and* coherently add up to THE ONE B-I-G IDEA.

I became obsessed (right word) with innovation . . . because my clients, in effect, begged me to. (This is a customer-driven book!) Quality is (way) up. Speed is (way) up. Product development time is (way) down. We've "reengineered" the plumber . . . and "empowered" the kitchen sink. Yet with global competition heating up by the picosecond, company after company . . . banks, insurers, Big Six accountancies, brokerages, office-furniture makers, packaged-goods firms, software and pharmaceutical houses, engineering services firms . . . tell me: MY SERVICE/PRODUCT IS BECOMING COMMODITIZED.

It takes about seven years to get a Ph.D. in economics from a leading school. But it's borderline fair to say you can capture the seven years in one sentence: IF THE OTHER GUY'S GETTING BETTER, THEN YOU'D BETTER BE GETTING BETTER FASTER THAN THAT OTHER GUY'S GETTING BETTER . . . OR YOU'RE GETTING WORSE.

Translation: It's innovation . . . stupid.

And . . . hint: "It" applies to my career (TP), your career, the six-person training department . . . and the 60,000-body behemoth.

* * *

Why are there so f-e-w books on . . . INNOVATION . . . and s-o-o-o many on teams/empowerment/reengineering/quality? (1) Beats me! (2) Too hard?

* * *

Well . . . THIS BOOK IS ABOUT . . . I-N-N-O-V-A-T-I-O-N. PERIOD.

* * *

Back to those 400 (mostly full-day) seminars in the last five years . . . since the publication of *Liberation Management.* I've administered a few beatings. (I'm old and increas-

*Forty-seven U.S. states, Brazil, Argentina, Chile, Ecuador, Malaysia, Hong Kong, Singapore, Thailand, the Philippines, South Korea, Australia, New Zealand, England, Scotland, Holland, Germany, Portugal, India, Saudi Arabia, United Arab Emirates, South Africa, Zimbabwe.

ingly impatient.) And I've been beaten up a few/many times. And I've . . . changed . . . and changed . . . and changed.

"They" call me inconsistent. I consider that a badge of honor. I.e.: I hope I've grown . . . and can therefore help you (a little) to grow (a little).

These are marvelously scary times. (Marvelous = Scary.) Ripe with . . . opportunity. (Marvelous = Scary = Opportunity.) Laden with . . . peril. (Marvelous = Scary = Opportunity = Perilous.)

* * *

I have no time to waste. You have no time to waste. SO LET US BEGIN WITHOUT FURTHER ADO.

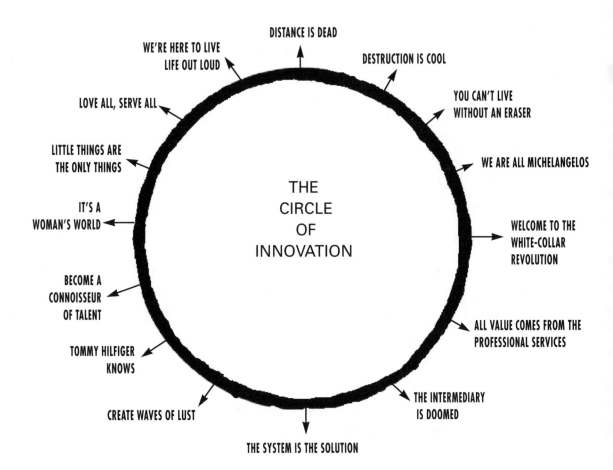

1 B-I-G IDEA (X15)

The Circle of Innovation is the overarching idea which animates this book. Here's a quick preview of the 15 stops along the way . . .

DISTANCE IS DEAD. We're all next-door neighbors. Incrementalism is innovation's worst enemy. Mid- to long-term: Business is about augmenting the top line . . . not cost minimization.

DESTRUCTION IS COOL! CDO . . . Chief Destruction Officer. Easier to KILL an organization—and repot it—than change it substantially. Learn to swallow it: DESTRUCTION IS JOB NO. 1 (before the competition does it to you).

YOU CAN'T LIVE WITHOUT AN ERASER. Forgetting—not learning—is the highest art. Think: ORGANIZED forgetting. STRATEGIC forgetfulness. How? Cherish WASTE . . . SILLINESS . . . FAILURE. I.e.: Ready. FIRE! Aim.

WE ARE ALL MICHELANGELOS. Convert every "jobholder" into a BUSINESS-PERSON. Convert every job into a BUSINESS. "Business" is a very different—and more encompassing—word than "empowerment." Keys: trust/respect/Michelangelos of Housekeeping/Michelangelos of Telemarketing. Boss as . . . RELENTLESS ARCHITECT OF THE POSSIBILITIES OF HUMAN BEINGS.

WELCOME TO THE WHITE-COLLAR REVOLUTION. IF YOU CAN'T SAY (SPECIFICALLY) WHY YOU MAKE YOUR COMPANY A BETTER PLACE . . . YOU'RE OUT! As of Now: ME, INC!/TAKE IMMEDIATE RESPONSIBILITY FOR CHANGE!/YOU (ME) ARE A BRAND. (Perform a PERSONAL BRAND EQUITY EVALUATION . . . NOW!) There are no guarantees . . . and that can be liberating (i.e., stomp out indentured servitude to BigCorp).

ALL VALUE COMES FROM THE PROFESSIONAL SERVICES. Make staff units The Vital Centers of Intellectual Capital Accumulation . . . rather than the prime sources of

bureaucratic drag. Tool: Turn Purchasing (HR, IS, Finance) into PURCHASING, INC.
. . . a full-fledged professional service firm . . . devoted to TRANSFORMATIONAL projects/awesome CLIENT service/WOW!

THE INTERMEDIARY IS DOOMED. (Big) organizations without employees. EVERY task your organization performs is performed BETTER (higher quality, faster, more imaginatively) by some hyper-fast specialist (somewhere) who lives/eats/sleeps/breathes the narrow task. FLAT is too modest a term. (By far.) We are gutting the "center" of vertical enterprises. THE INTERMEDIARY IS DYING/DEAD! Hail the disintermediated/network "organization". . . transparent to its customers (and all members of the value-creation chain).

THE SYSTEM IS THE SOLUTION. (1) Systems are the glue . . . in ephemeral/network "orgs." (2) Systems—great systems—are not about "nuts and bolts." They are/can be . . . BEAUTIFUL. Systems Engineering Dept.? NO! Dept. of Beauty?? YES!! It's W-A-Y beyond reengineering.

CREATE WAVES OF LUST. (Almost) everything works. Quality per se is not the advantage it once (recently) was. So: Just shout "NO!" to . . . commoditization (of anything)/me-too/look-alikes. Embrace: WOW!!!/lusted-after products and services! Ultimate sin: WHEN WE DO IT "RIGHT," IT'S STILL PRETTY ORDINARY.

TOMMY HILFIGER KNOWS. In a (very) crowded marketplace . . . branding is (far) more important than ever before. It is . . . THE AGE OF THE BRAND! (1) Anything can be branded (e.g., chicken, milk). (2) Branding is as much for the very wee outfit as for Levi's or Nike or Starbucks or Intel (Inside).

BECOME A CONNOISSEUR OF TALENT. RECRUIT DIVERSITY! HIRE CRAZIES! Make REVOLUTIONARY RENEWAL everyone's (LITERAL) Job No. 1. We are . . . ALL . . . RDAs . . . Rapidly Depreciating Assets. Therefore: (Continuing) Vitality = (Continuing) Commitment to (Bold/Formal) Renewal Programs . . . by . . . EVERYONE.

IT'S A WOMAN'S WORLD. Women purchase/are purchasing agents for well over half the U.S. GDP (commercial and consumer goods). Almost no BigCo. "gets it"—financial services, healthcare, autos, business services, etc., etc. I.e., "gets"catering-to-women-as-premier-purchasers. WHY?? It takes TOTAL TRANSFORMATION—not a "woman's initiative"—to take advantage of this bizarrely neglected COMMERCIAL OPPORTU-NITY NO. 1.

LITTLE THINGS ARE THE ONLY THINGS. As markets get more and more (and more) crowded . . . DESIGN is often the best "tool"— in services and manufacturing— for sustainable differentiation. Sad fact: Most companies do anything but OBSESS (e.g., Braun-like, Sony-like) on design. Personal design sensitization is Step No. 1: Home in on (OPEN YOUR EYES TO) the pervasive role that design plays in damn near every-thing—signage, forms, typeface, color (a big deal), etc., etc.

LOVE ALL, SERVE ALL. Even today (WHY? WHY?? WHY???) a ridiculously small number of sizable firms seek a sustainable edge through incredible service—Disney- or Caterpillar-style. To get from (tawdry) here to (Olympian) there takes a wholesale com-mitment to nothing less than reconceiving the way business is done in your market/niche.

WE'RE HERE TO LIVE LIFE OUT LOUD. Transformational leaders will eschew "hands off." They will be bizarrely focused . . . tell the truth . . . and live life on the LUNATIC FRINGE. I.e., revolutionary times call for revolutionary zeal/leaders.

* * *

15 IDEAS = 1 IDEA = INNOVATION/TOP-LINE OBSESSION/WOW!!

NOTE ON FORMAT

I illustrate my seminars with slides. You've asked for them time and again. SO HERE THEY ARE. The book purposefully retains the look and feel of my seminars. It is laid out in the main as slides . . . followed by explanatory text.

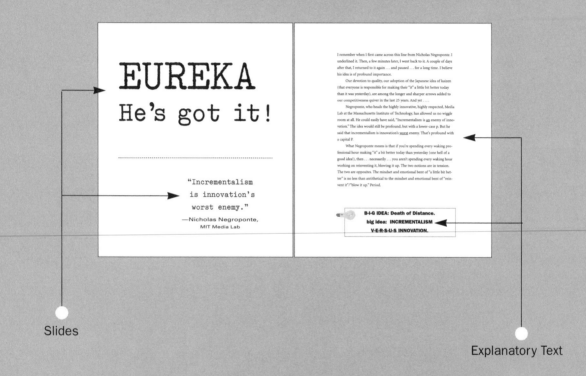

Slides

Explanatory Text

This is not the end! I will be updating this book with my weekly outpouring of new slides at my website: www.businessedge.net/tompeters. Join us for an ongoing, energetic dialogue. P-L-E-A-S-E.

READER'S GUIDE

Credo/Guiding Principles/Biases . . . or . . . Forestalling the Defenders of Drab

1. I love business. (And you??)

2. I think business is about emotion. Period. Cool products. Inspired service. People who give a damn. Leaders who are inflamed about the people they serve and the products they produce. Color by Technicolor! Dolby sound! (Tom Peters = Antithesis of Robert McNamara.)

3. I love . . . CAPITAL LETTERS. And !!! (exclamation marks . . . preferably more than one). Halfway is no way as far as I'm concerned. (I.e., Life's too short. Care deeply about your "it" . . . or don't bother to get out of the sack.)

4. I am a design freak. I don't think commerce is boring, economics is the Dismal Science. . . or that business books have to have the look and feel of the obit page of *The Daily Dull.*

5. I cherish inconsistency. A lot of what I say here contradicts what I said 15 years ago. Some of what I say here contradicts what I say here in other places. S-o-o-o? The world is inconsistent. All bets are off . . . and they never were on.

6. Business is a hoot. I hope this book is fun. (And that it scares the shit out of you.)

7. I am a frustrated academic. I like !!! and noisy quotes and pithy anecdotes. But . . . everything said here springs from solid research by me and (mostly) others.

8. I have lived most of my adult life in Silicon Valley. Silicon Valley is home to a ridiculously unfair share of demented dreamers. Silicon Valley is not normal. I am not normal. (But we won. Big. Right? I.e.: Maybe my/our biases oughta be your biases??)

9. I hope you love this book . . . or hate it. I will be devastated if you are lukewarm about it! (I hate Luke.)

10. I admit it. I have often been (v-e-r-y) wrong. And/but . . . 98 percent of my (grossest) errors have been errors/sins of conservatism . . . not errors/sins of excess. This book is probably wrong . . . far too mellow/far too modest in its predictions and prescriptions. Sorry!

TP
15 September 1997

Distance is Dead.

You've heard of the "global village."

I say a village is too big.

Try "global block."

Better yet, try "global mall."

"Carrying a call from London to New York costs virtually the same as carrying it from one house to the next. The death of distance . . . will probably be the single-most important economic force shaping society in the first half of the next century."
—*The Economist*

The global village is here . . . with a vengeance. No businessperson is, literally, more than six-tenths of a second (measured by the speed of light) away from any other businessperson. When I need a partner, I can just as easily look in Bangalore, India, as next door in my Silicon Valley neighborhood.

"The death of distance," *The Economist* continued, "will mean that any activity that relies on a screen or a telephone can be carried out anywhere in the world."

R.I.P. distance! Its passing means that services as varied as car design, home security, and healthcare delivery will be (already are!) as exportable as VCRs or automobiles. Airlines such as Swissair and British Airways are already sending their back-office work to India. And in Perth, in Western Australia, *The Economist* reports, "EMS Control Systems monitors the air-conditioning, lighting, lifts, and security in office blocks in Singapore, Malaysia, Sri Lanka, Indonesia, and Taiwan."

The death of distance marks the birth of (real) competition. We should all be feeling (white) hot under the (white) collar. Wages in the United States, Japan, Germany, Switzerland are . . . obscene. That is, ludicrously higher than the rest of the world. We like the relatively high wages. We Americans like the relatively high ranking (first place, these days) on the competitiveness tables. And if we want to continue to stay at or near the top, then we must be, as University of Southern California professor and expert on high-performing systems, Ed Lawler, puts it, working on the next act.

And the curtain is rising.

The world *is* catching up. More freedom! Higher standards of living! Hooray! But it also puts us, unmistakably, under the gun.

The death of distance struck a chord with me. No, struck a blow of thunder. Everything is changing. That is not an overstatement. It is a fact. We are in the midst of the most profound change since the beginning of the

Industrial Revolution, over two centuries ago . . . perhaps the most profound change since the Chinese more or less invented hierarchy thousands of years ago.

I'm serious!

The D-E-A-T-H of distance. Y-I-K-E-S!

 B-I-G IDEA: Death of Distance.

big idea: **WE ARE ALL NEXT-DOOR (NEXT-BED?)**

NEIGHBORS.

YIKES

The <u>nerds</u> have
won!

Bill Gates,
richest man
in the world!

When I began working as a management consultant at McKinsey & Co. in 1974, "we" (the professional service people—accountants, lawyers, consultants, ad agency denizens) were considered the PARASITES . . . living off the sweat of real people's brows.

Times have changed. And how!

The nerds have won! Bill Gates is the richest man in the world! It is the Age of Brainware. Now . . . the people who lift "things" (the . . . RAPIDLY . . . declining fraction) are the new parasites living off the carpal-tunnel syndrome of the computer programmers' perpetually strained keyboard hands.

Overstatement? I think not . . . (or barely).

 B-I-G IDEA: Death of Distance.

big idea: A-L-L VALUE FROM BRAINWARE!

Washed up at 21!

"Videogames are perfect training for life in fin-de-siècle America, where daily existence demands the ability to parse sixteen kinds of information being fired at you simultaneously from telephones, televisions, fax machines, pagers, personal digital assistants, voice messaging systems, postal delivery, office e-mail, and the Internet . . . . Those to the joystick born have a built-in advantage. Neo-Luddite polemics to the contrary, kids weaned on videogames are not attention-deficient, morally stunted, illiterate little zombies who massacre people en masse after playing too much *Mortal Kombat*. They're simply acclimated to a world that increasingly resembles some kind of arcade experience. From computer-generated weather reports to interactive kiosks at the local mega-mart, from Hollywood to the Pentagon, we are swimming in animated icons, special effects, and computer simulations."—J.C. Herz, *Joystick Nation*

Younger people are "more comfortable with technology than with a person," Jeffrey P. Luker of Andersen Consulting argues. Could it be true? Quite probably. No. Change that to . . . absolutely.

A New World "mental" order is being invented—at literally the speed of light. Who are today's technology experts? There are, as I see it, none older than 12. I'm kidding . . . barely. I started programming computers, with punch cards and pencils, as an engineering student at Cornell University in 1962. (CORC . . . Cornell Computing language.) I "get this stuff," to some degree, intellectually. But if you want to find someone who really gets it . . . watch an 8- or a 9- or a 10- or a 12-year-old attack (and I do mean *attack*) a new videogame. She or he gets it in the fingertips, intuitively.

Xerox's legendary Palo Alto Research Center (PARC) recently invited seven techno-savvy high-school students for a six-week brainstorming session called Workscapes of the Future. Can't wait to see (and buy) what they came up with!

Forget federal and state child-labor laws: If your information systems/information technology operation doesn't have a "senior executive" under the age of 15 . . . or at least under 25 . . . you're in trouble.

 B-I-G IDEA: Death of Distance.

big idea: THE YOUNG SHALL LEAD US!

Cray for

$199!

It was a little (tiny!) item in *Management Review*. Nintendo, we were informed, would soon be giving us (read: our nine-year-olds) a Game Boy, for $199, that has more computing power than the fastest Cray supercomputer of only 25 years ago. (You know . . . the one used by four-star generals to control missiles for the Strategic Air Command.)

So?

We are *all* in the technology business. *Travel-services organizations* (our reservation service is us). *Twelve-table restaurants* (our customer-preferences database is us). As well as, of course, *financial-services* (our communication and transaction systems are us). And any industry, as I said, that you can name. The computer revolution is now more than 50 years old . . . but what's *coming* makes what's *here* look Neolithic.

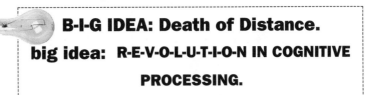

B-I-G IDEA: Death of Distance.

big idea: R-E-V-O-L-U-T-I-O-N IN COGNITIVE PROCESSING.

YIKES!

The cannibals (a.k.a. brainware players) are coming!

Stock market value of Microsoft + Intel > General Motors + Ford + Boeing + Kodak + Sears + J.P. Morgan + Caterpillar + Kellogg

A. Coca Cola: 18/115
    Merck: 17/78
    Microsoft: 6/71
    Intel: 16/62
    Disney: 19/42
    Oracle: 3/22

    B. Ford: 137/43
        GM: 169/42

C. Harley-Davidson: 1/4

It's the age of V-R-R-O-O-O-O-M! (Patent Pending)

Consider these statistics from the 1996 *Business Week* Global 1000, ranked by total stock market value. Coca-Cola's revenues were $18 billion . . . and its stock-market value was $115 billion. Merck: $17 billion in revenue, $78 billion in stock-market value. Microsoft: $6 billion in revenue, $71 billion in stock-market value. Intel: $16 billion in revenue, $62 billion in stock-market value. Disney: $19 billion in revenue, $42 billion in stock-market value. And Oracle: $3 billion in revenue, $22 billion in stock-market value.

Also on the list of 1,000 largest companies were a couple of names vaguely familiar to my fellow AARP-card carriers. Namely, Ford: $137 billion in revenue, $43 billion in stock-market value. And GM: $169 billion in revenue, $42 billion in stock-market value.

You don't have to be an astrophysicist to see the difference between the top and bottom halves of the list. The top half—Coca-Cola, Microsoft, Disney, and so on—are pure "players" in brainware. The bottom half are still lumpy-object purveyors, though automobiles are much "smarter" than they used to be.

Harley-Davidson, with revenues of about $1 billion and stock-market value of $4 billion, is an interesting and instructive anomaly. Yes, the Harley is, to many, the ULO (Ultimate Lumpy Object) . . . analogous, then, to Ford and GM. But Harley has much more in common with Disney and Coca-

Cola than with the big carmakers. Harley is selling, first, Harley-ism . . . and, second, that lumpy machine. That is, Harley clearly belongs to the (almost) pure brainware players.

Think about it. Marvel at it . . . *and* marvel at this: Harley-Davidson is trying to patent its . . . noise . . . its V-R-R-O-O-O-O-M. Why? The Japanese can't for the life of them . . . make noisy, powerful-sounding bikes. (Bless them.) So they "reverse engineered" Harley's sounds—that is, they've considered imbedding a sound generating chip in their engines to produce more Harley-like sounds. Getting wind of it, the U.S. bikemaker decided to protect its (VERY NOISY) machines (read protect its . . . INTELLECTUAL property). I've got to say it . . . Welcome to the age of V-R-R-O-O-O-O-M! (And the Japanese: They've learned about lawyers—!!—from the Americans and are . . . of course . . . challenging the patent!)

 B-I-G IDEA: Death of Distance.
big idea: VALUE = V-R-R-O-O-O-O-M!

YIKES!
You can't cut
your way to
success!

"Boosting profits through downsizing was easy; all executives had to do was take the heat from layoffs."

—G. William Dauphinais,
Price Waterhouse

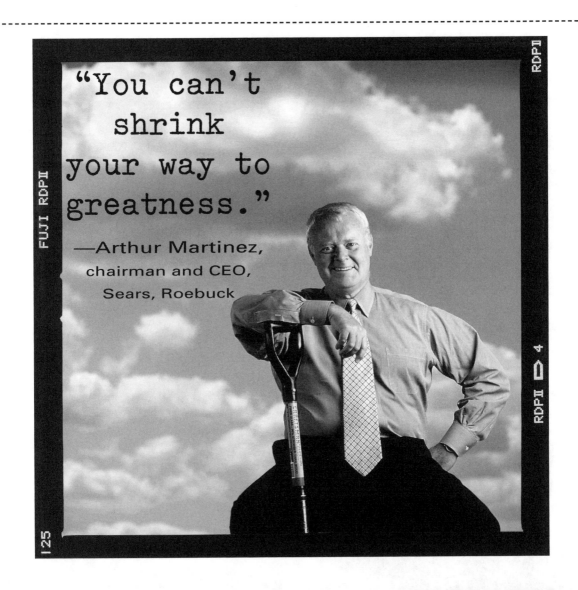

"You can't shrink your way to greatness."

—Arthur Martinez,
chairman and CEO,
Sears, Roebuck

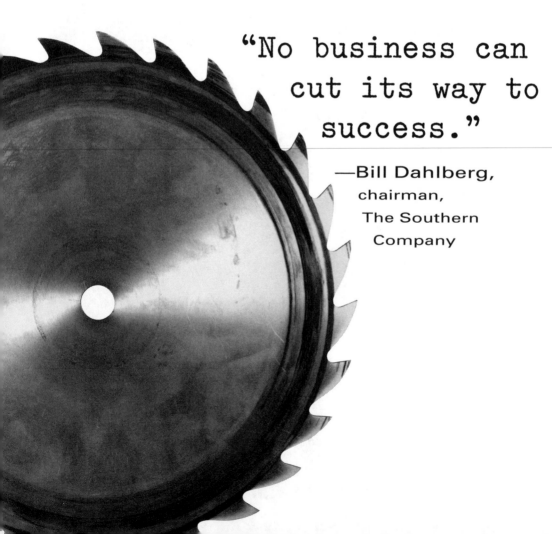

"In the final analysis, you can't continue to reduce costs and grow."

—Paul Cook,
founder, Raychem

"No business can cut its way to success."

—Bill Dahlberg,
chairman,
The Southern
Company

"Wall Street won't pay any more for raising profit margins on a stagnant sales base. The crucial issue has become how far does a company stretch for growth."

—Pankaj Ghemawat,
Harvard Business School

"For the past decade and a half, companies in every industry have obsessively devoted themselves to managing the supply side of their businesses, from manufacturing through distribution and pricing . . . . We have made enormous improvements in productivity. But opportunities and ideas to drive incremental growth are drying up. . . . As the 90s draw to a close, so will the viability of this strategy. Increasingly, companies will be forced to focus on the top line."

—Peter Georgescu,
chairman and CEO, Young & Rubicam

Of course, downsizing wasn't easy. And damn few executives I know took it lightly. (None relished it.) But I agree with William Dauphinais' remarks. And so does Arthur Martinez, Sears' much-admired chairman and CEO. And so does Paul Cook, founder of Raychem. And so does Bill Dahlberg, chairman and CEO of The Southern Company.

Dahlberg is leading a revolution at the giant electric utility. The company is too fat, and he's acting as dietician. But he acknowledges that cutting can take you only so far. And not that far at that.

Analysts on T-H-E S-T-R-E-E-T are becoming skeptical of downsizing-as-total-solution, too. In the long run, they argue, the real bottom line is the top line.

Revenue enhancement (new products, innovation in general) is the ticket. While relative costs must remain under control, and fat kept to a minimum, it's the builders, in the long haul, who will reap the rewards from Wall Street. Cutting jobs is hard work. Creating jobs is genius.

B-I-G IDEA: Death of Distance.
big idea: SHRINKING (CUTTING)
VS. GREATNESS.

YIKES!

You can't "improve" your way to success!

You don't leap
a chasm in 2
bounds.

—Chinese proverb

The chasm of change facing business—and me and you—is the equivalent of the Grand Canyon (and then some). Too many companies (and individuals) are trying to leap over it in 22, let alone 2, bounds. (Not that anything more than one matters.) It's not working. Think about it before y-o-u leap. Then leap.

To put it another way, it's my kaizen problem! Constant improvement in pursuit of perfection is admirable . . . to a point. But at some stage . . . and often earlier than imagined . . . PARTICULARLY IN THESE SIX SIGMA TIMES . . . (you remember Six Sigma, the VERY high-quality standard—3.4 defects-per-million-parts—popularized by Motorola) . . . pursuing perfection for perfection's sake can be a catastrophic mistake. It boils down to an almost inadvertent obsession with polishing yesterday's paradigm.

 B-I-G IDEA: Death of Distance.

big idea: QUESTION INCREMENTALISM.

EUREKA!
He's got it!

"Incrementalism
is innovation's
worst enemy."

—Nicholas Negroponte,
MIT Media Lab

I remember when I first came across this line from Nicholas Negroponte. I underlined it. Then, a few minutes later, I went back to it. A couple of days after that, I returned to it again . . . and paused . . . for a long time. I believe his idea is of profound importance.

Our devotion to quality, our adoption of the Japanese idea of kaizen (that everyone is responsible for making their "it" a little bit better today than it was yesterday), are among the longer and sharper arrows added to our competitiveness quiver in the last 25 years. And yet . . . .

Negroponte, who heads the highly innovative, highly respected Media Lab at the Massachusetts Institute of Technology, has allowed us no wiggle room at all. He could easily have said, "Incrementalism is *an* enemy of innovation." The idea would still be profound, but with a lower-case p. But he said that incrementalism is innovation's *worst* enemy. That's Profound . . . with a capital P.

What Negroponte means is that if you're spending every waking professional hour making "it" a bit better today than yesterday (one hell of a good idea!), then . . . necessarily . . . you aren't spending every waking hour working on reinventing it, blowing it up. The two notions are in tension. The two are opposites. The mindset and emotional bent of "a little bit better" is no less than antithetical to the mindset and emotional bent of "reinvent it"/"blow it up." Period.

B-I-G IDEA: Death of Distance.

big idea: INCREMENTALISM

V-E-R-S-U-S INNOVATION.

EUREKA!

"The only sustainable competitive advantage ..

They got it, too!

comes from out-innovating the competition."

—James Morse, management consultant

"Wealth in the new regime flows directly from innovation, not optimization; that is, wealth is not gained by perfecting the known, but by imperfectly seizing the unknown."

Kevin Kelly,
"New Rules for the New Economy," *Wired*

I have thousands (well, 30,000 actually) of pithy quotes for any and all occasions. It would be a lark to print out all of them. It's excruciatingly difficult to pick the one or two that best illustrate my message. But I've done it. And it's these: "The only sustainable competitive advantage comes from out-innovating the competition"/"Wealth in this new regime flows directly from innovation, not optimization; that is, wealth is not gained by perfecting the known, but by imperfectly seizing the unknown."

It's the oddest thing. Go to the business shelves of a sizable bookstore, and you will find hundreds of books: Dozens on TQM. More dozens on building teams. Dozens, again, on reengineering. What about innovation? On that topic, the shelves are virtually empty. Why?

I'm honestly not sure.

But this book (and the Circle of Innovation that animates it) is my shot at beginning to change that. The pursuit of COMPETITIVE ADVANTAGE = I-N-N-O-V-A-T-I-O-N. I BELIEVE IT. I (desperately) hope to convince you. (P.S. It holds for your career as much as for the vitality of the Finance Department.)

 B-I-G IDEA: Death of Distance.
big idea: I-N-N-O-V-A-T-E OR DIE!

EUREKA!
He's got it, too!
(And so should you!)

"Think revolution, not evolution."

—Richard Sullivan,
Senior Vice President, advertising, Home Depot

Richard Sullivan is the Vladimir Lenin, the Mao Tse-tung, and the Ernesto "Che" Guevara of business! And you?

B-I-G IDEA: Death of Distance.
big idea: THINK R-E-V-O-L-U-T-I-O-N.
P-E-R-I-O-D.

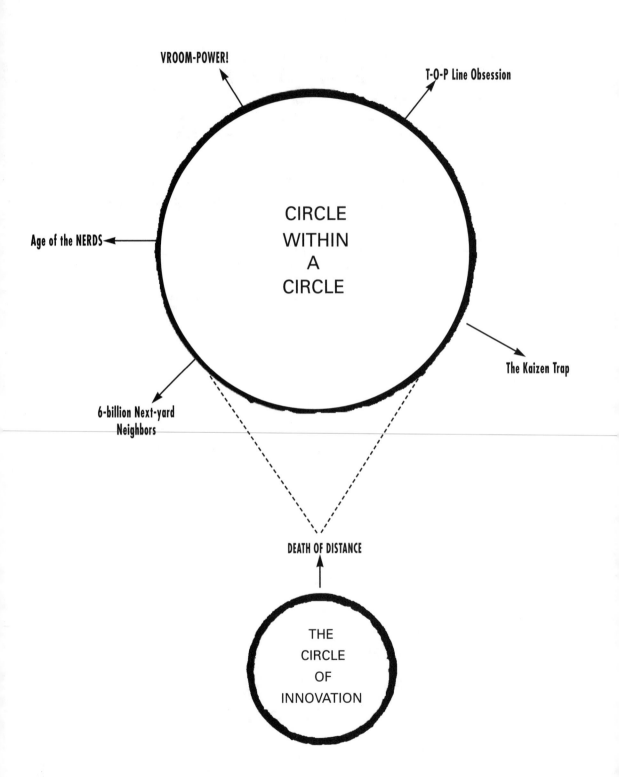

SEMANTICS ALERT No.1

Words are important.

Part of my effort is to put

new words into your mouth.

From this chapter:

Death of Distance

Information Age (still) in diapers

V-R-R-O-O-O-M = V-A-L-U-E

Nerd Nirvana

TOP-LINE Obsession

Cutting vs. Growing

Incrementalism vs. Innovation

Evolution vs. Revolution

Death of Distance. Nerds Have Won. Innovation Is It. This is the scene setter; and the next 14 chapters are a practical attempt to deal with the (enormous) challenges raised here.

Destruction is Cool!

How do you induce innovation?

SIMPLE: DECENTRALIZE!

What's the problem with decentralization?

It almost never works.

What's the solution?

Don't decentralize. Destroy!

Decentralization is hard to do.

(Just ask Bob Waterman.)

Fifteen years after the publication of *In Search of Excellence*, *Nikkei Business* asked my co-author Bob Waterman and me to contribute our lists of the big challenges facing business. Though Bob and I are great friends, and found it easy to work together on our book, the lists bore little resemblance to one another—except for the first item.

Both of us put real—and we did mean *real*—decentralization at the top of our lists. The point: After 50 (combined) years of watching organizations thrive and shrivel, we two held to one . . . and only one . . . basic belief: To loosen the reins, to allow a thousand flowers to bloom and a hundred schools contend, is the best way to sustain vigor in perilous, gyrating times.

B-I-G IDEA: It's easier to kill an organization than to change it. big idea: (REAL) DECENTRALIZATION USUALLY AIN'T.

Decentralization

is hard to do.
(Just ask Alfred Sloan.)

It's an old idea, and yet it remains new, mostly because we still haven't figured out how to make it work.

Big-time decentralization dates back to the 1920s. Henry Ford's little outfit was walloping Alfred Sloan's little outfit. Ford, creator of the first effective system of mass production, was giving every man (and for once I do mean man) the chance to own a car for a few hundred dollars—the Model T—and, as Ford apparently bragged, "in any color you want . . . as long as it's black."

Then Sloan had a profound—and profoundly simple—idea: to reorganize his company, General Motors, into divisions . . . the Chevrolet Division . . . the Buick Division . . . the Pontiac Division . . . and so on. Each division was an enterprise within the enterprise, with its own, distinct, even unique personality and character. Each would create and manage its own brand (a genuinely new concept at the time) and would attract a different type of customer and capture a different segment of the market. Sloan's tactic worked so well that, by the dawning of World War II, he had accelerated past Ford.

A brief update . . . and moral . . . to the story: GM nearly lost it again in the 1980s. Its independent divisions were independent in name only: Consumers (me!) couldn't tell the difference between a GMC Jimmy and a Chevrolet Blazer. Ford, with Taurus, Explorer, and other distinctive products, thrived.

Now, GM is setting about to challenge a spunky Ford once more by, you guessed it, really decentralizing. General Motors is promoting brand management within each of its divisions . . . and it's finding out how hard it is to *really* decentralize, to really create product families that are distinctive . . . in character and personality.

Decentralization is hard to do.
(Just ask the statisticians.)

Statisticians explain the difficulties of decentralization their way. Picture a five-division company, and suppose each division launches one new product this year. Statisticians would say that, under the principles of *true* decentralization, each product launch would be a "statistically independent try." That is, the products and product launches would be markedly different . . . meaning sometimes you win, and sometimes you lose.

But what the statisticians describe doesn't work in the world as I know it. The products and services of most businesses have a similar look and feel, no matter how decentralized their organization chart is . . . on paper.

Bottom line: A real decentralized organization is as hard to find as . . . well, a Tamagochi digital pet.

**B-I-G IDEA: It's easier to kill an organization than to change it.
big idea:
DECENTRALIZED UNIT = DISTINCTIVE CHARACTER.**

Decentralization is hard to do.

(Just ask the guys in the poly pants.)

Three or four times a year, my wallet trumps my soul, and I agree to take part in one of those great business traditions . . . the mid-winter, top-management, ultra-strategic, hyper-hyphenated "off-site" meeting. The chief executive sends me boxes of data about the company's troubles, and it all boils down to this: "We're facing an explosion of new competitors, an explosion of high-quality new products. Customers are pinching us, distributors are flexing their growing muscles, margins are sinking, and our product/service is becoming a commodity." "So," the CEO asks me, "how can we become more *innovative?*"

I confess I'm usually stumped. I walk into the conference room in Palm Beach or Palm Springs (it's always Palm something), on a mid-February day, at 7:50 a.m. In front of me are 150 managers, representing the top teams of 15 "autonomous" divisions in a "decentralized" $3-billion organization. In just a second, I have the answer: Of the 150 execs, 144 are between the ages of 48 and 59. (Or is it 49 and 49¼?) Of the 144, 137 are

OWMs—Old White Males. And of the 137 OWMs, 133 are wearing the traditional off-site garb: polyester lime-green golf pants.

I exaggerate . . . sorta!

The point: Members of the group look alike . . . talk alike . . . smell alike . . . eat the same foods . . . think the same thoughts . . . and probably have the same problems with their short games. It should come as no surprise that their products and services are anything but D-I-S-T-I-N-C-T IN CHARACTER AND PERSONALITY.

Is the company decentralized on paper? Of course! Is it decentralized in practice? Ho F------ Ho!

 B-I-G IDEA: It's easier to kill an organization than to change it.
big idea: THEY ALL WEAR POLY PANTS ≠ DECENTRALIZATION.

Decentralization is hard to do.

(Just ask Arie de Geus.)

"Low tolerance [for variety] is efficient, but it requires a strong set of hierarchical controls in order to minimize the use of resources. And it needs a stable world. It's a little like pruning roses. You decide to prune your roses short or long. If you prune long—if you are tolerant—you will certainly not be the best performer in the industry with highest return on investment. You may not have this year's largest roses. But you have considerably increased the chances that you will have roses every year. Tolerant pruning . . . gradually renews the plant over time and is more effective in a world you cannot control. I may not have the biggest roses, but I always have roses."

—Arie de Geus, former strategist, Royal Dutch Shell

The answer to the decentralization dilemma may lie in the rose garden. So says Royal Dutch Shell's fabled former head of strategic planning. (His perspicacity almost single-handedly made Shell . . . billions.)

De Geus has examined a handful of businesses that have thrived over the very long haul—e.g., DuPont, Hudson Bay Company, Mitsui, Sumitomo. And he finds that *the* key to their success is relatively loose reins. The l-o-n-g term top performers may not have been No. 1 in a given year or decade. But, decades in and decades out, they made relative monkeys out of the competition. Call it . . . true decentralization . . . or let 1,000 roses bloom.

B-I-G IDEA:
It's easier to kill an organization
than to change it.
big idea: LONGEVITY = TOLERANCE =
REAL DECENTRALIZATION.

Decentralization is hard to do.

(Just ask Mike Hannan and John Freeman.)

"Selection processes can only work on available diversity."

—Mike Hannan and John Freeman, authors, *Organizational Ecology*

A few years back, professors Michael Hannan and John Freeman wrote a meticulously researched, highly original book, *Organizational Ecology*. They studied the life and death of industries, the life and death of companies within industries. They applied mathematical modeling techniques from the biological and ecological sciences.

The book is a tough read. (That's an understatement.) But their conclusion, taken directly from ecology, is very understandable: "Selection processes can only work on available diversity." That is, all success boils down to accidents (new "tries" . . . or "available diversity").

What's the practical translation? Unless you do something, you don't know whether it will work. What a simplistic statement! Or: What a profound statement!

Most businesspeople think and think and think, plan and plan and plan, and seldom get around to "just doing it." But unless we're launching new tries, creating "available diversity" all the time, we won't have much to select from . . . in order to quickly adapt to a fast-changing world.

B-I-G IDEA: It's easier to kill an organization than to change it.
big idea: GOTTA INCREASE THAT NUMBER OF TRIES!

Synergy is a snare and a delusion.

(Just ask Bob Allen and Roger Enrico.)

"The complexity of trying to manage these different businesses began to overwhelm the advantages of integration."

—Robert E. Allen,
chairman and CEO, AT&T

"Roger Enrico's conundrum:
How does he compete with a singularly
focused, increasingly belligerent Coca-
Cola when he is preoccupied with fixing a
conglomerate?"—*Fortune*

On September 20, 1995, the chairman and chief executive officer of AT&T, Robert E. Allen, announced, without the help of the U.S. Department of Justice, the voluntary dismemberment of his company. Why? **While small isn't necessarily beautiful** (E. F. Schumacher notwithstanding), **very big is often very ugly . . . at a time when advantage goes to the quick and the spry.**

It's a lesson PepsiCo's chairman and CEO Roger Enrico has also learned. PepsiCo is one of my favorite companies (it has been since Bob Waterman and I wrote *In Search of Excellence*) and one of the most decentralized I have encountered. I count Enrico among the more brilliant marketers of our time and one of the great champions of internal entrepreneurship. But, in 1996, PepsiCo was hiccuping badly. Its enormous restaurant division (KFC, Taco Bell, Pizza Hut) was beset with problems. Coca-Cola, meanwhile, had spotted Enrico's distraction and was fizzing up the soft-drink wars. As energetic as he is, Enrico could eke only 24 hours out of a day, and he was spending much/most of it fixing restaurant operations. That left him damn little energy for fighting Coke.

Bottom line: Synergy is a snare and a delusion. It's difficult to manage one business well . . . let alone two or three!

B-I-G IDEA: It's easier to kill an organization than to change it. big idea: SYNERGY-SMINERGY.

Synergy
is a snare
and a
delusion.

(Just ask Sumner Redstone
and Nobuyuki Idei.)

"How Viacom's Deal for Blockbuster Chain Went Sour So Fast: Synergies Proved Illusory and Cultures Clashed."

—Headline, *The Wall Street Journal,*

February, 1997

"I don't understand the name of synergy."

—Nobuyuki Idei,
Sony

Blockbuster was a "can't miss" addition to Sumner Redstone's Viacom stable. Guess what? It missed. Ho hum. Sony got burned ... big time ... in Hollywood. Sony's Nobuyuki Idei says the problem is forgetting the one who brung you ... and mindlessly (and expensively!) pursuing synergy. He has a (very good!) point.

Synergy is a snare and a delusion.

(Just ask UAL and Sears and Baxter.)

Time and again in the last few years we have heard the word and its close kin . . . *one-stop shopping*. United Airlines, a decade or so ago, got together with a rental-car company (Hertz) . . . and a hotel chain (Westin) . . . so we could do all of our transportation-accommodation-vacationing-life (or so it seemed) through the one-stop shopping services of UAL. Except . . . it didn't work. And UAL management sold off Westin. And sold off Hertz. And . . . now . . . it's a helluva good airline. And UAL has plenty of synergistic *relationships* with car-rental companies . . . hotels . . . etc. But it doesn't *own* them. It (s-y-n-e-r-g-y . . . of the ownership variety) was a snare . . . and a dangerous/expensive/ego-centric delusion.

Ditto Sears. One-stop shopping. Pick up your washer and dryer. And a few pairs of underwear. And then get a home mortgage, a home loan, a few shares of stock, whatever. The flawed logic behind one-stop financial shopping cost Sears billions and distracted it from its main business.

Baxter International tried to play the same game in the healthcare supply business. Numerous divisions made best-in-world supplies. And then Baxter picked up American Hospital Supply . . . so it could distribute it all . . . seamlessly . . . along with other people's products . . . to hospitals. Turns out American Hospital Supply had a good distribution operation. And Baxter had a good product operation. But put the two together and you get . . . an energy-draining enterprise. Last year, management broke it up.

Last word: I'm all for synergy. That is . . . I'm all for relationships that allow one to leverage products or services through one channel or another. But owning it? As I said about UAL, synergy-of-the-ownership-flavor is almost always a snare and almost always a delusion.

None of this, of course, stops us: Witness today's entertainment "conglomerates" . . . combining "content" and "distribution." How much do you bet that breaking up will be surprisingly easy to do? SOON?? How's five years! Huh? That's Penn State Finance Professor J. Randall Woolridge's prediction . . . about the date of the split-up of Disney and ABC. As for me, I put the number at four.

Synergy is a snare and a delusion.

(Just ask Peter Job.)

> "Acquisitions are about buying
> market share. Our challenge
> is to create markets.
> There is a difference. . . ."
>
> —Peter Job, CEO, Reuters

It's true by definition. Big acquisitions mean buying a known quantity. Peter Job, Reuters chief, is clear about that . . . i.e., make a sizable acquisition and . . . YOU BUY MARKET SHARE. Reuters has grown . . . LIKE CRAZY . . . through organic growth/new-market creation. And you only do that if you work to create a garden where brand new species can grow.

A client agrees, praising Reuters as "one of the least-managed companies . . . [an] extraordinary concentration of very bright people, [engaged in] creative chaos." Hooray! In fact, Job admits to "having [no] grand strategy."

So what works?
Spin-offs!

"When asked recently to name just one big merger that has lived up to expectations, Leon Cooperman, former co-chairman of Goldman Sachs investment policy committee, answered,

'I'm sure that there are success stories out there, but at this moment I draw a blank.'"

—Mark L. Sirower,
author, *The Synergy Trap*

"Today's mergers
are tomorrow's spin-offs."

—- J. Randall Woolridge, finance professor, Penn State

"Acquiring
firms destroy
shareholder
value.
This is a
plain fact."

—Mark L. Sirower, author, *The Synergy Trap*

De-mergers

(of late):

3M

AT&T

Baxter International

D & B

Daimler-Benz

General Instrument

GM

ICI

ITT

Kodak

Marriott

Monsanto

PepsiCo

Rockwell

Sears

Westinghouse

Xerox

Equity carve-outs

Parent (e.g., Thermo-Electron, Enron, Genzyme, Safeguard Scientifics, The Limited, etc.): Operating center keeps more than 50 percent ownership; repeated carve-outs = "strategy."

Three-year compound annual shareholder return: Carve-outs, 37 percent; parent, 31 percent; Russell 2000 Index, 10 percent.

Stuff: Center must add explicit value: shareholder scrutiny; talent retention and motivation; investment flexibility for the center.

—*The McKinsey Quarterly*

Americans like big. Love big . . . or should I say B-I-G. And so the news is always those damn mergers. Put together NYNEX and Bell Atlantic . . . or Chase Manhattan and Chemical. Mate two dinosaurs in an effort to produce a herd of gazelles. But the real news is the *de*-mergers— that is, breaking up, which is increasingly not very hard to do.

De-mergers are an even bigger deal than they first appear. With rare exceptions, such as Lucent's split from AT&T, the spun-off unit is usually seen as a "dog" to be dumped. But, it turns out, let the dog out of the dog house—that is, free it from its corporate parent—and often the dog turns out to be a racing greyhound. Witness IBM's Lexmark, Kodak's Eastman Chemical, etc.

Business Week tells us that Barbara Goodstein of the investment banking firm Rothschild, Inc., is known on Wall Street as the spin-off princess. Her stock in trade is spin-offs, split-offs, carve-outs. And she has the numbers to back up her penchant. The spun-out, split-out, carved-out bits of large businesses, when sent on their own to the marketplace, have out-performed the fast-growing Standard & Poor's 500 by about 30 percent per annum . . . for years. Her logic? Spun-off bits are more focused on what they do, streamlined, and populated by newly motivated, highly incented, entrepreneurial manager-leaders.

Ms. Goodstein isn't alone in her approach. A recent analysis by McKinsey & Co. of "equity carve-outs" is revealing. Thermo-Electron has practiced the equity carve-out game for years, spinning out less than 50 percent public ownership in division after division. Some of its divisions have even spun out divisions . . . and some of the divisions spun out by divisions have spun out divisions. The company's objective is unabashed: Keep the entrepreneurial spirit alive . . . while maintaining some overall coherence to the enterprise. (Thermo is anything but an ITT-type conglomerate.)

The new McKinsey study focuses on Thermo . . . and Enron . . . and Genzyme . . . and Safeguard Scientifics . . . and The Limited. That is, businesses that choose . . . as a repeated strategy . . . to carve out less than 50 percent public ownership of sizable bits of the enterprise. But—again—the McKinsey research hardly champions old-style, unrelated conglomerates: In each case, the operating center aims to add explicit value by creating, at the very least, a strategic direction for the overall enterprise.

This halfway-house approach pays off. Over the three-year period McKinsey examined, compound annual shareholder return for the huge Russell 2000 Index was 10 percent. (The inclusive Russell 2000 is much more reliable than the small-sample Dow.) The carved-out bits of Thermo et al., on the other hand, provided a 37 percent compound annual shareholder return . . . and the parents (e.g., Thermo, Genzyme, Safeguard Scientifics) came away with a sparkling 31 percent.

The McKinsey analysts are inclined to attribute this exceptional performance of the parents to the carve out strategy per se. Among other things, it allows the parent to retain very top talent, that might be inclined to go its own way absent the opportunity to lead a "real" firm. It also allows the center exceptional investment flexibility (for, say, centralized R&D), since the divisions are, in effect, raising their own funds. The new division chiefs (cum CEOs of publicly-traded enterprises) are subject to real shareholder scrutiny . . . which tends to be a lot more motivating than oversight from the central strategic planning staff. There's a lot more to the story than this, but the idea is potent . . . and practiced by damn few at this point. It may provide a significant opportunity . . . in an age that begs for entrepreneurial spunk from our largest organizations.

So what works?
Acquiring talent!

In the midst of a London seminar, a Citicorp executive running a profitable part of the bank's Asian business came up and introduced himself. "You know what I call myself?" he asked with a grin. "No," I said. "A playground director," he answered.

"Excuse me," I mumbled.

"I hunt for the very best, often offbeat talent I can find. I give them the best technological tools available in the marketplace. Then I tell them to go out and raise hell, to go out and play in the world's financial markets. What else can I do?"

I like it. I love it!

Playground director! How else are you going to organize to survive in the late 1990s and the early part of the next century?

Microsoft gets it. Though a classic grow-from-within company, it has recently acquired dozens (!) of companies . . . and spent a billion and a half bucks in the process. Microsoft is . . . in effect . . . buying talent (and new ideas). That's great! Sure, there will be some/many losses (affordable!), some/many ho-hums, and . . . perhaps . . . a thimbleful of big wins that pay off the full $1.5 billion . . . perhaps several times over.

The MTA/Master of Talent Acquisition may be Cisco Systems, creator of a huge share of the "plumbing" for the Internet. The company has grown by leaps and bounds . . . largely by acquisition . . . but not of the Time Warner/Turner Broadcasting sort. Cisco unabashedly buys hot talent . . . and uses it to spark new, innovative businesses. According to *Fortune*, the company has systematized "the art of acquisition so that it's just another business process." For example, a designated Cisco team is developed to energize each start-up it acquires. Another part of its strategy: Cisco buys start-ups that are close to its headquarters; holding on to hot talent, perhaps surprisingly, means not forcing them to move.

Boil it down, and Cisco is basically purchasing major league talent from hot start-ups. Cisco is a Talent-Based Enterprise. Just like the Chicago Bulls. And the Baltimore Orioles. In this New World (Economic) Order, straight business . . . and baseball/basketball/Hollywood . . . are looking more and more alike. The "talent" part of things is getting more and more . . . and more . . . explicit.

High time!

 B-I-G IDEA: It's easier to kill an organization than to change it. big idea: ACQUIRE (HOT) TALENT !

So what works?

Acquiring talent!

The price of talent:

B.S.: $35,000

MBA(leading school): $100,000

After three years at McKinsey/PepsiCo:

$150,000 to 200,000

After start-up: $500,000 to 3 million

Post IPO: $100 million (or more)

It is . . . I repeat . . . the Age of the Talent-Based Enterprise. I.e.: THINK T-A-L-E-N-T. And if you're in the talent market, what's the price?

I figure it costs about $35,000 (give or take $10,000 either way) to acquire an employee with a bachelor of science. And if she/he has gone on to get an MBA at a leading school . . . well, the price tag soars to around $100,000.

If, following the MBA, she/he puts in a three-year apprenticeship at, say, McKinsey & Co. or PepsiCo . . . expect to pay $150,000 to $200,000 a year to buy the same, somewhat seasoned property.

And suppose she/he starts her/his own business . . . and it's showing signs of success? The price tag will probably range from $500,000 to $3 million a head. (Cisco Systems figures $2 million per body.) And if that start-up should go public . . . and you buy it as a small-but-hot company? Hey . . . the ante could jump to $10 million to $100 million per superstar. (Michael Jordan eat your heart out!)

Why is this a B-I-G deal? Simple. "Talent" is a B-I-G word. And a word that's very different from "worker" or "employee." Hollywood understands "talent." Theater companies understand "talent." So do professional sports teams. And professional service firms (e.g., McKinsey). But the large majority of traditional companies don't think "talent" . . . don't eat, sleep, breathe . . . TALENT. A "talent mindset" . . . à la Cisco Systems . . . is arguably a core strategic competence for any of us in the Age of the Talent-Based Enterprise.

B-I-G IDEA: It's easier to kill an organization than to change it. big idea: THINK . . . TALENT-BASED ENTERPRISE!

So what works?

The relentless pursuit of inefficiency!

"I believe in waste.
Waste is very important
in creativity."

—Alexander Liberman,
former (legendary!) editorial director,
Condé Nast

The mess is the message! Mess (economic) is quintessentially American. Silicon Valley is a mecca of mess. It's also a mecca of awesome success... that is the byproduct of an exceptional number of failures... vigorous tries that don't amount to anything... but feed the bubbling cauldron.

Mess is not inefficiency. As columnist/commentator George Will says, it is productive "'yeastiness' and creative fermentation." God bless America! God bless the mess! God bless the inefficiency!

Take Silicon Valley, arguably the most fertile economy in history. What's the region's secret? How about... waste and inefficiency? Dick Cavanaugh and Don Clifford, former partners of mine at McKinsey & Company, became the gurus of mid-sized growth companies in the early 1980s. Mid-sized growth companies, they reported, work like hell to negate the other guy's painstaking, decades-long pursuit of efficiency... by creating an innovation that is an order of magnitude beyond where that other guy has gotten. The objective, in effect: Put him out of business. Waste his factory. (Shutter it!) So, too, Silicon Valley. A new product comes along, leapfrogs what's already there, and puts a dozen companies and thousands of people out of business. (One of AT&T's biggest problems is that it's stuck with billions of dollars worth of copper wire, buried in the ground... in the age of fiber optics and wireless.)

Do it right the first time is insane advice. Nobody does anything... INTERESTING... right the first... or the twenty-first... or the forty-first... time. Doing the new means screwing around, trying stuff, and messing stuff up... again and again and again. That is... WASTE.

So how's your WQ? I.e., Waste Quotient? (No kidding!)

**B-I-G IDEA: It's easier to kill an organization than to change it.
big idea: WASTE RULES!
big idea: INEFFICIENCY RULES!**

So what works **best**?

Destruction!

"It's generally much easier to kill an organization than to change it substantially. Organisms by design are not made to adapt . . . beyond a certain point. Beyond that point, it's much easier to **kill them off** and start a new one than it is to **change them.**"

—Kevin Kelly,
author, *Out of Control*

Kevin Kelly says kill!

I say destroy!

Kelly, editor of *Wired* magazine, studies the new biology of machines, organizations, and communities. His book, *Out of Control,* remains one of my all-time favorites. I think—I know—he's got something to say to all of us.

What makes me so sure?

Every audience I speak to is made up of change agents . . . age 23 . . . age 43 . . . age 63 . . . junior human-resources professional . . . purchasing manager . . . chairwoman and chief executive officer. They're change agents all. (No exaggeration.)

And they need to understand that it's not a question of change. It's a question of d-e-s-t-r-u-c-t-i-o-n!

B-I-G IDEA: It's easier to kill an organization than to change it. big idea: DEATH!

So who works best?

CDO!

The Stewardship Problem

CW: Steward = Conservator

ME: Steward = Destroyer

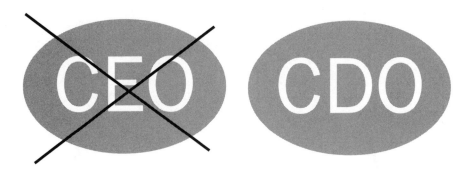

I sat down with a bunch of very senior Argentine executives recently. I told them . . . truthfully . . . that I had the greatest empathy for them. Their responsibilities are enormous. To a significant degree the working lives of thousands . . . indeed millions . . . were in their hands.

That's a daunting notion. The leader of anything has traditionally been thought of as a steward. That's a superb and moral idea. It's also a conservative notion. Or at least that's the way it's traditionally been translated. Conventional wisdom: Steward = Conservator.

I still buy the idea of stewardship. In fact, I think it's more important than ever. But . . . I don't think steward-as-conservator works any more. She or he is now responsible for living a new message . . . IF IT AIN'T BROKE, BREAK IT (OR SOMEBODY ELSE WILL BREAK IT FOR YOU!). In other words, the new definition is . . .

STEWARD = DESTROYER!

Think about it. Then change the boss's title from CEO (Chief Executive Officer) to CDO (Chief DESTRUCTION Officer)? Hint: This holds for the "CEO" (now CDO) of a 6-person department as well as the big cheese.

**B-I-G IDEA: It's easier to kill
an organization than to change it.
big idea: CDO.**

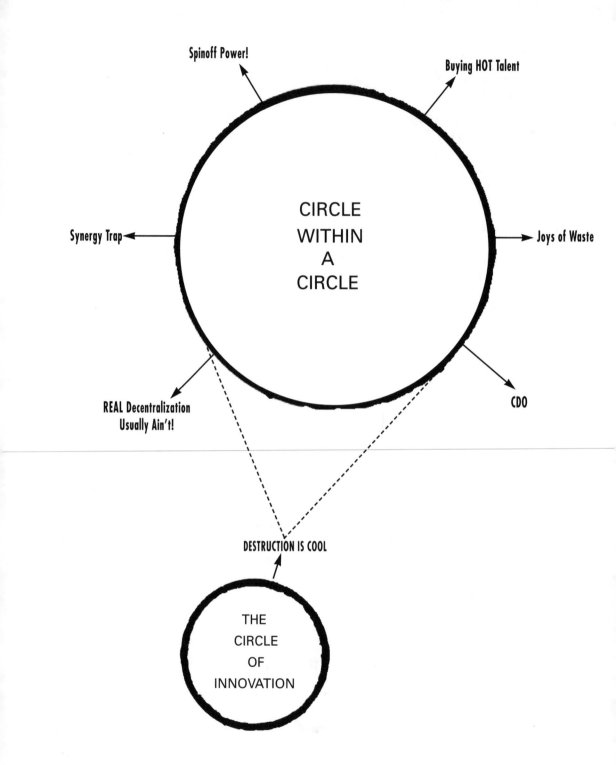

Spinoff Power!

Buying HOT Talent

CIRCLE
WITHIN
A
CIRCLE

Synergy Trap

Joys of Waste

REAL Decentralization
Usually Ain't!

CDO

DESTRUCTION IS COOL

THE
CIRCLE
OF
INNOVATION

SEMANTICS ALERT No. 2

Poly pants ≠ Divisionalization ≠ Decentralization

Synergy-Sminergy

Equity carve-outs

Playground Director

Talent (as in buying HOT)

Talent-Based Enterprise (Age of)

Joys of Waste + Inefficiency

Mess = Success

K-I-L-L

Destruction/CDO

The wide-angle lens is on the camera in this first "operational" chapter: We begin our look at innovation by taking a broad perspective.

Decentralization is the most potent weapon in the innovator's arsenal . . . and almost impossible to do (i.e., real . . . as opposed to paper . . . decentralization). Thus we raise the ante and champion death and destruction: Only the (very) paranoid survive. The language is harsh . . . and so are the challenges. The problems with accomplishing true, entrepreneurial decentralization run deep. Thus solutions cannot be half measures.

You Can't Live Without an Eraser.

(Very) hot management topic, circa 1994-7:

Organizational learning. Great idea . . . SORTA.

What word—in 1998—is more important than

learning? Easy: ORGANIZATIONAL FORGETTING!

What is much tougher than . . . learning? Easy:

FORGETTING!

Forget

"The problem
is never how
to get new,
innovative
thoughts into
your mind, but
how to get old
ones out."

—Dee Hock,
business visionary
and creator of Visa

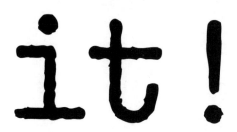

it !

Dee Hock founded what is probably the world's first trillion-dollar company —the Visa network. In a recent issue of *Fast Company*, Hock joins a select few in suggesting that the problem now facing business isn't learning, it's forgetting.

Organizational learning is one of the hottest management topics of the 1990s (some say even beyond). But I say forgetting is far more important. Forgetting is the key activity . . . the primary activity . . . these days. Cybernetics pioneer Gregory Bateson said it best: "You can't live without an eraser." Gentlemen and gentlewomen . . . are your erasers ready? They had better be.

 B-I-G IDEA: Innovation = Eraser Mania.
big idea: FORGET IT!

"The greatest difficulty in the world is not for people to accept new ideas, but to make them forget about old ideas."

—John Maynard Keynes, economist

A PERVERSE REACTION

"A pattern emphasized in the cases in this study is the degree to which powerful competitors not only resist innovative threats, but actually resist all efforts to understand them, preferring to further entrench their positions in the older products. This results in a surge of productivity and performance that may take the old technology to unheard-of heights. But in most cases, this is a sign of impending death."

—Jim Utterback,
author, *Mastering the Dynamics of Innovation*

Jim Utterback teaches at the Massachusetts Institute of Technology and is perhaps this country's (if not the world's) most meticulous student of innovation. In *Mastering the Dynamics of Innovation*, his summa, he provides an extraordinary set of case studies: integrated circuits, home computers, ice (yes, ice), electric lighting, glass, typewriters, commercial aircraft, and more. It's a distressing set of case studies. Time after time the industry leader reacts to the threat of change . . . by polishing yesterday's apple.

Time after time? Make that EVERY time!

Take the case of electric street lights. When the electric entrepreneurs arrived on the scene, circa 1880, they clearly had a (much) better idea. The gas-lighting monopolies awoke from a long, complacent slumber and they went to work. To get into electric lighting? Hardly! They strove to make gas lighting more efficient.

Their ploy paid off (for a fairly long while); many of the early electric-lighting entrepreneurs bit the dust. But the inevitable was, well, inevitable. As the electric boys' efficiencies increased, the big comeback of the gas gang proved, as Utterback says, nothing more than a blip, a last flicker.

B-I-G IDEA: Innovation = Eraser Mania.

big idea: THE PERILS OF POLISHING

YESTERDAY'S APPLE.

MCI (for)gets it!

"We run like mad and then
we change direction."
—Bert Roberts, chairman and CEO, MCI

"They're bloody fast."
—Peter Bonfield, CEO, British Telecom

"Big, agile company" is (almost) an oxymoron today. There are a few exceptions. Hewlett-Packard? Perhaps. 3M? Perhaps. Johnson & Johnson? Perhaps. And . . . for sure . . . MCI. I've studied the company for almost a decade now.

"We're quick to move forward and quick to pull back," says MCI chairman Bert Roberts, explaining his company's overall strategy. It's the truth. When MCI gets an idea, the idea champion grabs 30 or 40 people, finds an alliance partner . . . and locks the whole group, almost literally, into a small room for about 60 days . . . or less . . . and boom . . . a new product launched on the marketplace.

Ten months later, MCI's competitors are mostly still thinking, noodling, and appointing committees to examine the potential of the concept. Meanwhile, MCI has either scuttled its new try . . . or it's on version 11 . . . and on the verge of getting it right . . . occasionally (often, it turns out), very right.

That is precisely the MCI magic. As Peter Bonfield, CEO of the company's prospective new parent, British Telecom, says, it isn't at all unusual for MCI to get a product from concept to market . . . in a month. That's

probably 4 or 5 . . . or 9 or 10 . . . times faster than most of MCI's main rivals.

Run like mad . . . then change direction: Those six words may be all you need to know about turn-of-the-millennium business strategy. (Honest!)

Microsoft (for)gets it!

"I can't think of one corporation that has had this kind of success and after 20 years, just stopped and decided to reinvent itself from the ground up. What they're doing is decisive, quick, breathtaking."

—Jeffrey Katzenberg,
DreamWorks SKG, on Microsoft

Forgetting is tough for a successful business, especially one watched by anybody and everybody . . . the world over. Hence, my hat is (way) off to Microsoft's Bill Gates. In 1995, he bad-mouthed the Internet as a relatively useless fad. And then it became clear that the Internet had awesome potential . . . and Gates (and several thousand of his best friends/employees) dropped everything and, literally, reinvented Microsoft to attempt to be t-h-e Internet champ!

Having the guts to forget—that's the ticket in this roller-coaster world. Having the guts to eat (big) crow—especially if you're (arguably) the *loudest* crow in the world—is no mean feat. Winners will increasingly learn this gourmand discipline.

Banana Republic (for)gets it!

Banana Republic nearly slipped up. The company was trying to out-Gap the Gap, according to one executive.

So a couple of years ago management decided to stop that . . . and become the NEW Banana Republic. The company went upscale . . . worked on regaining a unique identity . . . and in 1996 same-store sales soared by 18 percent. Banana Republic literally threw out many/most baby parts along with the bath water . . . and reinvented itself from the ground up.

HURRAH!

B-I-G IDEA: Innovation = Eraser Mania.
big idea: THROW OUT BABY PARTS, TOO.

Lew Platt (for)gets it!

"Cannibalizing existing products is the way to remain the leader."

—Lew Platt,
chairman and CEO,
Hewlett-Packard

SOMEBODY ... is ... going to do you in. The only question: Will it be a competitor ... or YOU?

More companies have failed by trying to hold on to yesterday's franchise than by "confusing" customers with an explosion of interesting new products and services. I've heard all the excuses: "We don't want to wreck the current franchise." "But the profits are soaring on Model 9999X."

"Do you know what we're trying to do by holding back?" one irritated abrasives company executive (responsible for new ventures) informed me, "Protect a 35-year-old technology."

Yuck!

CANNIBALIZE ... YOURSELF ... AS ... QUICKLY ... AS ... YOU ... CAN. I.E., N-O-W.

* * *

Help wanted:　　**CEO as Hannibal Lecter.**

Silicon Valley (for)gets it!

SILICON VALLEY'S SUCCESS SECRETS

Tolerance of Failure
(It's a badge of honor.)

Tolerance of Treachery
(No such thing as loyalty.)

Pursuit of Risk
(Of 20 V.C.-funded startups, four go bankrupt, six lose money,
six do okay, three do well, one hits the jackpot.)

Willingness to Reinvest
(Cash flows into The Valley . . . and stays there.)

Enthusiasm for Change
("Obsolete ourselves or the competition will.")

Promotion on Merit
(Politics counts for little. Performance counts for all.)

Obsession with Product
(Find the "cool idea.")

Openness to Collaboration
(Generations last months . . . borrow and get going.)

Variety, Variety, Variety
(Mix fleeting with permanent.)

Anybody Can Play
("I can be rich.")

John Mickelthwaite, management editor for *The Economist*, recently produced a masterful summary of Silicon Valley's success secrets. (It's the best I've seen in 30 years.) To wit:

■ Failure tolerated. "Bankruptcy" in The Valley, Mickelthwaite writes, "is treated like a dueling scar in a Prussian officer's mess." It's no sin. It's almost a requisite. As a three-decade denizen of The Valley, I think it's an accurate statement . . . and maybe the most important one that Mickelthwaite makes. Another Valley commentator, Michael Malone, offers his own version of this: "Failure is Silicon Valley's No. 1 strength."
     Amen!

■ Treachery tolerated. Jumping from company to company . . . swapping secrets over brews or the latest-release Chardonnay . . . or across the Nautilus machines . . . The Valley is not the home to traditional loyalty. The ideas flow . . . and flow. Such Brownian motion is one of its success keys.

■ Risk seeking. One Valley venture capitalist lays out his expectations for any set of 20 investments: Four will go bankrupt, six will lose money, six will do okay, three will do well . . . and one will hit the jackpot. That is, there's hardly an expectation of a 1.000 batting average. Not even close!

■ Reinvest. The enormous positive cash flow generated in The Valley is . . . by and large . . . returned in reinvestments in new enterprises.

■ Enthusiasm for change. "Only the paranoid survive" is the fabled tradition, associated with those words by Intel's legendary chairman Andy Grove. Cannibalization is key . . . remember the word according to Hewlett-Packard chairman Lew Platt. "Obsolete ourselves or the competition will"—that's the way Mickelthwaite puts it.

■ Promotion on merit. There is substantial "openness to immigrants and to women," Mickelthwaite writes at one point. Understatement! If the immigrants split, The Valley would have to hang up a "Closed for Business" sign. In general, things are moving so fast that politics counts for little . . . performance counts for all. It's no small thing!!

■ Obsession with the product. The Valley, Mickelthwaite says, is hooked on "the cool idea." (That is, the latest cool idea.) The No. 1 characteristic of long-term innovators, according to a major study, is that they are "in love with their product." The "it" is it . . . in The Valley.

■ Collaboration. Generations are months. Sometimes weeks (at least in Internet World). The answer: Don't reinvent the wheel. Add your new (hopefully big) twist and quickly blend with tested bits borrowed from anyone and everyone.

■ Variety. The Valley consists of gazillions of fly-by-night outfits, here today . . . gone later today. And also a few Hewlett-Packards and Intels. It's the mix of the high-stature, in-it-for-the-long-haul firms and the overnight stars (most of whom become overnight flops) that, again, feeds that . . . ALL-IMPORTANT BROWNIAN MOTION.

■ Anybody can play. It's the old-fashioned American dream brought to life. "I can be rich"—Mickelthwaite says that each and every Valley denizen believes that. Perhaps an exaggeration. But not much of one.

I think this is a superb list. And I believe these 10 traits go a long way toward explaining The Valley's unique success. More important to this discussion: I believe this list can be translated—exactly—to the *individual enterprise*. Think about it! How does your company—or department—score on each of these 10 traits?? (In fact, try the following test . . . if you dare.)

My Department	Yes!	Sometimes	Never!
1. Failure is tolerated around here, even considered a good thing.			
2. Ideas flow readily, without hoarding by this person (dept.) or that.			
3. We're willing to swing for the fences and accept a relatively low batting average.			
4. We spend (time and money) heavily on investing in unit and individual renewal.			
5. We thrive on change.			
6. We are diversity freaks, and politics is rarely the basis for rewards or promotion.			
7. We groove on our service/product and are determined that it should be as cool as they come.			
8. We don't try to reinvent the wheel; we take a new idea and test it . . . fast.			
9. We're always working with others/outsiders on new projects, big and small.			
10. We think anyone can be a big winner.			

B-I-G IDEA: Innovation = Eraser Mania.
big idea: SILICON VALLEY TEST.

A quick guide to forgetting.

```
Innovation = Organized Forgetting
Innovation = Strategic Forgetfulness
```

Not to focus on forgetting is a mistake . . . perhaps mistake No. 1, for your division, your unit . . . and for you.

It's easy to say that learning something new drives out what's old. But it's not true!

IBM gravitated from mainframes to minicomputers and then to PCs. But its mainframe "mentality" continued to exist—and it brought Big Blue to the brink until Mr. Forget-It, Lou Gerstner, arrived. Likewise, U.S. automakers still haven't "forgotten" their attachment to big automobiles. In the case of General Motors, it took shock therapy—Saturn, the first separate GM subsidiary in 60 years—to get the company even near the road again.

If you're serious about innovation, you have to get serious . . . and systematic . . . about forgetting. Period.

How to do it?

How about this for starters?

1. Begin today: Put forgetting (USE THE WORD!) on your unit's top-of-the-mind agenda . . . on your top-of-the-mind agenda.

2. Make a list of your (your unit's, your division's, your company's) 10 core beliefs. Appoint a project team (include some of your best and brightest) to formally and systematically attack every one of those beliefs. It's more than a devil's-advocate trick: It's a matter of confronting (with a vengeance) the centerpiece of what got you to where you are.

3. Create a Strategic Forgetting Plan . . . call it that . . . and make it as detailed as your regular strategic plan.

Fine.

But we still haven't mined this idea for what it's worth . . . which is a lot. Keep reading . . . please. In fact I think of the rest of this chapter as nothing more (and nothing less) than a . . . QUICK GUIDE TO FORGETTING.

 **B-I-G IDEA: Innovation = Eraser Mania.**
big idea: STRATEGIC FORGETTING PLAN!

Forget hesitation!

"You miss 100 percent of the shots you don't take."
—Wayne Gretzky,
hockey great

Ready. Fire! Aim. . . . That's what pepper pot Ross Perot claims was his secret to taking EDS to the top.

Surely there are limits??

Well . . . I'm not so sure.

"But what about surgery?" That question (or one like it) often comes up during my seminars. And I have an answer: "Good point!"

That is . . . surgery is the . . . BEST . . . example of what I'm talking about. Surgery is the No. 1 trial-and-error game around . . . or that's what my surgeon friends tell me. Six billion folks on this planet = Six billion *different* bodies. Sure, people are similar, but each operation is different. Surgery requires a great memory (the shin bone's connected to . . .). But in the end it's an improv game.

Boris Yeltsin had bypass surgery. He was to be operated on by Russia's best. No doubt Russia's best have IQs as high as America's best. But there was a problem, reported in the press. The *best* cardiac surgeons in Russia are sequestered in the *best* institutes at which they are reserved, in effect, to perform surgery only on *v-e-r-y important* people. Net result: They don't perform many surgeries.

~~What's the magic of a cardiac cowboy like Michael DeBakey, by contrast?~~

NUMBERS! DeBakey has cracked open one hell of a lot more chests than his Russian counterparts! He's smart as hell, sure. But he's also a big winner at the "shots-at-goal" game. In fact, hard research suggests that the best predictor (by far) of a positive surgical outcome is the number of surgeries performed by the physician and her or his hospital. More evidence: Surgeons tell me that the greatest advances in surgery take place in times of . . . war. It's tragic, to be sure, but surgeons have less to lose: Try anything and try it fast is their sensible modus operandi.

Surgery: Its hallmark is trial, error, shots at the goal, improv! Go figure. Which is all another way of saying—as Perot and former PepsiCo chairman Wayne Calloway do—that: Strategy (of the winning sort) = Ready. Fire! Aim.

Forget blockbusters!

Beware the Coke trap!

I was talking to an executive in the pharmaceutical industry, and he said his company (which I won't identify . . . it was a private conversation) had a big problem. It needed to replace an enormously successful drug, then nearing the end of its patent protection. The company's de facto strategy was to pursue the Grand Slam Home Run . . . the discovery of the next BLOCKBUSTER . . . the next Coke.

Fact is, he explained, most drugs labeled blockbusters were so labeled after the fact; they were in reality the product of largely unanticipated pursuits that led to largely unanticipated findings. Most conscious pursuits of blockbusterism are, ironically, pursuits of the already known. Success, at best, amounts to a line extension.

(Logic: If you think it's going to be a big winner that's because you already understand "it" . . . which means that all your competitors understand "it," too. Products that spark new niches or industries—FedEx, CNN, Post-its, Ziplocs—end up being mostly used in ways that could not be imagined at the time of inception. That's the whole point.)

It's hardly limited to pharmaceuticals. Everyone wants to create a Coke. But Coke-ism was, in fact, largely an after-the-fact phenomenon. Success = Product of Variety. And . . . occasionally . . . that oddball variation takes off . . . for unexpected reasons . . . and you're in great shape . . . with the next Coke, Zantac, Tide, *Four Weddings and a Funeral*, Big Mac, Kleenex . . . .

Forget blockbusters!

"I would suggest that one support all forms of radical apps that show promise in changing the very nature of the business. Experiment!"

—Gordon Bell,
Microsoft Telepresence Research Group (and creator of Digital Equipment's VAX operating system)

"It's impossible to see what the products are going to be. That's why a solid information architecture based on encouraging and managing diversity, as opposed to containing diversity, has become so important."

—Steven Telleen,
IORG.COM

And if "forget it" holds anywhere (outside the surgery) . . . it's the Web.

The Web (1) will change everything; (2) we don't know how/when it will change everything; (3) so . . . per industry gurus Gordon Bell and Steven Telleen . . . EXPERIMENT!

Forget detail!

"Effective prototyping may be the most valuable 'core competence' an innovative organization can hope to have."

—Michael Schrage,
author and technology maven

It's one thing to say "run like mad and then change direction." Or urge: "Ready. Fire! Aim." Or: Just Do It. But how *do* you just do it? One technique stands head and shoulders above the pack: fast prototyping.

Michael Schrage, grand doyen of innovation, isn't given to overstatement, and yet he argues that a culture of rapid prototyping is *the* core competence among innovation's winners.

Schrage is onto something. A growing number of research studies suggest an iterative/prototyping approach beats a meticulous (Ready. Aim. Aim. Aim. Aim . . .) approach.

Schrage points to rapid-prototyping champs such as Hewlett-Packard, 3M, Microsoft, and Sony to make his point. At the latter, the mean time to prototype is an astonishing five days. (Yes . . . D-A-Y-S.) Competitors take several months, at best, to do the same.

Alas, rapid prototyping isn't amenable to a 10-quick-steps-that-you-can-start-tomorrow-morning approach. It's cultural.

Schrage says specification-driven companies require that every "i" be dotted and "t" be crossed before anything can be shown to the next level of management. Prototype-driven companies, by contrast, love to . . . PLAY. They are open to new ideas. They cherish quick-and-dirty tests and experiments. Free-flowing exchange around rough models is the norm. It's not that sloppy work is encouraged or tolerated; it's just that hasty experiments to gather some *real* data are "the way we do business around here."

Implementing a culture of rapid prototyping, then, is a subtle process. But it surprises many (most!) to realize that this one, apparently humble tool is anything but humble . . . or a tool. It is a way of life that arguably has an impact on a company's innovation potential more than any single idea/strategy. Call rapid prototyping . . . a culture . . . a strategy . . . a core competence. At least, begin by thinking about it . . . seriously . . . NOW. And acting on it . . . NOW. The following Prototyper's Laws may help you get going.

PROTOTYPER'S LAWS

1. Define a small, practical test in a page or less of text. Now.
2. Gather "found" materials on the (very) cheap.
3. Find a partner-customer who can provide a test site and act as a sounding board.
4. Set a (very) tight deadline of five working days . . . or a little less . . . or a little more . . . for the next (practical) step.
5. Conduct the test . . . ASAP.
6. De-brief and record results in a notebook (electronic or spiral bound).
7. Set the next test date . . . ASAP. (I.e., 5 days ± hence.)

Hint: This is what they taught you (or, at least, me) in 10th grade chemistry . . . which you/I/we forgot upon becoming a button-down businessperson.

B-I-G IDEA: Innovation = Eraser Mania.
big idea: PROTOTYPING (QUICK/CHEAP).

Forget $$$$!

Less than $10,000 . . . 34 percent
Less than $50,000 . . . 59 percent
Less than $100,000 . . . 75 percent

One *big* problem (on my top-five list) at *big* companies is the notion that, "We can't get started unless we can get *big* money." Writ small, this problem plagues tiny businesses—and 16-person departments—as well.

Inc. magazine, one of my favorite chroniclers of rogue companies, publishes an annual list of the 500 fastest-growing companies in the United States. The list isn't skewed toward biotech, software, or other exotic activities. It reflects the economy as a whole. It's got metal benders, fast-food companies, waste disposal enterprises, overnight-express companies, and so on.

Upon publication of one list, *Inc.* set about to find out how much money it took to start the companies. The numbers were startling: Fully a third came to life with less than $10,000, over half with less than $50,000, and three-quarters for less than $100,000. Don't get me wrong: To eventually roll out a company's product or service across the globe may take millions and the help of venture capitalists and kindly bankers. But to get the company going, to get its products or services into the hands of real customers . . . took, well, peanuts.

The message: Virtually anything . . . at Boeing . . . or Bob & Martha's Coffee Shop . . . or in the training department . . . can be tested, in the real world, for an astonishingly small amount of money. I really think that we can get a first reading on most any product or service for $10,000 or (much) less . . . and in six weeks or (much) less. At the small company or small department, the numbers are reduced further: It shouldn't take more than $500 and a couple of weeks to get a practical handle on a new concept. It's not a matter of thinking small. It's a matter of thinking big . . . and then thinking . . . T-E-S-T . . . and then thinking . . . N-O-W.

 B-I-G IDEA: Innovation = Eraser Mania.
big idea: DO "IT" ON THE CHEAP/NOW.

Forget Resources!

"But I'm only running an 11-person accounting shop," the seminar participant laments. "What can I do with these ideas?"

My answer: Who is the M-O-S-T indispensable person in the unit?
Barbara, you say. Well . . . toss her out. That is, send her off on a loosely
defined two-month project/"sabbatical." With a supplier. With a customer.
At a university. Traveling through Southeast Asia.

Make her a one-person skunkworks . . . out in pursuit of "finding
something neat/weird." "Bet you the $500 price of a ticket to this seminar," I
concluded, "that she comes back having done something interesting." Agree?
(If so . . . talk to Barbara . . . today.)

B-I-G IDEA: Innovation = Eraser Mania.

big idea: SEND-BARBARA-TO-THE-BOONDOCKS.

Forget
failure!

The 3 Fs
Fail
Forward
Fast

"In this company, you'll be fired for <u>not</u> making mistakes."

—Steve Ross,
late CEO, Time Warner

"If you are not bloodying your nose in today's warp speed economy, we have a name for you. Dead."

—*Forbes ASAP*

Years ago I had the privilege of introducing the late Sam Walton at an event honoring him. My remarks were supposed to last no more than a minute or two. What would I say?

I called Wal-Mart CEO David Glass, who had known Walton for almost 30 years.

"What would you say," I asked him, "if you had just a few seconds?" "The one thing about Sam that really stands out," Glass replied, "is he's not afraid to make mistakes, mess something up. He gets on with something new tomorrow morning. He doesn't waste time looking back."

Steve Ross, who parlayed a parking lot and a funeral home into, at the time of his death, the largest media conglomerate on earth (Time Warner), had the same view.

It's too bad that most of us don't.

Funny thing is, at age five, we got it! Mom and Dad gave us a bike for Christmas. An hour later we were out in the driveway with our three best friends. We tried to ride the bike. Fell off. Skinned both knees. Made asses of ourselves in front of our peers. But at five we understood: The deal is . . . get up on the bike again . . . NOW!

Then we became "businessmen" and "businesswomen." We learn that mistakes are to be avoided at all costs. "Do it right the first time" becomes our mantra.

Warren Bennis, perhaps our greatest student of leadership, interviewed leaders in the public, private, and nonprofit sectors for his book *Leaders*. These men and women had only three or four traits in common. One was: Each had made severe mistakes and bounced back from them.

Bottom line: Mistakes are not the "spice" of life. Mistakes *are* life. Mistakes are not to be tolerated. They are to be *encouraged*. (And, mostly,

> Bottom line: Mistakes are not the "spice" of life. Mistakes *are* life. Mistakes are not to be tolerated. They are to be *encouraged*. (And, mostly, the bigger the better.)

the bigger the better.)

Failure is the *only* precursor to success. (O-N-L-Y.) BIG failure . . . in turn . . . is the *only* precursor to BIG success. (O-N-L-Y redux.) Screw up. Get up. Try again. Quickly. Or, as one high-tech exec brilliantly put it to me, "Our strategy is 'fail . . . forward . . . fast.'"

I like it.

I LOVE IT!

 B-I-G IDEA: Innovation = Eraser Mania.

big idea: FAIL. FORWARD. FAST.

Forget rules!

"If you play by the rules there's no chance your name will enter the list with Stanley Marcus, Richard Branson, Wayne Huizenga, and Donna Karan."

—Retail industry executive, at AmericasMart

I was giving a speech to, mostly, youngish retail buyers . . . at Atlanta's AmericasMart manufacturers' showroom. I was asked a question by an old pro (read . . . tired/jaded?): "How do you deal with the conservative incentive systems that buyers face, the ones that punish failure . . . and barely reward success?"

I felt an immediate surge of anger. I wanted to tell him that wise folks . . . WOULD-BE VISIONARIES . . . ignore the damn incentive systems. And then someone else made the point for me: "If you play by the rules there's no chance that your name will enter the list with Stanley Marcus, Richard Branson, Wayne Huizenga, and Donna Karan." I could have hugged him . . . kissed him.

THAT'S EXACTLY THE POINT! Sticking your neck way out . . . does not guarantee success. (Understatement.) But to FAIL TO STICK YOUR NECK WAY OUT . . . does guarantee . . . beyond a shadow of a doubt . . . that you will never be a Stanley Marcus or Donna Karan. The mad do often (usually!) fail. Yet they are responsible for ALL the world's great successes.

Think about it. Then . . . choose sides.

At AmericasMart, I also gave my trademark "too much commoditiza-tion," "too many me-too products" pitch. And then I laid it on the line.

"If you walk out of this Market," I said uncompromisingly, "without having picked up some weird stuff, without having followed your nose, without great anxiety about a few of your purchases, you will have gotten no return for the blisters on your feet. You will have pissed away a matchless opportunity." And I meant it. The retail world is staggering. Not because incomes are low. (They aren't.) Not because the economy is in a trough. (It isn't.) But mostly because look-alikeism is rampant.

How do I know? I also attended AmericasMart as a member of a start-up company. I wandered the floors. I got my full share of blisters. Most of what I saw was insipid. A little bit of what I saw made me squirm. (That's the definition of exciting, isn't it? Exciting = MAKES YOU SQUIRM.) And I bought some stuff that was "far out." I planned to introduce it . . . soon . . . in my startup's one retail outlet. Why? Precisely *because* that stuff made me squirm. It was interesting. It made me stretch. It wasn't what "people are buying" . . . yet.

It probably won't sell. THAT'S JUST FINE. But if I hadn't bought the stuff that made me uncomfortable . . . I wouldn't even have tried. (And I'd have the damned blisters anyway.)

B-I-G IDEA: Innovation = Eraser Mania.
big idea: RULES ARE FOR FOOLS.

Forget propriety!

"All great
truths begin as
blasphemies."
—George Bernard Shaw

"If people
did not
sometimes do
silly things,
nothing
intelligent
would ever
get done."
—Ludwig Wittgenstein

Think deeply about it: We don't *need* any innovation. By definition.

Take the wheel. Did we need it? Of course not! Society, such as it was before the wheel, was—by definition—designed for wheel-less-ness. And you and I can both guess what happened to the guy who invented the wheel: Other guys in the cave trashed him: "Look at George. He uses the wheel. Real men carry rocks on their backs." Or some such.

All innovations are silly.

All of us wish to be innovators. So . . . be silly! *No kidding*!! This is neither an amusing point . . . nor a trivial one. It's at the heart of innovation.

Quite simply . . . as a member of the 7-person purchasing department, the 11-person finance department, the 4-person marketing department, the 8-person human resources department . . . if you haven't done something silly in the last 24, 48, 96, 120 hours . . . then . . . by definition you have wasted your time.

Sound a little strong? I really don't think it is. Post-it Notes were silly. (Very.) The fax machine was silly. (Very.) FedEx was silly. (Very.) CNN was silly. (Very.) The World Wide Web was silly . . . way back in . . . 1995. And so is that little idea in the back of your mind that just doesn't feel quite right . . . .

Let it out! Think survival! Be silly! Or as G.B. Shaw said . . . blasphemous!

 B-I-G IDEA: Innovation = Eraser Mania.
big idea: IT'S SILLY, STUPID!

Forget Professional!

Epithet No. 1:

Thoroughly professional . . .

but not provocative

Given: We are all in the professional services business. (Ninety percent of us, even in manufacturing, work in "services"—IS, HR, finance, marketing, logistics, engineering, etc.)

Question: What is the essence of professional service delivery . . . in 1998?

During my seminars I extol—to the heavens—the virtue of exciting failures (planned "silliness"). I often get attacked for it. I remember one seminar where the first question came from a Big Six accounting partner, "But, Tom, my clients won't accept failures. What should I do?"

I must admit . . . I lost it.

Won't accept failures? When I look back at my professional service delivery career at McKinsey, I find that I was involved in about a dozen major projects. I think we earned our pay in every case. (Batting average: 12 for 12 . . . or 1.000.) But, with the advantage of hindsight, I believe that only in two or three of my dozen cases did we really act as catalysts for fundamental change. And, for me as well as for a firm as well reputed as McKinsey, I think that "catalyst for fundamental change" is the only worthwhile measure . . . and that 2 for 12 (.167) is a miserable Big-League (a.k.a. me, McKinsey) batting average.

Thence what I say to every professional service delivery person (well over 90 percent of my seminar attendees, remember): My No. 1 epithet, in 1997: "Thoroughly 'professional' but not provocative." My theory, and you will never budge me on this: Professional service delivery people (including the 26-year-old trainer in the nine-person training department) are paid to provoke. *Period.*

Dot the "i's," cross the "t's," check the facts . . . of course that's important. I have to "show up" for my seminars, despite thunderstorms, blizzards, ice storms, the flu. If I don't show up, I don't get paid. *But I don't get paid to show up.* I get paid to push, nudge, cajole . . . in short, to provoke.

And I fervently believe . . . in 1998 . . . that what's true for me is true for you. As I said . . . *period.*

 B-I-G IDEA: Innovation = Eraser Mania.

big idea: PAID TO PROVOKE.

Forget
balance!

CEO (IQ of 180):
Ms. Crazy!

CFO (IQ 180):
Mr. Conservative!

There's more to life than innovation. (Even I will admit that.) I run my own small business . . . and covering the payroll is a *very* big deal. The system/infrastructure/finances in any enterprise must be v-e-r-y buttoned down. That is . . . we seek "balance" between innovation and infrastructure/system/finance.

Or do we? In fact I think we shouldn't. Forget . . . balance. Embrace instead . . . TENSION.

I hit upon the word at a seminar where I was chastised for being the archenemy of order. I said, "Look, I understand the importance of both ideas . . . innovation and infrastructure/finances. But I propose to address it is as follows: I want a chief executive officer, brighter than hell, charging off, due west, at a thousand miles an hour. . . in pursuit of the bold, the brave, and the innovative. And I want a CFO, equally bright, charging off . . . also at a thousand miles an hour . . . due east. I want them to fight. I want them to shout. I want them to be in constant . . . TENSION."

During a subsequent break, I was delighted when a senior Michigan police official attending the seminar asked me to sign a page in his notepad. On it was written, in large capital letters . . . "BALANCE SUCKS!"

 B-I-G IDEA: Innovation = Eraser Mania.

big idea: TENSION!!

Forget
consensus!

"If you have two
people who think
the same, <u>fire</u>
one of them.
What do you need
duplication for?"

—Jerry Krause,
general manager, Chicago Bulls

I've said it a lot . . . to 26-year-old, first-time supervisors . . . to 36-year-old entrepreneurs . . . to 56-year-old executive vice presidents: "The most important person who reports to you is the one who most vigorously disagrees with you, who has the guts to disagree with you."

The translation of this sentiment, courtesy the extraordinarily successful general manager of the Chicago Bulls basketball team, Jerry Krause: "If you have two people who think the same, fire one of them. What do you need duplication for?" Krause was talking about himself and masterful Bulls' coach Phil Jackson. The two have very different views of the world. (Understatement.) And that contrast is all-important! Hint: "All-important" does not mean easy. And it surely doesn't mean serene.

B-I-G IDEA: Innovation = Eraser Mania.

big idea: 3 HEARTY CHEERS FOR THE ONES

WHO DISAGREE WITH YOU.

Forget consensus!

Keeper of the Flame of Creation
(Brahma = Creator)

Keeper of the Flame of Preservation
(Vishnu = Preserver)

Keeper of the Flame of Destruction
(Shiva = Destroyer)

Creator

Preserver

Destroyer

I spend a lot of time in India. To learn my way around, I read up, at least a bit, on Hinduism. Its three principal gods are Brahma (creator), Vishnu (preserver), and Shiva (destroyer). This troika describes just about all you need to know about business (or perhaps anything else . . . as the Hindus would have it).

Every enterprise, public or private, is about balancing system/infrastructure/regularity/consistency . . . i.e., preservation and remembering . . . and inventing the new . . . i.e., creation . . . and forgetting the old . . . i.e., destruction.

Should every company have three equal co-presidents: Co-president for Creation, Co-president for Preservation, Co-president for Destruction? In fact, maybe the 10-person unit ought to have these three positions more or less formally created: Keeper of the Flame of Creation, Keeper of the Flame of Preservation, Keeper of the Flame of Destruction.

Hint: I'm *very* serious about this, and the feedback I've gotten from those who have tried to apply it is very positive. There are two problems that the notion aims to amend. First, no one can effectively encompass all three of these mindsets; the emotional make-up of the preserver, for instance, is antithetical to the emotional make-up of the destroyer. Second, in most organizations, preservation gets de facto (very) top billing, with creation (a distant) second and destruction (an off-the-charts) third.

 B-I-G IDEA: Innovation = Eraser Mania.
big idea: THINK . . . BRAHMA/VISHNU/SHIVA.

Forget right and wrong!

"There is always the danger
that big, successful companies
become arrogant. . . . They start
to think they know the right answers,
which is never true because there are
no right answers. If you deal with
contemporary art, it'll teach you
very fast that there are many answers
and some of them are wrong and right
at the same time."

— Peter Littmann, CEO, Hugo Boss

Well said! Enough said!

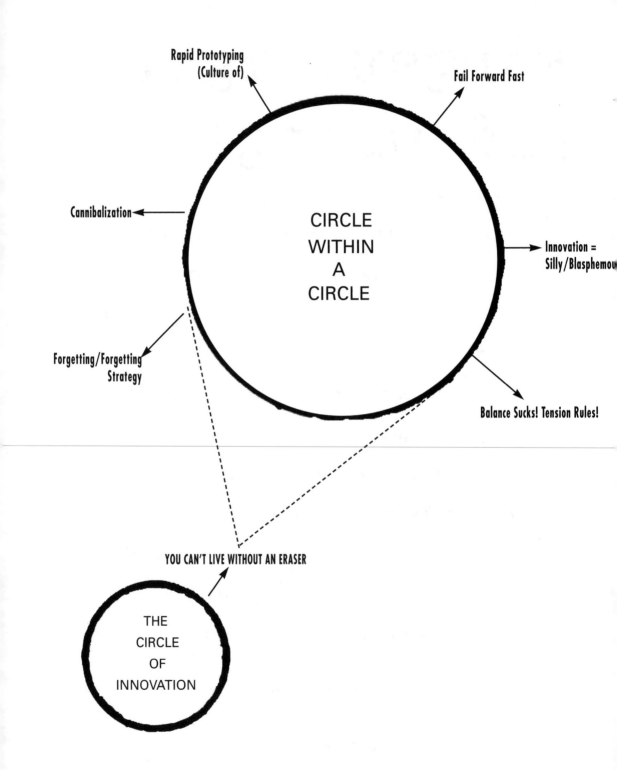

Rapid Prototyping
(Culture of)

Fail Forward Fast

Cannibalization

CIRCLE
WITHIN
A
CIRCLE

Innovation =
Silly/Blasphemou

Forgetting/Forgetting
Strategy

Balance Sucks! Tension Rules!

YOU CAN'T LIVE WITHOUT AN ERASER

THE
CIRCLE
OF
INNOVATION

SEMANTICS ALERT No. 3

Forgetting/Forgetfulness
Run like mad . . . then change direction
Cannibalize!
Silicon Valley Test
Strategic Forgetting Plan
Ready. Fire! Aim.
Crack more chests
Just say no . . . to blockbusters
CULTURE of Prototyping/Prototyping as
Core Competence/Prototyping STRATEGY
Forget $$$$
Send-Barbara-to-the-boondocks
Fail. Forward. Fast.
Mistakes = Life
Big Success α Big Failure
Rules are for fools
Innovation = SILLY (!!)
Innovation = Blasphemous (!!)
Balance Stinks!
Think: Brahma/Vishnu/Shiva

The wide-angle lens is replaced with a close-up lens. We're still working through innovation-as-"real" decentralization ... but have examined strategies that can be applied at the small unit/individual level: e.g., programs such as rapid prototyping ... aimed at "organized forgetting."

We are all Michelangelos.

Business—at its heart and at its best—is about service, growth, and (yes, I'll say it again) i-n-n-o-v-a-t-i-o-n. So why, goes my argument, can't we achieve the ultimate in real decentralization, why can't every person become a businessperson? Why can't each of us be a business unit of one? Answer: We can!

Down with empowerment!
Up with the
b-u-s-i-n-e-s-s-p-e-r-s-o-n!
Up with the Unit of One!

"Ultimately our strategy is all about creating an organization of 15,000 effective businesspeople, where everybody thinks about the future, everybody amazes customers, everybody manages the bottom line. It's the ultimate accountability strategy."

—Chris Turner,
Learning Person, Xerox Business Services

Businesspeople! Businessperson!

Chris Turner, businessperson (Learning Person . . . that's the title on her business card) at now-billion-dollar Xerox Business Services (XBS), gets it. Everyone in the joint (soon to be, she claims, 40,000 folks) needs, Turner says, to be a businessperson.

Why? XBS is the EDS and the Andersen Consulting of photocopying/document management. A few years ago Xerox joined the growing numbers of companies wrapping a B-I-G service around a product. It convinced scores of customers to outsource their entire photocopying/document management operations to Xerox Business Services.

Thence, most XBSers are (far) away from home . . . on customer premises . . . aiming to deliver an innovative/efficient/complex service (document management, which entails the streamlining of paper-generating business processes, meaning all of them). Thus, XBS wants everyone to be a *salesperson* . . . a *reengineering guru* (that's what document management really is) . . . an *efficiency freak* . . . in short a full-fledged businesswoman/businessman . . . who also happens to be an XBSer.

The idea of employee-as-businessperson, employee-as-"free agent" ... knows no bounds AT ALL. Let's see...

Superstar businessperson: Virginia Azuela

In 1994, I broke all the rules of business book writing . . . and published full-page pictures of *my* superstars. None was a Fortune 1000 CEO . . . and none was more important than Virginia Azuela, a housekeeper at the Ritz-Carlton Hotel in San Francisco.

Ms. Azuela . . . and the bellhop who picks up your bags . . . and the doorman who hails you a cab . . . are authorized . . . on the spot . . . no sign-offs from above . . . to spend up to $2,000 to fix any customer's problem. That's right . . . $2,000! I know lots of people with exalted titles (like Vice President), who can't spend $2,000 without six signatures!

My point: With that big grant of spending authority, the Ritz-Carlton has turned Ms. Azuela into the de facto Chief Operating Officer, Entrepreneur-in-Chief of her floor in the hotel. She "owns" that floor (Azuela, Inc. . . . a wholly-owned subsidiary of the Ritz San Francisco). She is not a h-o-u-s-e-k-e-e-p-e-r . . . she's a no-baloney businessperson . . . a bona fide business unit of one!

**B-I-G IDEA: Innovation =
Michelangelos All.
big idea: AZUELA, INC.**

Superstar businesspeople:
Lakeland Care Pairs

Some other Azuelian superstars ply their trade at the 897-bed Lakeland Regional Medical Center (RMC) in Lakeland, Florida. It's a pioneer in "patient-focused care," one of the most promising concepts in acute-care delivery today.

Lakeland, in effect, broke itself up into 40-bed, patient-focused minihospitals. They are self-contained (labs, admissions, etc.) except for the absence of a few pieces of ultra-expensive capital equipment that are shared by all units. More interesting: The *mini*hospitals, in turn, are made up of *micro*hospitals. At the heart of the microhospitals are entrepreneurial teams—*business units of two*—known as Care Pairs. A Care Pair is a registered nurse and a technician. After only a few weeks of cross-training, Care Pairs can perform 90 percent of pre- and post-operative requirements for five to seven patients.

(The V-E-R-Y big deal: In the average giant hospital, it's common to find 500 or more non-medical specialty job classifications. Lakeland RMC has, in effect, collapsed the 500 to . . . ONE . . . Care Pair member.)

What's more, using computers with custom-designed software called Care Link, the Care Pairs can act as de facto quarterbacks for the 10 percent of a patient's activity they can't perform themselves. (I.E., THEY REALLY ARE A BUSINESS UNIT.)

Do business units of one (or two) work?

RESULTS: RITZ-CARLTON
Malcolm Baldrige National
Quality Award.

RESULTS: LAKELAND

Routine test turnaround time:
157 minutes to 48 minutes.

Fewest patient falls, lowest
medication error rate.

Physician satisfaction up,
patient satisfaction up.

Costs significantly down.

Care Pair direct time with patients:
More than doubled!

Employees encountered in a multi-day stay:
13, versus 53.

In the case of the Ritz-Carlton, business units of one definitely work. The company is one of the rare service firms to win a Malcolm Baldrige National Quality Award.

In the case of Lakeland, the answer is also a loud-and-clear "yes." In its first minihospitals, average test turnaround time quickly dropped from 157 minutes to 48 minutes. Fewer patient falls were reported. Medication error rates dropped. Physician and patient satisfaction shot up.

But the two most important indicators were these: The Care Pairs more than doubled their direct patient-contact time. And, in the course of a multi-day stay, the average patient encountered 13 Lakeland employees, down significantly from 53 in the not-so-distant past.

Some numbers!

B-I-G IDEA: Innovation =
Michelangelos All.
big idea: COLLAPSE 500 JOB CATEGORIES TO . . . 1.

Q: Can every job be businessed?

A: Yes! (With nerve and imagination.)

Business-ing = The process of turning every job into a business, every worker into a businessperson, a business unit of one.

What does it take "to business"?

Imagination!

Do you have it? Bill Charland, a Denver-based career consultant, claims everyone has it. He provides a simple, yet intriguing (and I believe powerful) model of organization, which he calls the "emerging diamond" or "diamond on end."

The upper tip of the diamond is a tiny complement of managers, all of whom double as functional experts of the first order. The bottom tip is a tiny number of clerical workers. (Some several-thousand-person organizations have eliminated *all* clerical jobs—for example, VeriFone, the 4,000-person producer of transaction-processing software and hardware systems.)

Charland's main point: You can transform 98, 99, or 99.8 percent of workers into autonomous businesspersons. To wit: Azuela, Inc. (and friends) at the Ritz-Carlton . . . the Care Pairs Inc. at Lakeland RMC . . . and Chris Turner and the gang of 15,000 BPs at XBS.

If there is a Chief Evangelist for this businessing schtick, it's Jack Stack . . . charismatic (and pragmatic!) boss of down-and-dirty Springfield Remanufacturing of Springfield, Missouri. Springfield takes worn-out

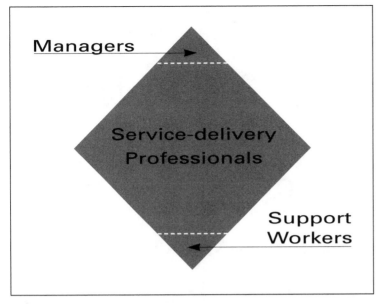

Managers

Service-delivery
Professionals

Support
Workers

motors from cars, trucks, bulldozers, and other heavy equipment and rebuilds them, saving the parts they can, replacing the ones they can't. Jack was sick and tired of demoralized, old industrial firms and wanted to get everyone at Springfield in on the action. His ingenious idea: TEACH EVERYONE TO PLAY "THE GREAT GAME OF BUSINESS." That is, he exposes everyone to the company's own financial statements and shows employees exactly how their efforts influence the P&L and balance sheets.

Stack is on an unabashed crusade for what he calls open-book management. Since his company took up the game in 1983, sales have skyrocketed 20,000 percent!

Go, Jack!

I.e.: We all can ... AND MUST ... learn to be businesspeople ... not merely "empowered" jobholders.

B-I-G IDEA: Innovation = Michelangelos All.
big idea: LEARN TO PLAY THE GREAT GAME
OF BUSINESS.

Businesspersons of housekeeping!

Michelangelos of housekeeping...
...and hairstyling!

"Ours is the most incredible industry in which to pursue a career. We touch people—physically and emotionally—and change their lives by helping them to improve their image. We give them a whole new lease on life."

—Michael C. Hemphill,
North American Hairstylist of the Year, 1997, *BeautyInc.*

"Can you imagine," a hotel manager once asked me, "Michelangelos of housekeeping?" Then he added, "If you can't, you ought to get the hell out of the hospitality business."

MICHELANGELOS OF HOUSEKEEPING. YES! I L-O-V-E THAT! What about Michelangelos of *parking* . . . Michelangelos of *accounts receivable?* Michelangelos of *plumbing?* Michelangelos of *selling?* Michelangelos of *hairstyling?* Michelangelos of _ _ _ _ _ _ _ ? (You fill in the blanks.)

Businesspersons of
telemarketing!

Michelangelos of
telemarketing!

At a recent seminar, I was going on (and on!) about "turning every job into a business," and "turning every person into a businessperson." But, one participant asked, what about a high-turnover, cannon-fodder job like telemarketing? "NO DIFFERENCE" . . . I loudly asserted. I meant it! The telemarketer deals with scores of folks every day. It's just like being a waiter or a waitress in a restaurant. Each of those customers/people is unique. Each is coming off a good, bad, or indifferent day. The telemarketers have an opportunity to make their 45 seconds (or four or five minutes) with that person into a special, memorable, enlightening experience. (Or not.)

Bottom line: A telemarketer is not a telemarketer is not a telemarketer. Bottom line redux: Telemarketer-as-Businessperson . . . Michelangelos of Telemarketing . . . NOT SUCH A SILLY IDEA!

Businesspersons of

e-v-e-r-y-d-a-m-n
t-h-i-n-g!

Michelangelos of

e-v-e-r-y-d-a-m-n-t-h-i-n-g!

There's no excuse for not being great.

 **B-I-G IDEA: Innovation =
Michelangelos All.
big idea: TELEMARKETING STARS/HEROES.**

What's the bottom line on this
every-person-a-businessperson,
every-person-a-Michelangelo
approach?

Awesome customer
service!

Reason for switching to a competitor: Contact from old supplier's personnel was poor in quality — 49 percent.

—Forum Corporation

One explanation of the importance of every-person-a-businessperson comes from turnaround champ Barry Gibbons, who was CEO of Burger King for several years and, while there, crafted a major comeback against his tough-as-gristle competitor . . . McDonald's.

In *This Indecision Is Final*, Gibbons writes that "70 to 90 percent of decisions not to repeat a purchase of anything are not about the product or price. They are about some dimension of service." His observation is consistent with the quantitative research from the Forum Corporation of Cambridge, Massachusetts.

Forum examined the motivations of customers who defected from 14 major service and manufacturing businesses. Fifteen percent left because of

> 70 percent of customers bail because of the look/feel/smell/taste of doing business with a company.

quality problems, as defined in technical terms (e.g., shorter MTBF . . . mean time between failures). Another 15 percent defected because they found a less expensive alternative. Twenty percent departed because of "too little contact and individual attention" from the prior service or product provider; and almost half, 49 percent, left because contact from the old supplier's personnel was "poor in quality."

That's the data as presented by Forum researchers. I would collapse the third and fourth categories, in which case we could say:

■ 15 percent of customers scooted for technical quality reasons.
■ 15 percent took off because of price.
■ 70 percent bailed because of the look/feel/smell/taste of doing business with a company.

So?? Drum roll. Enter . . . what? Bill Charland's diamond-on-end . . . with 99 percent plus of employees turned into de facto independent-service providers. Virginia Azuela . . . housekeeper-turned-COO of her floor at the Ritz. The Care Pairs/micro hospitals at Lakeland. Chris Turner's XBS businesspersons. That is: This every-person-a-businessperson/every-job-a-business approach is PERFECTLY designed to deal with the data set generated by Forum. That is: The whole damn idea is to transmit the zeal and customer intimacy of Mom and Pop, Inc., owners of the corner coffee shop or copy shop, to all 15,000 XBSers. The Care Pair "owns" their 5 to 7 patients . . . just as Mom and Pop own their 20-square-block trading area in downtown Kansas City . . . *if* they don't screw up.

Something that matters!

"What brings people to their gift of service [to the church] is a desire to do something that—perhaps unlike their day job...matters."

—Charles Trueheart

In a cover article for the *The Atlantic Monthly*, author Charles Trueheart comments on rising church attendance in the United States and . . . better yet . . . a sharp rise in community service by congregation members.

Hooray! Or . . . about 98 percent "hooray."

I was snapped to attention by Trueheart's "something that—perhaps unlike their day job . . . matters." Don't get me wrong, I'm delighted, along with Colin Powell, at the rise in and rising awareness of the importance of community service. It's just that . . . .

I see "something that—perhaps unlike their day job . . . matters" as an out-and-out condemnation of those who manage people—*and* those of us who write about it!

Business (and public service in the public sector) ought to be about . . . service . . . growth . . . innovation. I.E., THAT DAMN DAY JOB SHOULD MATTER! IT S-H-O-U-L-D BE AIMED AT CARING AND ATTENTIVENESS AND INCREASING HUMAN POTENTIAL (yours, mine, our colleagues', our customers'). I'm 54. I'm no dewey-eyed youngster. But I think that it is JOB NO. 1 for A-L-L bosses to damn well make sure that the day job is something that A-L-L of their employees can BRAG ABOUT to kids, spouses, neighbors, significant others.

Agree??? (If you don't . . . write for a refund.)

1. What does it take to lead an organization of businesspersons?

> "What creates trust, in the end,
> is the leader's manifest respect
> for the followers."
>
> —Jim O'Toole,
> author, *Leading Change*

Big words! E-N-O-R-M-O-U-S words!

Jim O'Toole is one of the world's premier students of leadership. I first experienced his kind of respect 30 years ago. The field wasn't business; it was battle.

Serving as a (very junior) officer in Vietnam I noticed, at least subconsciously, that people of my rank seemed to come in two varieties: those who hung out at the officer's club, sucked up to their seniors, and constantly yanked the chain of command; and those who hung out with their soldiers, their sailors, their airmen, their Marines. With this second group, I'm not talking about fraternizing. I'm speaking of respect . . . admiration . . . and appreciation . . . in the deepest senses of those marvelous words. As far as I was concerned (then and now), that first group (the suck-ups) were literally not worth the powder to blow them to hell.

But back to my friend O'Toole: Do you routinely exhibit, in ways small and large, "manifest respect for the followers"? Do you routinely see Michelangelos of Housekeeping/Telemarketing? Do "their" day jobs . . . matter? Look in the mirror. Look now. Look *long*. Look *hard*. What kind of leader are you?

T-H-I-N-K A-B-O-U-T I-T. P-L-E-A-S-E!

2. What does it take to lead an organization of businesspersons?

"In essence, the leadership
challenge is to provide the 'glue'
to cohere independent units in a
world characterized by forces of
entropy and fragmentation.
Only one element has been
identified as powerful enough
to overcome the centrifugal
forces, and that is trust."
—Jim O'Toole, author, *Leading Change*

In my seminars, I pause when I get to this quote. I spend a few minutes on it, then I announce, "Everything I have said before, everything I will subsequently say, hinges on this one, single remark."

Why? I think O'Toole gets it exactly right. He's addressing *the* paradox of our age. It's a paradox futurist John Naisbitt addressed, too, in his seminal book *Megatrends*. Naisbitt talked about "high tech, high touch." Meaning . . . paradoxically. . . the higher the tech and the more dispersed the networks, the more important the touch or . . . per O'Toole . . . trust. How about this: *high tech, high trust.*

So? What do we do about trust *operationally?* How do we start? At the very least, we can take it seriously, put it on the agenda, put it on the t-o-p of the agenda, keep it at the top of the agenda, treat it as a hard issue, not a soft one.

TRUST = V-E-R-Y HARD.

**B-I-G IDEA: Innovation = Michelangelos All.
big idea: T-R-U-S-T = H-A-R-D STUFF.**

3. What does it take to lead an organization of businesspersons?

"I set as the goal the
maximum capacity
that people have—I settle
for no less. I make myself
a relentless architect
of the possibilities of
human beings."

—Benjamin Zander, conductor,
Boston Philharmonic

"A relentless architect of the possibilities of human beings." Lovely. And I'm not at all sure how *I* stack up against this standard. It's a tough one (perhaps the toughest imaginable).

What's the take-home value from this quote? (Take-home value = What books and seminars are all about.) It is a (VERY) practical test . . . that you should take . . . RIGHT NOW. Boss (or non-boss) the question is the same: How do you stack up on the RAHP (relentless-architect-of-human-possibilities) Scale?

THINK ABOUT IT! What the hell else is leadership all about? Words *are* important: RELENTLESS ARCHITECT OF THE POSSIBILITIES OF HUMAN BEINGS. What an aspiration!! Breathtaking . . . LITERALLY. (At least it takes *my* breath away.)

4. What does it take to lead an organization of businesspersons?

"The best thing a leader can do for a Great Group is to allow its members to discover their own greatness."

—Warren Bennis and Patricia Ward Biederman, *Organizing Genius*

"Should we use group or individual incentives?" the seminar participant asks. He's one of many who's gone team-bananas, as I call it, in the last few years.

Using my friend and leadership guru Warren Bennis as teacher, I responded: "Exactly the wrong question."

That is . . . it ain't either-or . . . damn it. Take sports or the theater. Precision execution is a must . . . yet great coaching/directing is about turning even the bit player into a high-impact individual who performs on a plane she or he could never have imagined before. Teamwork + Quirky (Great) Individual Performance = Great Group. Team *versus* individual? No . . . no . . . N-E-V-E-R!

5. What does it take to lead an organization of businesspersons?

"In the digital age, as we move into
quicker and quicker exchanges of
information . . . and re-inventions
of the world of work, our organizations and our careers in action will
become more and more closely aligned
with the jazz ensemble. . . . We
will find ourselves improvising with
greater and greater confidence
and fearing less and less the
imaginative power of the individual
committed to enriching the whole."

—Stanley Crouch, *Forbes ASAP*

I am a fan of imagery, an assiduous collector of images/metaphors. That's because in times like these (read *traumatic times like these*), pictures are our most practical guides, our real strategic plans. And I like this quote from social commentator Stanley Crouch, writing in *Forbes ASAP*. The jazz ensemble is a marvelous model. What makes a jazz group special is its skills at improvisation.

Look at another Crouch phrase: "fearing less and less the imaginative power of the individual." Every concertmaster understands it. So does . . . especially . . . the leader (and there is one!) of the jazz ensemble: Respecting the power/potency of individuality may be challenge No. 1 in the years ahead . . . in this, the Age of Brainware, the Age of Creativity.

6. What does it take to lead an organization of businesspersons?

Coach/Conductor

Can't do the "work."

Script (no variation: Ibsen = Ibsen).

Be All That You Can Be/
Be MORE than you could imagine.

Mozart's 41st: 62,423d time . . .
<u>and</u> new/original/fresh.

(Very) Loose – (Very) Tight

Sports

Symphony

Theater

Surgery

War

Business

Life

"Chaordic" (Dee Hock)

The football coach: Game plan! Precision execution! X's and O's on a black-board. The symphony conductor: A score . . . invariant for 200 years. Precision in execution . . . again.

What can we learn about business from a coach or conductor? First, they can't do the work! One of the biggest problems a "typical supervisor" has is that she or he is ready to jump in (after all, he was the best accountant when he was promoted) with a second's notice, to do the work of an employee, thus gutting, often unintentionally, that employee's sense of own-ership/control. The results are invariably . . . disastrous.

The wonderful news for the football coach: He can't throw the ball as well as his quarterback. Can't block as well as his left tackle. And the con-ductor? Can't play the violin nearly as well as his first violinist. Thus, the coach/conductor has a-b-s-o-l-u-t-e-l-y no alternative but to develop oth-ers. It's develop others . . . or else.

And more. You think of the director or conductor's work as following a script. Ibsen is Ibsen. Mozart is Mozart. And that's true, to a point. You're not allowed to fool around with Ibsen's lines . . . or Mozart's score.

On the other hand, the world of a theater director or football coach or symphony conductor is the classic stage for . . . as they say in the U.S. Army . . . "Be all that you can be." More than that: Be *more* than you could *imagine*. The magic of great coaching (soon-to-be Hall of Fame quarterback Joe Montana and his mentor, San Francisco Hall of Fame coach Bill Walsh) is that Walsh took full advantage of Montana's unique strengths to create something that neither could imagine. True, Walsh has a well-deserved rep-utation as a "quarterback's coach." But he and Montana were always at each other's throats . . . and each made the other one greater than either one alone could have been. That is, the essence of great coaching/playing and directing/acting (Martin Scorsese and Robert De Niro in *Raging Bull*) is . . . ALWAYS . . . stretching beyond what is imaginable. That is . . . it's all about innovation.

Or put another way, the next performance . . . somewhere on earth . . . of Mozart's fabulous 41st ("Jupiter") is probably the 202,423rd performance of that symphony. But what will make it special, in the hands of a modern-day Leonard Bernstein, is that the 202,423rd interpretation is new/original/fresh . . . even though, in one (very) limited sense, it's true to the original score.

Coaching and conducting and direction are about . . . innovating . . . about originality . . . about freshness . . . or, as I like to say, about loose and tight.

Excellence . . . and I'll be the first to acknowledge it . . . really is about loose and tight: The most creative activities (symphony, theater, sports, surgery) *demand* loose and tight. So does war: Go to basic training. Learn to duck at the sound of a shot . . . without holding a committee meeting. Create plans. But the essence of war is . . . chaos. And the essence of success . . . in war/amidst chaos . . . is opportunism and improvisation.

> Coaching and conducting and direction are about . . . innovating . . . about originality . . . about freshness . . . or, as I like to say, about loose and tight.

So, too, with business. A great hotel has a buttoned-down budgetary process. I'm the first to champion it. (Hey, I'm a small businessperson myself!) But an "excellent hotel" is not at all the same as an excellent budget. Excellent hotel = Surprises/Stuns/Amazes/Cheers up you (me!)after a (very) long plane ride.

Visa founder, Dee Hock, talks about systems that combine chaos and order. Within the Visa family, for example, a few basics must be executed with absolute precision. On the other hand, members are free/encouraged to improvise on many marketing dimensions.

Loose. Tight. Combine the two. Chaos and order. "Chaordic," per Dee Hock.

Life. Tight *is* good! (Great.) Loose *is* good! (Great.) The two are complements, not either/or, not enemies.

Azuela-ism, care
pair-ism is
impossible without
abiding respect
for/trust
in the increasingly
dispersed
front-line team.

B-I-G IDEA: Innovation = Michelangelos All.

big idea: TIGHT and LOOSE/LOOSE and TIGHT.

Do you have the nerve?

	Not so sure	Sorta	Absolutely!
1. I believe that "every person can become a BUSINESSPERSON."			
2. Respect for/trust in front-line employees is sky high around here.			
3. I believe in "Michelangelos of HOUSEKEEPING" (etc.).			
4. My employees "believe their day jobs . . . MATTER."			
5. I am an "Architect of the Possibilities of Human Beings."			
6. I help every employee "discover her/his own greatness."			

Do you have the **nerve** (you'd better) to take . . . the LEADER'S ACID TEST?

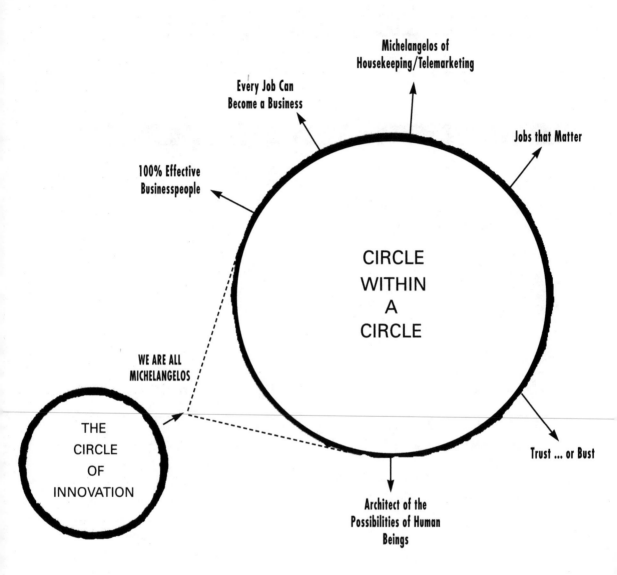

Michelangelos of
Housekeeping/Telemarketing

Every Job Can
Become a Business

Jobs that Matter

100% Effective
Businesspeople

CIRCLE
WITHIN
A
CIRCLE

WE ARE ALL
MICHELANGELOS

THE
CIRCLE
OF
INNOVATION

Trust ... or Bust

Architect of the
Possibilities of Human
Beings

SEMANTICS ALERT No. 4

Every person a businessperson

Every job a business/Business Units of 1

Azuela Inc.

The Great Game of Business

Michelangelos of Telemarketing

A "day job" that MATTERS!

MANIFEST RESPECT FOR THE FOLLOWERS

Trust = Hard

RELENTLESS ARCHITECTS OF THE POSSIBILITIES

OF HUMAN BEINGS

In Chapter 4 the close-up lens is given another twist. The new focus: the "decentralized" individual . . . that is, the/every "jobholder" as full-fledged businessperson.

Welcome to the White-Collar Revolution.

Change lenses. Snap in the 400-mm zoom. ZOOM . . . to you . . . to me . . . to the besieged (at last) WHITE-COLLAR PROFESSIONAL . . . that is, 90 percent of us, even if we do wear (blue) 501s to work. ■ The age of ISBC . . . Indentured Servitude to BigCorp . . . for life . . . is over. Think liberation . . . P-L-E-A-S-E!

Why a white-collar revolution?

The government says 75 percent
of us work in the service sector.
I say the government is <u>**nuts!**</u>

Sure, 75 percent of us work in the officially-labeled service sector, but . . .

Fact is, somewhere in the neighborhood of 90 percent of those who labor in so-called manufacturing actually work in services—that is, white-collar professional jobs such as accounting, human resources, purchasing, logistics, marketing, sales, engineering, information systems, and so on . . . and on.

For the last 20 years (maybe 60 or 70, depending on how you count), we have worried ourselves to a frazzle about blue-collar productivity. Fine. But, truth is, we have largely ignored white-collar productivity. Now, with new technologies in hand and the globe shrinking, our full attention is appropriately aimed at collars colored . . . white. And so it is just that: a white-collar revolution.

"Your four o'clock is here."

Reengineering-pioneer Michael Hammer got it right a few years ago when he said the first several decades of the computer revolution amounted to "paving the cow paths," using new technologies to automate yesterday's outdated methods ("allow us to make yesterday's mistakes faster than ever," according to one information systems/information technology manager). Now, we are beginning to completely reconceive organizations. A Wal-Mart, a Microsoft, a VeriFone simply isn't "shaped" like its organizational predecessors. Entirely new ways of "doing things" are beginning to emerge. And the white-collar job—that is, 90+ percent of all jobs—are squarely in the cross hairs of the emerging economy's sites.

Viva revolution! *(Hint I: You have no choice.) (Hint II: The inevitable white-collar revolution is going to make yesterday's blue-collar revolution look like v-e-r-y small change.)*

B-I-G IDEA: The White-Collar Revolution is Now!
big idea: YOU/ME (FINALLY) ARE DESIGNATED TARGETS OF THE PRODUCTIVITY-IMPROVEMENT CRUSADERS.

Why a white-collar revolution?

Can a fraction be a
metaphor?

This one is:

58.6/60

In 1980 Percy Barnevik left his job as boss of the U.S. arm of the Swedish-toolmaker Sandvik, and went home (or, in typical Swedish fashion, was "called home") to take over the reins at the giant heavy engineering firm, ASEA.

There, he inherited a 2,000-person headquarters. Remember, we're talking about Sweden, a country with labor mobility of about zero. Yet, rapidly, the headquarters was pruned to . . . 200!

In 1987, Barnevik merged ASEA with Switzerland's Brown Boveri to create the world's leading electrical engineering firm. With the merger, Barnevik inherited Brown Boveri's headquarters staff of 4,000 . . . again in a country with very low labor mobility. Six months later, headquarters head count was down to . . . you guessed it . . . 200!

Add the 2,000 at ASEA and the 4,000 at Brown Boveri and you have a combined corporate staff of 6,000. Today, the 200,000-person +, $35 billion in revenue ABB Asea Brown Boveri is run by a headquarters staff of just 140, housed in a nondescript building in Zurich. That is . . . 5,860 of 6,000 senior staff professionals (vice presidents, etc.) went bye-bye . . . or 58.6 out of every 60.

This fraction (58.6/60) is "for real". . . and it's "for real" in countries with traditionally low labor mobility. Barnevik discovered that 58.6 out of every 60 of his "best and brightest" (senior staff professionals) were excess baggage.

His experience sends a B-I-G message.

Viva 58.6/60! *(Hint I: If it hasn't happened to your outfit . . . it will.) (Hint II: And it will . . . with perhaps a 5- to 20-year lag . . . happen in the public sector, too. Call it technological determinism.)*

B-I-G IDEA: The White-Collar Revolution is Now!

big idea: 59 OUT OF 60 OF THE LIKES OF YOU AND ME ARE AT BIG RISK. (OK, 58.6.)

Why a white-collar
revolution?

"If you can't say why you actually make your company a better place,

you're out."

—Cynthia Kellams, businesswoman, consultant, expert on middle management

---

In my seminars I make an outrageous claim: that this brief quote from a former Towers, Perrin consultant is one of the most important sentences in the English language. Outrageous? Yes, it's outrageous . . . but relative to your and my professional careers . . . it really just may be . . . THE MOST IMPORTANT SENTENCE IN THE ENGLISH LANGUAGE.

Look at it this way: If a 20-year-old waiter or waitress shows up for work late six days straight, we fire him or her . . . with justification. (Right?) If a staff purchasing professional, age 49, making $63,800 a year, habitually shows up tardy a day a week, and is half "tuned out" two of the other four days, we say, "Well, that's old Joe." And we give him an 8, instead of a perfect

10, on his annual evaluation. (Right?)

The reason Percy Barnevik was able to cut his corporate staff at ABB from 6,000 to 140, I suspect, is that most of the 5,860 couldn't answer the implied question: HOW HAVE YOU MADE YOUR COM-PANY A BETTER PLACE?

It's the New World Order. And it's affecting all of us . . . waiter . . . house painter . . . staff professional, age 24 . . . staff professional, age 54. All of us . . . EACH AND EVERY DAY . . . have got to deal with Kellams' Dictum (as I call it): "If you can't say why you actually make your company a better place, you're out."

Viva Cynthia Kellams! *(Hint: It can be liberating as hell if your mindset is right . . . read on.)*

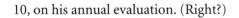

B-I-G IDEA:

The White-Collar Revolution is Now!

big idea: PERFORM/MAKE A MEASURABLE

DIFFERENCE . . . OR . . . SAYONARA.

Why a white-collar revolution? THINK TIME!

Time is (almost) all there is!

"If you're not working on your ideal day, you're working on someone else's."

—Marjorie Blanchard, career consultant

Time is all there is!

True? Of course! Simplistic? Of course! But we S-T-I-L-L F-A-I-L T-O L-I-V-E T-H-E I-M-P-L-I-C-A-T-I-O-N-S.

Not long ago, I was listening to a presentation by premier career consultant Marjorie Blanchard. She was going on and on . . . and on . . . about time management. I've always hated those time management "things"—e.g., elaborate daytimers.

But she got to me. She convinced me that taking a time-management course is probably a good/great idea for most of us (e.g., me). Time is all there is. It's obvious . . .

IT-IS-DEAD-FLAT-INSANELY-OBVIOUS. And yet day after day gets pissed away. A distraction here . . . a distraction there . . . and the frigging day is gone. We end up not working on the "it" that could distinguish our three-year tenure as head of the distribution center . . . or whatever.

Okay, okay . . . what I'm saying is not new. But I think in this era . . . which has all of us increasingly running around like chickens with our heads cut off . . . thinking every day (at the beginning of the day . . . per Marjorie Blanchard) about the time-management issues/OPPORTUNITIES that confront us is a (v-e-r-y) good idea.

Thanks, Marjorie! (And I am gonna try!)

Blanchard also suggests we begin the day by spending a few minutes contemplating what a good day would look like for us—that is, how we would manage to get some things done that moved our critical agenda items along. She calls it "imagining your ideal day."

And then, she adds, take stock in the middle of the day: "If you're not working on your ideal day, you're working on someone else's." It's a (v-e-r-y) powerful/profound notion. It doesn't urge you to . . . ignore the boss. It doesn't urge you to . . . be selfish. She argues that you have legitimate priorities . . . and that those priorities probably make sense. (For you. For your organization.) So get them on the day's agenda.

Don't let the day slip by. (Again.) Don't let distraction after distraction . . . after distraction . . . lead to the end of another day in which important projects don't get attended to. (Again.) Remember: IF YOU'RE NOT WORKING ON Y-O-U-R IDEAL DAY, YOU'RE WORKING ON SOMEONE ELSE'S.

B-I-G IDEA:

The White-Collar Revolution is Now!

big idea: MAKE EVERY DAY COUNT . . . DESPITE

THE BULLSHIT OF EVERYDAY LIFE.

Why a white-collar revolution? THINK CHOICE!

Choice is (almost) all there is!

"We must spread the gospel
that there is no gospel to
spare us the pain of choosing
at every step."

—Benjamin Cardozo,
U.S. Supreme Court Justice, 1920s

"The word upon which all
adventure, all exhilaration,
all meaning, all honor
depends. In the beginning
was the word and the word
was CHOICE."

Tom Robbins,
author, *Still Life with Woodpecker*

In 1900, 50 percent of Americans were self-employed. By 1977, that number had shrivelled to 7 percent. Now it's back up to about 16 percent. I think, in fact, the period from about 1900 to 1975 will soon be seen as an anomaly, a time when large numbers of us worked, more or less for life, for small numbers of big corporations. Truth is, most members of my father's generation, and even my generation, were, in effect, "indentured servants to the 'generals'"—General Electric, General Motors, General Mills, General Dynamics, etc. We let them guide our careers. We gave them our lives!

Justice Cardozo speaks of a United States that Ralph Waldo Emerson understood well, a United States based on the idea of self-reliance. I think that's liberating as hell.

When I look in the mirror, I don't see the "U.S. Navy" or "McKinsey"

Oh, for the days when we could sit on the 42nd floor of the corporate tower, from nine to five, passing memos from the left side of the desk to the right . . .

or "some general." I see, for better or for worse (a little, or a lot, of each), Tom Peters. It's up to me. It's my choices that count in the end. Liberation? That's the ultimate in liberation: to see yourself, and nothing but yourself, in the mirror. Selfish? Of course! But it also means—absent reliance on those big-company payrolls—responsibility and accountability. To get it done. To serve. To create. To grow. Everyday.

I call it the Gardener/Painter Test. If the gardener or house painter screws up today, the customer may not invite him back tomorrow. He's history! And via word of mouth, he's quickly history over a 10-square-mile area. The same has not been true for the white-collar denizens at big company havens. Now it is!

There's another piece to this, too. And the way I put it is rather snide: It's what I call "the false nostalgia for shitty jobs phenomenon." Or: "Oh, for the days when we could sit on the 42d floor of the corporate tower, from nine to five, passing memos from the left side of the desk to the right . . . 40 years running." A life? I think it sucks! I'll take Emerson! I want to see *me* in that mirror!

CHOICE! It is your life! Choice! Choice! You are in charge! No one else is! (No shit.) Choice is Imperative/Axiom/Law No. 1 for the 1990s . . . and for the New Millennium.

> **B-I-G IDEA:**
> **The White-Collar Revolution is Now!**
> **big idea: CHOOSE . . . OR DIE (PROFESSIONALLY).**

Why a white-collar revolution? THINK POWER!

Power is (almost) all there is!

Powerlessness is a state of mind.

If you think you are powerless,

<u>you are</u>.

"The thing women have got to
learn is that nobody gives you
power. You just take it."
—Roseanne Barr,
author, actress, comedian, producer, philosopher

I worked with AT&T in the early 1980s, just before its (first) breakup. Its middle managers let me have it. "Most of the people you quote," one said, "are like Sam Walton of Wal-Mart and Jack Welch of General Electric. They run the show! What if you're stuck in the middle?"

I had to admit it was a damn good question. And it's a question, given what I do for a living, that I have revisited virtually every day since. Truth is, I don't really have a great answer, although I think I do have a good answer.

In short: Powerlessness is a state of mind. Age 18 or 68, if you think you're powerless . . . you are.

Helpful? It's no "12 steps to salvation," but the statement does have one attribute: It's bone honest!

When my AT&T friends, stuck in the middle of a dozen or more layers of organization, started beating on me, I thought back to a parallel situation. After a two-year stint in Vietnam in 1966 and 1967, I was "promoted" to the real war zone . . . the Pentagon. I worked for a lieutenant commander, Joe Key. (Lieutenant commanders, for those who don't know the Navy system, are junior-plus middle managers. Put another way, to declare that lieutenant commanders come a dime-a-dozen in the Pentagon is to grotesquely overvalue lieutenant commanders.)

My boss . . . "powerless" Joe Key . . . got things done. Got them done creatively. Got them done fast. More creatively, and often two or three times faster than people who had—literally—twice his seniority.

How?

At the time (I was age 25), management theory wasn't one of my top 10 (hell, top 50) priorities. I was fascinated by Joe's effectiveness, but didn't analyze it in detail until 15 years later . . . when the gang from AT&T got on my case.

The only conclusion I can come to is this: It never even occurred, almost literally, to Joe Key that he was a mere lieutenant commander! In his mind, he was on a mission, and nothing would get in the way of that mission. He was an admiral . . . who just hadn't bothered to sew the fat gold stripes onto his sleeves. If Joe needed an answer to a question that only "the admiral" had . . . he walked into the admiral's office . . . and asked. And invariably got a reply. In the two years I carried Joe's bags, I was stunned at how much support (fiscal and moral) he got for the units (Navy Seabees) he represented. His two secrets:

■ **Networking.** "Networking" has become a staple of the businessperson's language. Overused, in fact. But long before networking was even in the management/business lingo, Joe was the consummate networker. It seemed as though he had taken every admiral's aide in the building, for example, out to lunch in the last six months. In short, he had that 23,000-employee, five-sided gray monster on the Potomac wired for action.

■ **State of mind.** Powerless? Don't make me laugh! Joe had enormous power . . . because he couldn't find any reason why he shouldn't. I do, honestly, think it's just about that simple . . . and complex.

Subsequently, as I've thought more about it, and observed more, I have noticed that what I call a JKA/Joe Key Attitude is present in a handful of 15-year-olds, absent in most; present in a handful of 42-year-olds, absent in most; and present in a handful of 56-year-olds . . . and, unfortunately, absent in most.

One last point I'd like to make on the subject of power: Those who succeed . . . male or female . . . are usually those who "go for it," who grab it even when it's inappropriate (grab it especially when it's inappropriate).

I know women are more relationship oriented than men. They try not to upset a single applecart. That's all well and good. (Mostly good.)

On the other hand, it does hurt on the dimension Roseanne Barr points to: Women . . . more than men . . . "have got to learn . . . that nobody gives you power . . . you just take it."   AMEN!!

Why a white-collar revolution? THINK AUTHORITY

Authority is (almost) all there is!

Authority is a state of mind.

How much formal authority did Mohandas Gandhi have?

My most profound "authority" epiphany (and I think it does deserve that rather pretentious word) occurred, embarrassingly, at the ripe old age of 52. While reading a book by John F. Kennedy School of Government professor Ronald Heifitz, *Leadership Without Easy Answers,* I came across a novel—to me—chapter title: "Leading Without Authority." His examples got me thinking. Got me thinking . . . in retrospect . . . about the obvious.

Consider: In 1935, how much formal authority did Mohandas Gandhi have? (That's right, the fellow who created the largest democracy in the world.) In 1959, how much formal authority did Dr. Martin Luther King, Jr. have? And in 1985, how much authority was vested in Vaclav Havel . . . who led the liberation, just a handful of years later, of Czechoslovakia? And as late as 1988, say, how much formal authority did the man we now call P-r-e-s-i-d-e-n-t Nelson Mandela have?

In all four cases, the answer is . . . none . . . or damn little. In fact, about all these four supermen had in common was jail time. (No surprise: People who piss off the establishment tend to get relegated to corporate Siberia, if not the real thing.)

Let me put it another way: MANY/MOST GENUINELY SIGNIFICANT ACCOMPLISHMENTS—SUCH AS THE CIVIL RIGHTS MOVEMENT—THAT HAVE HAPPENED IN THIS CENTURY HAVE BEEN SPARKED BY PEOPLE WITH LITTLE/NO FORMAL "ORG-CHART" AUTHORITY.

When I'm in Atlanta, and I'm heading out to the airport, I usually ask the cab driver to stop by tiny, nondescript Ebenezer Baptist Church. It's my way of showing respect for Dr. King . . . and also for this idea. From that modest beginning, where King's only followers were his father's parishioners, came what may be the single greatest accomplishment in this country in the past 50 years: the Civil Rights movement.

You may argue that your mission—and mine—isn't as profound as Dr. King's or President Mandela's. I buy that, obviously. But thinking about what those people accomplished does suggest that calling-card/job-title authority isn't all there is! King, Mandela, Havel, Gandhi: Each had a mission, a vision, extraordinary integrity, persistence. Very tough hides. And absent those fancy calling-cards (in all four cases) came profound, global change . . . which has made our world a better place.

In other words: . . . don't tell me: "I can't do it, I'm stuck in the middle." (And believe it or not, I've actually had vice presidents of sizable corporations tell me precisely that.) Nonsense! I.E., BULLSHIT! Your lack of authority is in your head! (DAMN IT!)

B-I-G IDEA:
The White-Collar Revolution is Now!
big idea: POWER = MINDSET.
POWER (LACK THEREOF) = MINDSET.

Why a white-collar revolution? THINK RESPONSIBILITY

Responsibility is (almost) all there is!

Down with Dilbert!

"If I don't do something, nothing is going to get better."
—Nathaniel Branden,
author and psychologist, *Taking Responsibility: Self-Reliance and the Accountable Life*

"If we embrace self-responsibility not merely as a personal preference but as a philosophical principle, logically we commit ourselves to a profoundly important moral idea."

—Nathaniel Branden,
author, *Taking Responsibility: Self-Reliance and the Accountable Life*

Taking responsibility, not giving in wholesale to cynicism in even the (apparently) crappiest of settings, is about something more than you and me. Branden says it. I believe it: It is a moral issue. It is about society/community/family. It is a philosophical issue: To give in to "the jerks" is . . . literally . . . to deny one's own will . . . TO DENY THE ESSENCE OF WHAT IT MEANS TO BE A HUMAN BEING.

To read *Dilbert* and laugh . . . that's okay. (I do.) But deny what makes us human . . . that is a moral outrage!

Whether your boss is a jerk, whether your company is populated with a bunch of idiots . . . it is your career. You are the one who has to look in the mirror at age 60—if you're lucky enough to make it that far—and ask yourself what you have contributed to peers, community, the welfare of the world. We particularly do so in our choice of a job. (Hey . . . it's where we spend most of our waking hours.) The issue is ... then ... shall we invest in that job? It is a huge question. Very near the central meaning of human-ness.

I'm not urging you to hang in there in hopeless situations. Taking Branden's/my advice may well mean job shifts, company shifts ... with some regularity. A job-for-life is no longer the norm. Yes, company loyalty to employees isn't what it used to be. On the other hand, I'm not all that sure that what it used to be was all that great: It was mostly a matter, as I've said, of indentured servitude on our part ... in return for loyalty on their part. Too many big company people ... even today ... act as if they are ter-rified to change jobs.

That's no way to live.   And you are in charge!

B-I-G IDEA:

The White-Collar Revolution is Now!

big idea: TAKE YOUR LIFE BACK FROM "THEM."

Why a white-collar revolution?
THINK SELF-MOTIVATION!

Self-motivation is (almost)

all there is!

Driver: "So why are you doing this, anyway?"
Me: "Because I said I would."
Driver: "Who did you say it to?"
Me: "Myself."

—Ffyona Campbell,
author, *On Foot through Africa*

Between April 2, 1991, and September 1, 1993, Ffyona Campbell *(pictured left)* walked every step—16,088 kilometers—from Cape Town to Tangier. Traveling (walking) through jungles, deserts, and a 400-mile-wide mine field, she earned the label "the greatest walker of them all" from legendary polar traveler, Sir Ranulph Fiennes.

Why did Campbell do it? Why does anyone do "it"? To please the boss? To get a raise? To get a promotion? No! Or at least "no" is what the best of the best would say. The best elementary school teachers. The best violinists. And . . . the greatest walker of them all.

The only motivation that's really worth talking about is SELF-MOTIVATION. Quit bitching about your life. Listen to Roseanne! Listen to Ffyona Campbell! Take your life back from . . .
THE GENERALS.

Why a white-collar revolution? THINK... NEW AMERICAN PROFESSIONAL

The New American Professional is (almost) all there is!

THE NEW AMERICAN PROFESSIONAL:

1. Distinctive (towering) competence

2. Projects-is-life

3. Client-service obsessed (measurable)

4. Networker extraordinaire!

5. Emersonian/Me, Inc./ Be Your Own Rock/ NO (frigging) GENERALS!

I call her/him the New American Professional. NAP. The "forgotten 90 percent" . . . those who work in Information Systems, Human Resources, Purchasing, Finance, Marketing . . . the white-collar professionals (post-reengineering) whose creativity/organization effectiveness is barely mentioned on the pages of business/management textbooks.

So who is this Renaissance Woman (Man)?

- First, she/he is good (very good!) at . . . SOMETHING. That is, there is no excuse for anyone not being renowned (at least at a local/regional level) for something. Back in my days as consultant at McKinsey & Co., there was an insistent demand for good project work . . . and a long-term demand that one achieve "towering competence" . . . at something or other. Made sense/makes sense to me. (The competition is ever so much hotter these days . . . and that's an understatement!)

- Next: Projects-is-life. The project, the nugget, the atom-of-life . . . something with a beginning, an end, a signature . . . and an implemented outcome. That's what life is. In any job! (And if it ain't that way . . . change it . . . NOW.)

- The NAP (New American Professional . . . remember) is client-service obsessed. And "obsessed" further means that she/he isn't content until the delighted client has seen measurable results.

- Next up . . . the NAP is a networker extraordinaire. She/he is constantly working to expand and maintain her/his Rolodex network . . . particularly via contacts from outside (far outside) the "parent" organization.

- Finally, the NAP takes her/his life back from it/"them" . . . and returns to the basic U.S. value . . . ignored for the last 70 years during the reign of BBE (Big Bureaucratic Enterprise). That is . . . SELF-RELIANCE. I also call the approach Me, Inc. You're Chairperson/CEO/Entrepreneur-in-Chief of your own professional service firm, even if you inadvertently happen to be on somebody's payroll . . . at the moment. Selfish . . . what else are you going to be in the face of the "downsizing"/"reengineering"? And selfless . . . Me, Inc. is only a successful "company" if customers are served . . . VERY WELL . . . and . . . VERY IMAGINATIVELY . . . and . . . VERY MEMORABLY.

Prudential is running a series of ads with the lovely tag line . . . "Be your own rock." I LOVE IT. (Dreyfus' "Rule Your Kingdom" gets high marks, too.) Or the way I most prefer to put it . . . NO GENERALS! That is, stamp out indentured servitude to (General) Mills, (General) Motors, (General) Electric, (General) Dynamics.

Remember or perish . . . NO GENERALS.   BE YOUR OWN ROCK. SELF-RELIANCE. ME, INC. All hail the liberated New American Professional!

This is strong language. From someone who knows. LISTEN UP! P-L-E-A-S-E!

B-I-G IDEA:

The White-Collar Revolution is Now!

big idea: BE YOUR OWN ROCK . . .

RULE YOUR KINGDOM.

Why a white-collar revolution? THINK RÉSUMÉ!

Résumés are (almost) all there is.

My former employer, management consultants McKinsey & Co., are damned good at what they do (and have been for more than 50 years). But they are also typical of professional service firms. So . . .consider a typical third-year McKinsey consultant . . . call her Jane Dokes. She's no bionic woman, but she is good enough to hold onto her job.

It's December 31, 1997. Ms. Dokes is reviewing what she has been up to for the past 12 months. Namely . . .

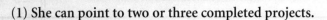

(1) She can point to two or three completed projects.

(2) She can enumerate, qualitatively and possibly quantitatively, the benefits delivered to her clients in each of those projects.

(3) She can provide references—names, addresses, e-mail addresses, phone numbers, fax numbers—of living human beings . . . called clients . . . who will testify to the fact that she was alive . . . and doing good work . . . during the past year.

(4) She can explain (precisely) what she has learned that's new and how it makes her more valuable on the labor market for her skill-set.

(5) She can point to a measurably fatter paper/electronic Rolodex, in which the preponderance of the new entries will come from outside her firm rather than in. And . . .

(6) Should she so wish, for whatever reason, at year's end she can work up a résumé/curriculum vitae that is noticeably/discernibly/distinctly different than her résumé/curriculum vitae would have been on December 31 of the previous year.

Your/my ultimate question: Can you/I/we pass the McKRT . . . or McKinsey Résumé Test? It is one of the toughest queries that you must answer. The upshot of this: THINK RÉSUMÉ. OBSESS RÉSUMÉ.

 B-I-G IDEA: The White-Collar Revolution is Now!
big idea: YOU = YOUR (IMPROVING) RÉSUMÉ.

Why a white-collar revolution? THINK BRAGGABLES!

Y.O.U.

"I drag my myth around with me."
—Orson Welles

Suppose Nike boots out its ad agency. Suddenly, dozens of "creatives" from its former agency hit the pavement—on Madison Avenue in Manhattan, or wherever. Picture them in your mind: carrying those oversized, leather-encased portfolios . . . that enclose the storyboards from their previous ad campaigns. Those story boards—in a tangible (and ultimate) way—are themselves! Those are their projects.

Those are their braggables. I LOVE THAT IMAGE.

So . . . what are your braggables for the last 12 months? (Six months? Three months?) Are you working assiduously . . . RIGHT NOW . . . on a potential "braggable"? If not . . . get a life . . . reformulate the project . . . or find something else to do. Braggables . . . that's the (only) deal.

> **B-I-G IDEA:**
> **The White-Collar Revolution is Now!**
> **big idea:** IF YOUR CURRENT "IT" ISN'T POTENTIALLY
> MEMORABLE . . . DROP IT/FIX (REFORMULATE) IT . . . NOW.

Why a white-collar revolution? THINK BRAND!

Brand is (almost) all there is!

Brand! Or: Brand! Brand! Brand!

Sure it has to do with Procter & Gamble. Nike. Coke. Ford. Intel. But it also has to do . . . IF YOU ARE WISE . . . with you.

The downsizers haven't quit. They're still climbing over the side. Your odds of surviving and making your career at one company are low.

How do you stand out from a crowd? You stand out by working on . . . BRAND EQUITY . . . an explicit focus on development of YOUR brand equity.

Dennis Rodman understands! Martha Stewart understands! Management-guru Michael Hammer understands! Mega-media mogul Oprah Winfrey understands! Golf legend Jack Nicklaus understands!

Rick Kaminski understands!

Rick spends 25 percent of his time signing autographs. How about you?

Kaminski is known as "the Peanut Man," according to *The Seattle Post-Intelligencer.* He plies his trade—with matchless skill and pizzaz—in the stands at Seattle Mariners' home games.

Peanut-vendor Kaminski warms up with stretching exercises and practice tosses of 30 bags of peanuts. (A Mariners scout has clocked his accurate throws at 72 mph.) The job is no cakewalk. Kaminski told the paper it takes a good working knowledge of physics: "You have competing visual angles. You have the horizontal curvature of the dome, and the vertical concaves of the roof and the slanting stands."

Rick Kaminski could obviously teach the course: Call it Advanced Personal Brand Building.

Rick = Brand. (Do you?)

Why a white-collar revolution? THINK Y-O-U!

You are (almost) all there is!

YOUR PBE (PERSONAL BRAND EQUITY TEST)

1. I am known for (2-4 items); by next year at this time, I plan also to be known for (1-2 items).

---

2. My current project is provocative and challenging to me in the following (1-3 ways).

---

3. New learnings in the last 90 days include (1-3 items).

---

4. My public (local/regional/national/global) "visibility program" consists of (2-4 items).

---

5. Important new additions to my Rolodex in the last 90 days are (2-5 names).

---

6. Important relationships nurtured in the last 90 days include (1-3 names).

---

7. My principal "résumé enhancement activity" for the next 60-90 days is (1 item).

---

8. My résumé is specifically different than last year's at this time in the following (1-3 ways).

Think of yourself as a brand. You are! The 19-year-old waiter or waitress at McDonald's is. (Just like the Peanut Man.) And so, too, is the 38-year-old professional in purchasing at Rubbermaid.

Think brand! Think PBE . . . Personal Brand Equity! WORK ON IT! The list above may halp you begin to think about your own brand equity. I call it: THE PERSONAL BRAND EQUITY TEST.

Or: The creation—and maintenance—of a BRAND CALLED YOU . . .
Or: Brand U.

Or: The founding of Me, Inc. . . . a one-person professional service firm . . . aimed at standing (way) out in a (big) crowd.

Hint: As for Nike or Levi's, Brand U's brand equity is always . . . going up . . . or going down . . . in a crowded, competitive market. It is never, ever stable.

The words and phrases above are self-evident. TAKE THIS SERIOUS-LY . . . IT'S ABOUT YOUR PROFESSIONAL LIFE OR DEATH. You ("new security") = Personal Brand Equity.

One final note: I introduced this idea in the middle of 1996. To my surprise, it became—overnight—my most requested slide. To my even greater surprise, it was as much a "best-seller" in Malaysia and Australia . . . and among senior British Civil Service execs . . . as in the United States.

"Life is either a daring adventure, or nothing."

—Helen Keller

Why a white-collar revolution? THINK Y-O-U!

"There is a vitality, a life force, a quickening that is translated through you into action, and because there is only one of you in all time, this expression is unique. And if you block it, it will never exist through any medium and be lost. It is not your business to determine how good it is nor how it compares with other expressions. It is your business to keep it yours, clearly and directly."

—Martha Graham

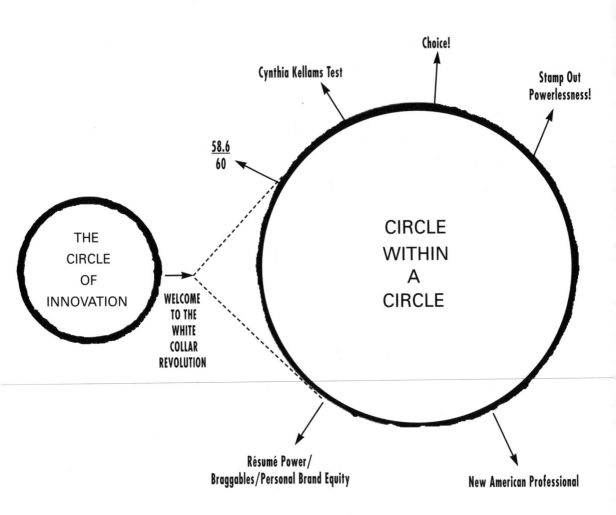

THE CIRCLE OF INNOVATION

WELCOME TO THE WHITE COLLAR REVOLUTION

$\frac{58.6}{60}$

Cynthia Kellams Test

Choice!

Stamp Out Powerlessness!

CIRCLE WITHIN A CIRCLE

Résumé Power/ Braggables/Personal Brand Equity

New American Professional

SEMANTICS ALERT No. 5

58.6/60

White Collar Revolution

Cynthia Kellams Test

The Gospel of Choice

Powerlessness is a State of Mind

Leading Without Authority

Be Your Own Rock

Me, Inc.

NAP (New American Professional)

McKinsey Résumé Test

Braggables

Personal Brand Equity Test

The focus on innovation = "decentralized"/"businessed" individual in general is turned now to the productivity target-of-choice: the white-collar staff professional. The question we try to answer: How do we transform him/her from "bureaucrat"/"corporate impedance" to "talent"/prime source of intellectual value added?

All Value Comes from the Professional Services.

Jog down to your local bookstore.

Check the business shelves.

Bet 1: 10 or more books on creating the self-managing *factory* work team.

Bet 2: *No* books on creating

the GREAT Purchasing Department . . .

the GREAT Finance Department . . .

the GREAT Engineering Department.

Why? Beats me. But let's fix the problem . . . .

A show of hands, please.

We're all in the professional service business ... Right!?

To my surprise, seminar audiences from Little Rock to Lisbon, Toledo to Taipei, always give me a strong, unflinching "yes" to this question. Why? Most of the departments they work for are de facto professional service firms ... that just don't happen to be listed in the Yellow Pages. The purchasing department is a professional service firm. So, too, the marketing department. And the finance department. And the human resources department. And the logistics unit. Etc.

Formal professional service firm people are hell-bent on improvement ... and revolution ... just like everybody else. Nonetheless, the average staff department can learn a lot (a helluva lot) from the average professional service firm.

Professional service delivery is pure, raw brainwork. The assets of professional service firms aren't "hard." (They rarely own the buildings they occupy ... or their computers ... or even the plants in the entry way.) It all boils down to the expertise of its people, masses of them, booking, in some cases, BILLIONS OF DOLLARS in revenues.

My goal is to help you learn from the best of the best: real, top-flight professional service firms (KPMG, Deloitte & Touche, IDEO, Andersen Consulting, McKinsey). And my suggestion is that you seriously consider ... NOW ... transforming your department, your unit into a professional service firm.

Must we be "bureaucratic drag"?

"All growth will come from intellectually based services."
—James Brian Quinn

"All value chain elements are . . . SERVICES."
—James Brian Quinn

"All services can be OUTSOURCED."
—James Brian Quinn

"We give up competitiveness to the extent that ANY service task is not equal to Best-in-World standard."
—James Brian Quinn

The dust has settled on your major, two-year reengineering project. And? If you survived . . . you still work in something called . . . human resources . . . or purchasing . . . or finance . . . or information systems. Right?

Since time immemorial such "staff departments" have been considered bureaucratic drag. Or . . . overhead. Or . . . action-impedance units. No more. Or, rather: It won't do.

The/we nerds have won (Chapter 1).

WHAT IF . . .

What if "those" staff activities—purchasing, finance, etc.—could become the primary sources of value added? What if? Instead I claim: What's the alternative?

James Brian Quinn, Buchanan Professor Emeritus of Management at Dartmouth's Amos Tuck School of Business, wrote the bible on knowledge-based enterprise . . . *Intelligent Enterprise.* All (A-L-L) growth and all (A-L-L) value, he asserts, will emanate from the services . . . e.g., redux: purchasing, information systems, finance.

Moreover, Quinn adds, any company concedes competitiveness if any service activity in its value chain (again, purchasing, HR, logistics, etc.) is less than the best-in-the-world.

The nerds have won. But so far it's mostly been a hollow victory. The object of this chapter: Getting on with the services' value-added revolution.

This chapter is divided into two parts—a kit for converting your department/unit into a professional service firm and a kit for creating and managing projects.

 B-I-G IDEA: Professional Services, Inc. big idea: GETTING (WAY) BEYOND STAFF-DEPART-MENT-AS-BUREAUCRATIC DRAG.

PSF 1.0/CONVERSION KIT

Turn your Department into a Professional Service Firm

PSF 1.0

or

Professional Service Firm
Conversion Kit/
Release 1.0

What follows is a kit. I call it PSF 1.0. Since I introduced the idea a year ago, hundreds of people have requested my PSF 1.0 material . . . and dozens have reported putting it into practice. The ideas are taken from my 23-year career in professional services (McKinsey & Co., The Tom Peters Group) and from hundreds of discussions with professional service denizens.

So here goes:

1. T-h-i-n-k Inc. You're no longer manager of purchasing. You're de facto/de jure transformed into Managing Partner of Purchasing, Inc., a full-fledged professional service firm.

Not so fast/not that easy, you reply. Well . . . I disagree. Maybe you can't incorporate today . . . or tomorrow. But you know (who doesn't in your shoes?) that the powers that be are considering outsourcing . . . training, information systems, whatever. So gather your gang and at least begin the psychological process of creating a for-profit "firm" as a substitute for your department. WHAT'S STOPPING YOU?

2. T-h-i-n-k client! Professional service firms live and breathe for their clients. Case in (personal) point: I reported to work at McKinsey in early December 1974. Two hours after showing up I was on a client-service team. I remained on such teams continuously until two hours before I left for good in 1981.

Life = Client Service. Period.

Problem is, the denizens of the average purchasing (finance, human resources . . . you fill in the blank) department rarely view the people they serve as clients. Fact is, I'll bet you the price of this book that if I spent three hours interviewing people in your "department" . . . I'd not hear the term client once. (P.S. I've tried this on several occasions. My wallet is still untouched.)

3. **Visit every client** (i.e., department, division, and so on). Start a dialogue. Review past work. Examine results. Did you do exciting/memorable work? Did your work have a lasting impact? Was your work p-r-o-f-e-s-s-i-o-n-a-l?

Years ago, my *In Search of Excellence* co-author Bob Waterman began his tenure as managing director of McKinsey's Australian offices by calling on past clients. In several instances, he unearthed slipshod work. His immediate response: Do the work over . . . gratis. What an impact that had on everyone.

4. **Turn every job into a project.** Life in a professional service firm is about the development and execution of projects.

Projects!

Projects!!

Projects!!!

ALL work can be converted to project work. No task is so rote, so mundane that it can't be turned into a project . . . WITH SIGNIFICANT VALUE-ADDED POTENTIAL. If you think otherwise . . . you've got a (big)

problem. One hundred percent of everyone's time should be taken up by . . . P-R-O-J-E-C-T-S. For example: A pal of mine at McKinsey converted a silly little clean-up-the-library task into a strategic project to assess knowledge-development practices throughout the $2-billion firm. "All" it takes is (lots of) imagination!

5. **Put together a Current Projects List . . . or CPL.** Post it prominently. Carry it with you. Obsess about it. Your Current Projects List = You. It is the department-turned-professional-service-firm. Keep your unit's project list on your computer . . . in the upper left-hand drawer of your desk . . . in your briefcase . . . in your pocket . . . under your pillow . . . or at least on your bedside table. Pull it out . . . and talk it up . . . at every opportunity.

Remember my BIG semantics crusade: I am trying to screw around with your head. I am trying to turn you into a . . . **Raving Project Fanatic. Period. Project = Stuff Done = Client Work = Résumé enhancers = Most (or A-L-L) economic value added in the modern/emerging economy.**

6. **Conduct a weekly Current Projects Review.** Post everyone's coming milestones prominently (and electronically). Make everyone conscious of milestone-progress/project-outcomes. Make the completion of milestones, no matter how small, an event to celebrate. Ring a bell. Bring in cupcakes or pizza. Leave a card on the desks of those who got the task done (on time).

7. **Score, quantitatively, every project on excitement . . . urgency . . . and transformation potential.** Work hand-in-glove with your clients to up the excitement score, the urgency score, and the project's transformation-potential score. Never allow project work to become rote work. I was blessed early in my McKinsey sojourn with a senior partner, Allen Puckett, who had the ability to turn the silliest damned task into a Harrison Ford-like quest for the Holy Grail. He kept his young consultants perpetually turned on . . . and always delivered unique value to even his most humdrum clients.

8. **Think portfolio quality.** The professional service firm is its project "portfolio." So am I! So are you! Right now I'm working on print and Web versions of this book, my memoir, a speech I'm giving on Monday. (i.e., day after tomorrow). These are my projects du jour/de l'année. They are me. How many are special? How many are pushing me to the limit? How many are taking me in new directions? How many will make a big difference to my clients? How many are gutsy? How many are boring? The answers to these questions constitute my business strategy. I.e., think project portfolio. Project portfolio quality = Life.

9. **Do whatever it takes.** Projects are about outcomes . . . about getting things done. The project team is the heart and soul of the professional service organization. And: Trust me . . . a lifelong professional service denizen . . . it is everyone's sacred duty to help out a project team that's in a crunch. P-E-R-I-O-D.

I call this a "rush-to-the-scene-of-the-crime" culture. Gary Withers, chief of the brilliant marketing services firm Imagination, has made this a mainstay of his organization. He encourages—no, demands—individualism and entrepreneurship. Yet no one I've met is as zealous about nurturing a rush-to-the-scene-of-the-crime culture.

Nobody—starting with Withers—is "too senior" to run the copy machine or get coffee (2:00 a.m.) when a project team needs help. And if the team screwed up big-time? Doesn't matter! Who doesn't screw up regularly? I repeat: IT'S YOUR SACRED DUTY TO HELP OTHER TEAMS IN A CRUNCH NO MATTER HOW DAMN BUSY YOU ARE.

10. **Transfer your skills to clients.** Excellence in professional service delivery is about leaving a legacy. Surely you've heard the old adage: Give a person a fish, and you feed him for a day. Teach a person to fish, and you feed him for a lifetime. That holds in spades for professional services.

I once made the mistake of saying that client service was the sine qua non of professional services . . . with one exception . . . the internal audit department. An IBM auditor came up to me afterwards: "Nice talk, Tom. But you revealed your ignorance about auditing. Our object is not to 'catch people.' It is to teach them a lasting reverence for orderly books and records."

Amen! Professional Service Excellence = Teaching/Transferring Excellence.

11. **Include the client on every project team.** McKinsey has just learned it (though we experimented with it in my time). If knowledge transfer is the professional service giver's greatest legacy . . . well . . . you need . . . transferees. In fact, my old pal Bob Waterman, post-McKinsey, has made this the signature of Waterman & Associates . . . working cheek-by-jowl with clients . . . every step of the way . . . to teach/model an approach to problem solving . . . as much as to provide THE SOLUTION.

12. **Insist that clients evaluate "your" people and "their" people on each project.** What gets evaluated gets done! Take a page from Deloitte & Touche's book. Evaluate managers (de facto professional service firm partners) on their ability to create exciting/urgent/transformative projects, manage client relationships, and generate measurable implementation effectiveness. Emphasize client satisfaction in performance evaluation immediately after . . . and long (L-O-N-G = Years!) after . . . a project is over.

13. **Bring in outsiders.** Everyone on a professional service team ought to be developing at least a substantial local/regional reputation. That is, aim to be the best there is. On the other hand . . . it's insane to believe there aren't fabulous folks outside the team. To a large extent, the great professional service firm is as great as its network of outsiders (other consulting organizations, academics, or sterling individuals with world-class reputations). Those "world's best" outsiders should regularly/routinely be involved with many (maybe all) projects. My best pals at McKinsey were marked by one trait: an amazing set of contacts in global academia. (Very) smart though they all were, they were never too proud to shamelessly seek best-in-galaxy advice.

14. **T-h-i-n-k marketing.** Partners in professional service firms are marketers. Marketing = Project Development. Marketing = Relationship Management. Marketing = The guts to go for other than the easy solution. Marketing = Reputation Development. Begin . . . in your staff department . . . to . . . T-H-I-N-K M-A-R-K-E-T-I-N-G.

15. T-h-i-n-k **research and development.** It's everyone's province. (DAMN IT!) Many of the ideas that are transforming business today come from unlikely places . . . logistics and distribution (talk about revolution!) . . . finance (i.e., the value of intangible assets) . . . human resources. IT'S OBVIOUS . . . to me . . . that research and development is at least as important in distribution and logistics as it is in the laboratory!!

Test: If the HR/IS/Purchasing/Finance boss can't describe . . . in great detail . . . the bold R&D program going on in his or her department . . . THEN SHE/HE SHOULD BE REMOVED FROM HER/HIS POSITION . . . TODAY. (Am I making myself clear?)

16. **Turn your CPL/Current Projects List into a research-and-development test ground.** Create projects that allow you to conduct effective research and development as you work on them. I admit it: I learned computer simulation modeling at Getty Oil's expense. It was a strategy project on oil exploration. (McKinsey redux.) And that pal of mine—Allen Puckett—was determined to push the state of the art in simulation modeling for the world's oil fields. If we "lost," we'd cost the client a few thousand bucks; if we "won," we could add hundreds of millions to the bottom line . . . literally.

17. **Devote a large share of gross revenues to knowledge development.** Arthur Andersen has poured mega-bucks into an ongoing advertising campaign that features, as giant Andersen's No. 1 Competitive Advantage . . . GBP. That is, Global Best Practices . . . the output of Andersen's extraordinary, systematized knowledge accumulation process.

18. **Establish clear, tough incentives for contributing and sharing knowledge . . . even if it distracts from today's project.** Bottom line: "Community stuff" (sharing) is as important as "project stuff" . . . and that should be unmistakably reinforced in the evaluation process. Starting time: NOW. No ifs, ands, or buts.

Hey . . . it's the life I lived at McKinsey for 7+ years. Your project stressed you to the breaking point . . . and beyond. Yet the ethos was clear: Drop whatever you are doing . . . to share unstintingly with others. And if you don't/didn't, the bogeyman (annual evaluator) is gonna get you!

19. Train! Train! Train! Projects-is-us . . . so PROJECT-TRAINING-IS-US. Aim much/most of your training efforts specifically at project management and project membership. Between construction companies, ad agencies, and Big Six accountancies (among others), there's a lot of knowledge "out there" about project creation/project management/project membership. Projects are art. (Everything important is.) Still, there are a hundred tricks-of-the-ancient-trade worth learning. Why is it, then, that I find project training AWOL in most training-department curricula?

20. Train in project creation. The idea is to train everyone to turn the most mundane "assignment" into a transformational project. All the best consultants I know are . . . truly . . . artists at this. (And not just for the bucks . . . they get bored stiff if they're not doing something "neat.") Gary Withers (remember . . . Imagination) is the best of the best: He can convert the most mundane "marketing assignment" into an excuse for reinventing the world (of, say, retailing).

21. Train in problem solving. The consultants Kepner-Tregoe have made a fortune teaching . . . THE BASICS OF PROBLEM ANALYSIS . . . to the likes of Hewlett-Packard, Chrysler, Johnson & Johnson, Honda (U.S. and Japan), and Harley-Davidson. (Not bad.) Andersen, McKinsey, Boston Consulting Group (BCG) et al. pride themselves on their approach to sizing up hopelessly complex problems and piercing the fog . . . quickly . . . to say something of (great) value. So? My experience (clearly) suggests that such patentable approaches to situation analysis are utterly foreign to the average "department." Which is to say . . . OPPORTUNITY LURKS . . . via development of a distinctive approach to scoping ambiguous situations.

22. **Train in implementation.** Getting consultants squarely focused on implementation is a monumental and critical task, a top-of-the-agenda task . . . FOREVER. Deloitte & Touche consultants have created a valuable core competence out of being . . . BORING. That is, the firm prides itself on not being as "sexy" as McKinsey or BCG . . . but on sticking around until the dirty work (a.k.a. implementation of the brilliant-on-paper solution) is done.

23. **Train in client relations and client development.** Remember: Client relations/client development *is* professional service marketing . . . but it's not smarmy. That is, à la McKinsey or Chiat/Day, you can't deliver real client impact until you've been around awhile. So focusing on joint (you and client) problem analysis and joint implementation as a key skill/core competence is (VERY) legit.

24. **Train in "Rolodexing."** Make no mistake about it! A good consultant is only as good as the quality and quantity of his/her Rolodex. How about an ongoing course/seminar titled "Rolodex Development"? *Hint: I'm serious!*

25. **Challenge! Challenge! Challenge!** Professional service firms are like the National Basketball Association in at least one (big) respect: They are their talent. People are everything. Nothing else matters.

Sure . . . I know that everybody says that. But look at recruiting (of front-line consultants) at McKinsey: The v-e-r-y senior members of the firm literally devote weeks each year to it. Like the general managers of pro-sports franchises, McKinsey et al. understand that . . . ho hum (!) . . . what they will be five years from now is today's new talent.

26. **Rigorously evaluate "talent" after every project.** Up or out: Either survive and thrive . . . or . . . away you go!

Oy vey! It's t-o-u-g-h out there. "Up or out" has long been standard fare at many professional service firms . . . including almost all law firms. Tough? Yes. Fair? I guess I'm inclined to say . . . more or less . . . yes. OK . . . Y-E-S. House cleaners gotta do it! House painters gotta do it! House builders gotta do it! Why not professional staffers? You're only as good (or as bad) as your last gig. Meryl Streep knows. Harrison Ford knows. Jessica Lange knows. And you must, too.

27. **Be G-R-E-A-T!** As I see it, everyone who works in a professional service firm should cultivate at least a local/regional reputation (best project-management trainer in the Northeast!) . . . and quite possibly a national/global reputation. One big reason: We can no longer afford to keep hangers-on on the payroll. If you aren't determined—UTTERLY DETERMINED—to stand out, you're history. Remember Cynthia Kellams: IF YOU CAN'T SAY (PRECISELY—my addition) HOW YOU MAKE YOUR COMPANY A BETTER PLACE . . . YOU'RE OUT. Remember: 58.6/60.

28. **Think WOW!** There is (absolutely, positively) no reason why professional service firms should not . . . as a matter of course . . . be about WOW! Simple point: Why the hell bother to get out of bed in the morning if your objective is not . . . WOW! Or: Holy Maloney! Or: Neat! Or: Over the top! These are precisely the terms that should apply to the completion of any project . . . at Accounting, Inc. . . . Purchasing, Inc. . . . Marketing, Inc. . . . whatever . . . whoever . . . wherever . . . whenever.

Professional service need not be boring! Take the case of Jose Ignacio (Inaki) Lopez. Sure, he might end up in jail for stealing General Motors' secrets and taking them to Volkswagen. But that proves my point. HE AIN'T BORING! Lopez may have saved GM and VW. Yes, literally S-A-V-E-D! He was crazy (and that's the highest praise I can give anyone . . . particularly in purchasing!). He put his GM gang on a "warrior diet" and made them into crusaders. I LOVE IT!! No . . . if he broke the law, I don't condone his behavior. But I do love his flamboyance . . . and particularly the fact that his brand of flamboyance was practiced in P-U-R-C-H-A-S-I-N-G. Yes . . . WOW! does go . . . PERFECTLY . . . with . . . PURCHASING.

And with . . . information systems. Consider Max Hopper. He . . . more than any single individual . . . reinvented the airline industry following deregulation. As American Airlines' information systems guru, Hopper created "dynamic pricing" . . . the ever-changing price-model that gave American a several-year jump over the competition.(WOW!)

And WOW! goes with . . . logistics. First Gus Pagonis won the Gulf War for George Bush, Colin Powell, and Norman Schwarzkopf: He was the magician/logistics guy who moved half the planet (or so it seemed) to the desert . . .almost overnight . . . and almost flawlessly. Now he's doing the same for . . . Sears.

Purchasing and WOW? ✓✓
IS and WOW? ✓✓
Logistics and WOW ✓✓
Etc. and WOW ✓✓

If you don't see it that way . . . YOU have a problem. (Sorry.)

1. Think Inc.

2. Think client.

3. Visit every client.

4. Turn every job into a project.

5. Put together a Current Projects List (CPL).

6. Conduct a weekly Current Projects Review.

7. Score, quantitatively, every project on excitement, urgency, and transformation potential.

8. Think portfolio quality.

9. Do whatever it takes.

10. Transfer your skills to clients.

11. Include the client on every project team.

12. Insist that clients evaluate "your" people and "their" people on each project.

13. Bring in outsiders.

14. Think marketing.

15. Think research and development.

16. Turn your Current Projects List into a research-and-development test ground.

17. Devote a large share of gross revenues to knowledge development.

18. Establish clear, tough incentives for contributing and sharing knowledge.

19. Train! Train! Train!

20. Train in project creation.

21. Train in problem solving.

22. Train in implementation.

23. **Train in client relations and client development.**

24. Train in "Rolodexing."

25. Challenge! Challenge! Challenge!

26. Rigorously evaluate "talent" after every project.

27. Be Great!

28. Think WOW!

The Five Ps of
PSF 1.0

Projectization

Professionalization

Provocation

Partnership

Performance

To sum up PSF 1.0:

1. Transform everything into scintillating projects. Call it . . . PROJECTIZATION.

2. Turn everyone into a self-sufficient, de facto "independent" consultant . . . fabulously good at . . . something. Call it . . . PROFESSIONALIZATION.

3. Routinely push clients . . . hard . . . to places they could never have imagined. Call it . . . PROVOCATION.

4. Do everything with the explicit objective of transferring knowledge and self-sufficiency to clients. Call it . . . PARTNERSHIP.

5. Make things happen! Leave a lasting legacy! Call it . . . PERFORMANCE.

We **can** do it, Tom!

Here was a typical response I got to one of my PSF 1.0 riffs. This one came from Sue Newton, training manager for Asda Stores in the United Kingdom:

Dear Tom:

1) We have used the PSF 1.0/Conversion Kit to "projectize" our team. We have, at first attempt, 43 projects in progress and each has been assigned a leader. Every member of the team is a leader for at least one project, including our admin team members and they were particularly excited/daunted by the idea! Every project must have others involved from outside the team and for all of them we have established "what a good job looks like" which must include the WOW!

2) I have done a "quick and dirty" training session on project management, but we are going to work up an ABW (Asda Best Way) of project management to help new team members—we don't know what it is yet but it's project No. 1!!

3) We are preparing our project board.

4) We are using Cynthia Kellams' view—"If you can't say why you actually make your company a better place, you're out"—as the basis for our existence, and are going to use the McKinsey "CV" approach at appraisal.

Sue

> **B-I-G IDEA: Professional Services, Inc.**
> **big idea: CONVERT YOUR DEPARTMENT . . . NOW**
> **. . . INTO PURCHASING, INC. (ETC.)**
> **big idea: PURCHASING, INC. (ETC.) = WOW, INC.**

PC 1.0/PROJECT CREATION KIT

Turn every job into a project.

Projects are the nuggets . . . the atoms . . . the basic particles. (Of PSF 1.0. Of life . . . in the new economy.) Time and again I'm asked, "How do we b-e-g-i-n?" My reply: T-H-I-N-K P-R-O-J-E-C-T. Projects ("projectization") is like breathing to me and professional service firm folks in general. And, I've found, it's like Greek to many/most others. Hence . . . in response to popular demand . . . my complement to PSF 1.0 . . . the Project Creation/ Conversion Kit . . . or PC 1.0.

1. Begin with what you are doing . . . right now. IS IT A P-R-O-J-E-C-T? How do you know? PROJECTS ARE DEFINED IN TERMS OF SPECIFIC/TIME-BOUND OUTCOMES. What will constitute a good result? And when? (Write it down . . . NOW.) A bad result? And when? (Write it down . . . NOW.) A WOW! (memorable) result? And when? (Write it down . . . NOW.) Projects are "chunks" . . . "doables" . . . THINGS WITH FINITE TIME HORIZONS THAT WILL RESULT IN MEASURABLE END PRODUCTS.

2. Projects are about milestones. About finite benchmarks. About tests . . . (VERY) RAPID/(VERY) PRACTICAL TESTS. So . . . the most important project questions . . . are about . . . NEXT MILESTONES. When is the next milestone? And the next? And the next? The next 5 to 10? Likewise: When is the first road test? The next road test? With insiders? With outsiders? The "next test" answer had better be . . . WITHIN THE NEXT 10 WORKING

DAYS. (No matter how complex the project . . . something can be partially piloted in the next few/10-or-fewer days.)

3. Effective projects are about . . . EFFECTIVE CLIENT INVOLVEMENT. Thence, these questions . . . WHICH MUST BE ANSWERED: When was the last time you talked to the client? (The answer had damn well be "yesterday"/"today." Constant contact is a must.) Likewise: How much time did you/have you spent . . . WITH THE CLIENT . . . scoping out the project? And: Do you continue to hone the definition of the project . . . DAILY . . . with the client?

4. While clients are important, so are weird/wacky/creative/interesting outside inputs. Thence: What interesting (kinky!) outsiders have you worked with on the project? An answer of "fewer than three or four" is . . . TOTALLY UNACCEPTABLE! You are as good as the interesting/kinky/weird/ fascinating/unexpected/counter-intuitive inputs to your project.

***

Very first step: Take whatever you are working on . . . right now . . . and begin today to shape it into a scintillating project . . . using the criteria above.

B-I-G IDEA: Professional Services, Inc.

big idea: TURN "IT" (A-N-Y "IT") INTO A PROJECT . . .

STARTING N-O-W.

YOU/I/WE ARE . . . AT RISK

YOU & I VS. SOFTWARE "AGENTS"

"Clerks trained to take consumers through interviews while software linked to a vast constantly updated database makes sophisticated choices have already replaced skilled professionals at technologically savvy service companies."

—Walter Russell Mead,
presidential fellow,
World Policy Institute

Why do "this stuff" . . . i.e. PSF 1.0/PC 1.0? Simple. You can be replaced by a software agent!

In numerous companies, as Walter Russell Mead says, "skilled professionals" are quickly being replaced . . . en masse . . . by $8.00 per hour clerks supported by advanced software systems . . . a.k.a. white-collar robots.

What's the alternative?

Simple . . . become a VALUE ADDED PROJECTS FREAK. Enter . . . PSF 1.0/PC 1.0.

B-I-G IDEA: Professional Services, Inc.

big idea: THE WHITE-COLLAR ROBOTS ARE COMING.

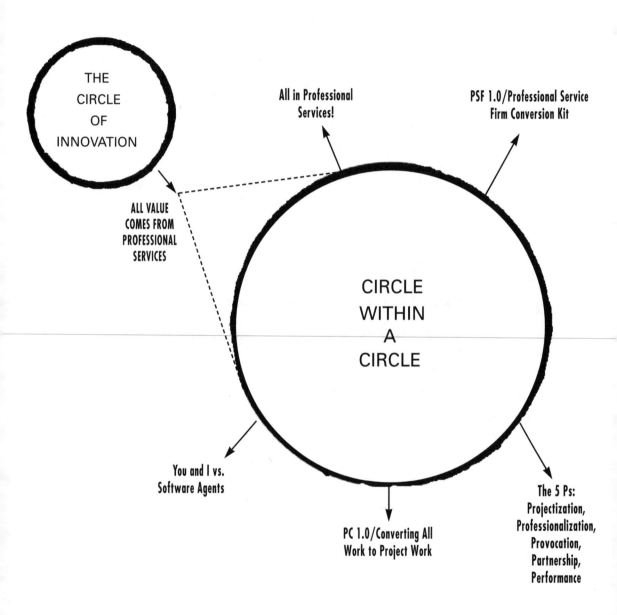

THE
CIRCLE
OF
INNOVATION

All in Professional
Services!

PSF 1.0/Professional Service
Firm Conversion Kit

ALL VALUE
COMES FROM
PROFESSIONAL
SERVICES

CIRCLE
WITHIN
A
CIRCLE

You and I vs.
Software Agents

PC 1.0/Converting All
Work to Project Work

The 5 Ps:
Projectization,
Professionalization,
Provocation,
Partnership,
Performance

SEMANTICS ALERT No. 6

All value = Services

Professional Services = Me. (Period.)

PSF 1.0/Conversion Kit

Purchasing (Etc.), Inc.

T-H-I-N-K C-L-I-E-N-T

T-H-I-N-K P-R-O-J-E-C-T

T-H-I-N-K Transformational project

T-H-I-N-K R & D in Purchasing (etc.)

W-O-W! (as in . . . PROFESSIONAL SERVICES)

UP . . . or . . . O-U-T (Sorry.)

The 5 Ps: Projectization, Professionalization, Provocation,
Partnership, Performance

PC 1.0/Conversion Kit

You/I vs. Software Agents

So far our thrust has been on disintegration: destruction/decentraliza-
tion (real)/forgetting/jobholder-to-businessperson/individual staff professional to value-adding "brand." Now the approach is flip flopped
as we reintegrate . . . starting by reconceiving the much-maligned
"staff" department's role to that of de facto (de jure?) professional
service firm and prime source of economic value added.

The Intermediary is Doomed.

Welcome to . . . organizations without employees . . . organizations
without walls and metes and bounds . . . organizations that are so
seamlessly entwined with customers and suppliers that "them" and
"us" are indiscernible. Before you proceed, I'd suggest a seatbelt . . .
or a slug of Johnny Walker . . . .

What the hell is an organization now?

"The intermediary is doomed: Technology strips him of effectiveness. This flattening of the vertical order . . . is already clear."

—Pat McGovern,
chairman, International Data Group

"Free: Landmark Tower, 31 Stories, As Is."

—headline, *The Wall Street Journal*, December 1996, on Alcoa's inability to get rid of its corporate headquarters

"'Disintermediation'—It's all about cutting out
the middle processes, the huge distribution
costs associated with simply issuing
[an airline] ticket. Those costs can be up to
50 percent of the ticket itself."

—Barry Saxton, vice president, Rosenbluth International

Disintermediation Transparency

"On the one hand, eliminating the middleman would result in lower costs, increased sales, and greater customer satisfaction; on the other hand, we're the middleman."

Two all-important words for the 1990s and beyond: disintermediation—removing layer upon layer of "intermediary" in the supplier-producer-buyer chain; and transparency—making the organization's inner workings apparent and malleable to customers and suppliers.

The short and the long of it: Organizations, as we have known them for hundreds of years, are disappearing. Literally.

What the hell is an organization? It used to be about buildings. (Don't tell Alcoa.) About departments. About fat payrolls. Now . . . it seems that it's not.

Buildings are tumbling. Boundaries are vanishing. Temps . . . with LL.D.s . . . are coming. Where "you" start and where "I" stop are no longer clear. Where "I" stop and where "you" start are no longer clear.

How far will it go?

Very far.

F-L-A-T (disintermediated) orgs . . . the watchword of the 80s and 90s. F-L-A-T (disintermediated) value chain . . . the watchword of the late 90s and first decade of century 21. Then . . . F-L-A-T society (Ross Perot's electronic democracy, etc.)? Who knows?

B-I-G IDEA: Innovation = Organizations are Disappearing!
big idea: ORGANIZATIONS AS WE'VE KNOWN THEM ARE LOSING THEIR SHAPE AND SUBSTANCE . . . LITERALLY.

What the hell is an organization now?

It's Banc One!

Automatic Teller Machines (ATMs). The "business end" is a humble 2'x2'6"
metal maw. But the most advanced ones these days have supplanted as many
as a half-dozen layers of bankers. ATMs are one part of a large class that Bell
Labs' Nobel Laureate Arno Penzias calls . . . CIRCUMVENTION MECHA-
NISMS. (The intermediary is DOOMED . . . redux.)

Via the ATM, Penzias writes in *Harmony: Business, Technology & Life
After Paperwork,* "a customer bypasses the human chain that began at the
teller's cage and ended with the keeper of the bank's general ledger." And it's
just gathering way: Banc One in Huntington, West Virginia, is testing a
Personal Automated Loan Machine, nicknamed PAL, that will evaporate
most of its loan department. Customers insert their cards, punch in their
PINs, and apply for a loan of up to . . . $10,000. In 10 minutes, the ATM
accepts or rejects the application. And: It can issue a check on the spot!

What the hell is an organization now?

It's
Campbell
Soup!

Campbell Soup recently announced Intelligent Cuisine . . . healthy fare developed with and endorsed by the American Heart Association and the American Diabetes Association. The (big) catch: Campbell won't peddle its tins in the local Safeway or Albertson's. Instead, the goods will go directly to select (needy) customers via UPS. A tiny drop in the (big) soup bowl . . . but one more indication of new (disintermediated) things to come.

B-I-G IDEA:
Innovation = Organizations
are Disappearing!
big idea: WHO NEEDS GROCERY STORES?
NOT CAMPBELL. NOT THE CONSUMER.
(MORE OR LESS . . . PERHAPS MORE THAN
LESS IN 10 YEARS.)

What the hell is an organization now?

It's
Wells Fargo!

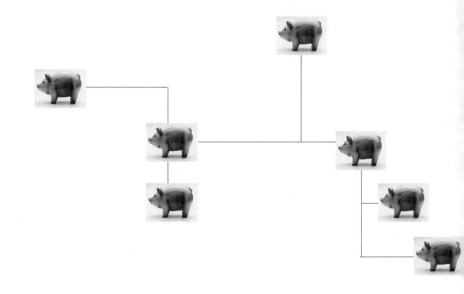

Among the multitude of bankers . . . Wells Fargo seems to get it. It's closing (lots of) branches . . . and opening (lots of) branches. That is, it's closing traditional branches, which cost a million bucks to set up, and opening a large number of "minibanks."

You'll find the new minibanks, which cost $250,000 (and do house human beings), inside the likes of Safeway, Chevron, Wal-Mart, Target, and Thrifty Payless. The net result: In California alone, Wells will double its 526 retail outlets by 1998!

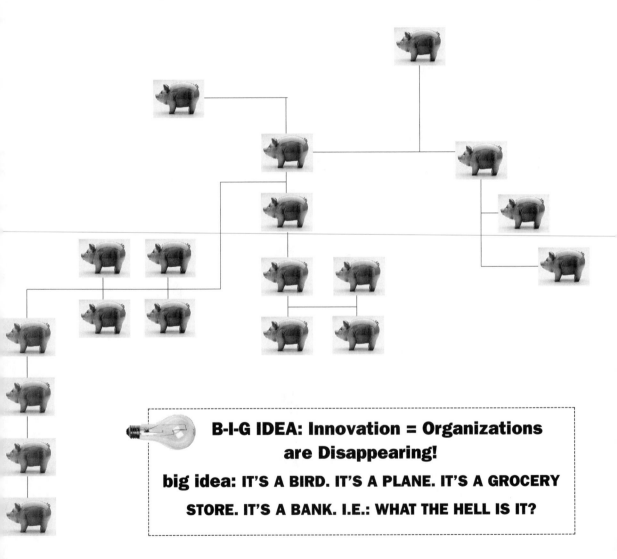

B-I-G IDEA: Innovation = Organizations are Disappearing!

big idea: IT'S A BIRD. IT'S A PLANE. IT'S A GROCERY STORE. IT'S A BANK. I.E.: WHAT THE HELL IS IT?

What the hell is an organization now?

"Organizations will be critically important in the world, but as organizers, not employers."

—Charles Handy,
consultant and author

A New World (Organizational) Order dawns worldwide. It isn't Silicon Valley. It is Kuala Lumpur. June 1997. The manufacturing executive comes up to me at break. (I've just been through "organizers . . . not employers.") He is Malaysian of Chinese ancestry. And a little sheepish.

"Dr. Peters, you rang a bell. And now I want your help."

"I'll try," I said.

"I've been thinking seriously about outsourcing, well, everything. You've given me the motivation to really consider taking the plunge. What criteria would you suggest I use to select partners?"

YE GADS! OUTSOURCE E-V-E-R-Y-T-H-I-N-G? (That is . . . it really is a New World Organizational Order . . . as in . . . WHAT THE HELL IS AN ORGANIZATION THESE DAYS?)

The old world order (and it was orderly): You've got a thorny problem in Latin American project finance. Where to find the answer? "Go to the 14th floor." A difficult issue involving human resources relative to temporary workers? "Head for 26." That is . . . to deal with the finance problem, go to the "finance floor" . . . with the HR problem, up to the "HR floor."

The underlying assumption: Regardless of the nature/complexity/ uniqueness of the problem/any problem, the best resources . . . on earth . . . live on our 14th/26th/17th/5th/etc. floor.

What shocking arrogance!

That is . . . the logic of bygone days was . . . to take advantage of a resource you need to own it (i.e., have the person on the payroll . . . and ensconced in your tower). Today's new logic: You're a damn fool if you own it! Access to the best resources . . . from anywhere and everywhere . . . instantly . . . is the W-H-O-L-E D-A-M-N P-O-I-N-T.

"Organizers . . . not employers" is how U.K.-based management consultant and author Charles Handy puts it. What does he mean? Where one organization "starts" and another "ends" is becoming increasingly murky.

Example: Production-organization genius Inaki Lopez (the executive who left GM for VW . . . and then left VW) created an entirely new automotive organization. VW's plant in Brazil is really "nothing more" than a "hotel" for subsystem vendors. That is, various subsystem vendors run large sections of the plant. VW "simply" puts the bunch together . . . and produces cars.

Contrast VW/Brazil with the old Ford, and you see how the world has changed. Not so many decades ago, Ford owned the grazing land . . . on which the sheep grazed . . . from which the wool came . . . that went into the then wool seat slipcovers of its cars. The theory was: In order to be a good carmaker . . . you also have to be a good shepherd!

(By the same logic, I should own a publishing house to produce my books. Hey . . . some newspaper companies still own forest-products companies. Trees = Pulp = Paper. Talk about stupid!)

I repeat, find the (absolute) best partners—on a temporary or, at most, semi-permanent basis—and work with them to exploit a (probably fleeting) opportunity in the marketplace. Then recreate yourself/your alliances structure to take advantage of the next (probably fleeting) opportunity.

It's organization all right. But . . . organization-as-floating-crap-game/ever-shifting-network. Bye-bye organizational boundaries! Bye-bye "organization" . . . as-we've-known-it-for-the-last-250 (or so)-years! Hello . . . HOLY SHIT!

B-I-G IDEA: Innovation = Organizations are Disappearing!

big idea: BIG ORGANIZATION . . . NO PEOPLE . . . NO PIPE DREAM.

What the hell is an organization now?

B-I-G . . . Small . . . ????

"Giant" Marriott?

"Bitsy" PPS?

E-T-C.

What is big? What is small?

The answer, I contend, is anything but obvious.

Case-in-Point I: I was giving a fundraising speech in Irvine, California. Noon. The traffic was awful! A thousand cars squirmed into the Marriott . . . in about 15 minutes.

It was a spectacle . . . a wonderful spectacle! The parking valets were dressed in spiffy uniforms. They ran back and forth to the cars. Yet they remained unfailingly polite. Late as I arrived (not good for a speaker), I stopped and watched the valets at work. (I have done the same when I saw a brick layer doing a magnificent job. And I'm a total sucker for great pizza-dough flippers. I'm sure you've got similar favorite showstoppers.)

In my speech, I commented on what I had witnessed. Pointing to a couple of tables populated by folks from The Walt Disney Company, I said, "I know you at Disney do everything better than anybody else on the planet when it comes to handling people. But I think even you would admit our friends at Marriott did a terrific job at getting us all into this hall in short order." The audience applauded, suggesting I was not the only one who had observed this feat of parking artistry. I admit I was proud of myself for remembering to thank our Marriott hosts.

After my talk, a young man introduced himself. "I'm Paul Paliska," he said. "Along with my brother Stephen, I'm the founder of Professional Parking Services, Inc. [PPS], the folks who actually parked those cars today."

Time for egg all over my face!

And time for a (big) lesson learned.

One of the major

issues in so-called event parking is insurance associated with stolen CD players, dinged doors, etc. So . . . who gets the lower insurance rates? "Giant" Marriott or "bitsy" PPS? Or, to put it differently: Who's bigger? "Giant" Marriott? "Bitsy" PPS?

You guessed it. (I hope.) When it comes to its super specialty, event parking, PPS has a more extensive/proven track record than multibillion dollar Marriott corporation. So relative to this issue . . . unequivocally . . . PPS Inc. is the bigger.

Case-in-point II: "You've been asked to speak to CBIS," my events coordinator told me.

"Huh?" was my brilliant reply. Followed by: "What's a CBIS?"

The unenlightening response: Cincinnati Bell Information Systems, a subsidiary of Cincinnati Bell.

More information followed. CBIS pulled in $480 million in revenue in 1996. And it's growing fast. A genuine global superstar. Its niche . . . billing for cable television and wireless telephones. It's simply the best-of-the-best . . . with clients such as AT&T, British Telecom, Nippon Telegraph and Telephone, IBM, Cox Broadcasting, and Time Warner.

(Oh . . . you haven't heard of them either? For shame.)

Case-in-point III: And if you haven't heard of PPS or CBIS . . . I suppose you haven't heard of the pride of Lee, Massachusetts, either. Ta da: Color for Realtors. They call themselves "The Way Coolest Real Estate Color Printer in the USA." I call them . . . POWERHOUSE.

Fact is, they are—clearly—the way coolest real estate color printer in the United States. Their periodic promo material—the one I have in hand is a 64-page booklet—is outta this world. Loaded to the gunnels with brilliant examples of tools to assist realtors in soliciting business. Post-card kits (hundreds of tested examples). Closing-gift-kit suggestions. Etc. All supplied by Color for Realtors . . . who use the world's most advanced printing technology . . . and currently serve 64,224 realtors in the U.S.A. I could go on . . . and on. Like CBIS and PPS and . . . and . . . and . . . they are the best-of-the-best/the biggest-of-the-big and more. They've taken a "trivial" task and completely redefined it as high art/awesome delivery.

The larger point: What is an organization . . . AT&T or Marv and Martha's Print Shop? It is nothing more (or less) than a . . . collection of tasks. Accounting tasks. Housekeeping tasks. Billing chores. Prototype-building activities.

And when it comes to virtually any task . . . some(little)one . . . some(little)where . . . is probably . . . enormous. (Remember, "The Way Coolest Real Estate Color Printer in the USA.") . . . even though "they" might have only a handful of people (or one person!) compared to giant Marriott, AT&T, etc.

And if you are perfectly honest . . . a scary thought in this instance . . . you'll perhaps conclude that, like my Kuala Lumpur associate, you can (!)/should(?) subcontract every subtask to some awesome specialist which is, in fact, better than the gang on 5,17,23 (as in the 5th, 17th, or 23d floor of your tower).

Big? Small? Go figure. Or, rather, go refigure.

B-I-G IDEA: Innovation = Organizations are Disappearing!

big idea: SMALL = BIG.

THE CONCEPT: PERVASIVE/INCLUSIVE.

What the hell is an organization now?

It's ME!

MY STRATEGIC ALLIANCE SECRETS:

BEST-IN-WORLD

(WSB, HSM, WYNCOM)

PERSONAL CHEMISTRY

(!!!)

TRUST

(SOFT = HARD!!!)

TIME

(Rome wasn't built . . .)

RECIPROCITY

(True equals)

RESULTS

(They can't carry me . . . very long;
and I can't carry them . . . very long)

INVESTMENT

(Spend time on relationships!)

PEOPLE

(Not exclusively "top-to-top")

I'm going to be arrogant/egocentric. My life . . . my becoming a brand . . . is driven by the choice and maintenance of extraordinary alliance partners. Here's my short list of "secrets" (secrets-no-more):

■ Best-in-World

I give about 40 or so public seminars in the United States each year. My partner for all of them (yes . . . all my eggs in one basket) is WYNCOM, a Lexington, Kentucky, firm that earned the 33rd spot on the 1996 *Inc.* 500 list of fastest-growing companies. Years ago, WYNCOM founders Larry and Bunny Holman came up with what turned out to be a fabulous idea: Fade into the background and co-sponsor seminars with college and university executive education programs. Nobody has succeeded in copying Larry and Bunny! They're simply the best.

My other seminars are booked mostly through the Washington Speakers Bureau (WSB). Harry Rhodes and Bernie Swain built it from nothing to BIW (best-in-world). Along the way they used integrity and a passion for execution to reinvent what had been a mostly sleazy industry descended from the world of old Manhattan theater agents. I was an early client. They're (simply) great. (Lucky me.) In South America, I team up with José Salibi Neto . . . whose organization, HSM, has been written up in many direct-marketing books as . . . ho hum (NOT) . . . best-in-world.

BIW. That's key to alliance success.

■ Personal Chemistry

Strategic alliances are about individual capability, but they're also about people working together for each other's good. So personal chemistry counts . . . a lot. Bunny and Larry at WYNCOM. Harry and Bernie at WSB. José at HSM. Etc. The personal chemistry is . . . well . . . great!

■ <u>Trust</u>

The soft(est) stuff is the hard(est) stuff. There are a lot of shysters in the world. Far short of that, there are corner-cutters. Years ago, Harry Quadracci, the iconoclastic chief executive officer of extraordinary printer Quad/Graphics, told me: "Never do business with people you don't trust. Life's too short." I listened to his words. I listened closely. And I'm a true believer. Larry, Bunny, Harry, Bernie, José . . . and various others . . . well . . . I TRUST THEM . . . literally . . . with my life.

■ <u>Time</u>

No serious relationship is built in a day . . . with a roommate/spouse . . . or a commercial alliance partner. In the cases I mentioned we got along well from the start, but we learned to love/trust each other . . . over time. Choosing an alliance partner is a time issue . . . not just a logical/rational/analytic/core-competence issue.

> "Never do business with people you don't trust. Life's too short."
>
> Harry Quadracci,
> Quad/Graphics

■ <u>Reciprocity</u>

All of my alliance partners are my true equals. They are the best at what they do, and I'm reasonably good at what I do. No relationship between non-equals is a genuine strategic alliance. Period.

■ <u>Results</u>

My "trust" grew as my partners and I delivered the goods for one another. Small change at first. (Like dating.) Bigger change later. (Like marriage.) Also, I understand that my partners can't carry me . . . for long, anyway. And I'm not big enough to carry them for long. They've got to perform. I've got to perform. There's some altruism involved . . . but not all that much. We're all grownups . . . we all get it. Results count!

■ <u>Investment</u>

It's a pleasure, not a pain, to invest in a core relationship. But even if it were largely a pain, I would still do it. These relationships are invaluable—personally, emotionally, financially, strategically—to me. Therefore, they are worth (lots of) effort.

■ <u>People</u>

Strategic alliances aren't about strategic synergy between one boss man/woman and another boss woman/man (though it may start there). They are about integrating "your" organization from top to bottom with "their" organization. This task not only involves the people who work "for" me, in my own company; it also involves me being involved with the folks in my partners' organizations . . . many steps down the line. "Down" that line is "up" the line . . . when it comes to critical implementation issues!

My list is hardly exhaustive, but it's a start. It underscores the human—and performance—dimensions of turning an alliance-on-paper into a genuine strategic alliance.

I'll also admit that the evidence presented here is anecdotal. One case . . . ME. But there is a pro-from-Dover who plays on this field. His name is Jordan Lewis. And we agree.

In the carefully researched *The Connected Corporation*, Lewis examines newfangled supplier-producer relations at their best . . . at Motorola, Chrysler, Marks & Spencer, and so on.

The computer is <u>not</u> the point . . .
The point:
HUMAN RELATIONSHIPS.

↓

Okay?

Most interesting (to me): THIS IS A S-O-F-T BOOK. "Interfirm links," Lewis writes at one point, "are broad, deep, unique." The magic words/ideas that come up . . . again and again . . . and again . . . in the book: trust/commitment/compatible cultures/long-haul/partnerships/simple contracts/top-to-bottom relationships/cross-functional integration/information sharing/joint continuous-improvement programs/etc./etc. And believe it or not: "Information technology" is not in Lewis' book's index! Circa 1996!

True, Lewis talks about EDI (electronic data interchange) and the like. The computer is hardly AWOL. But the point is . . . the computer is not the point . . . even if it is a matchless/revolutionary enabling device. The point: HUMAN RELATIONSHIPS. Okay?

B-I-G IDEA: Innovation = Organizations are Disappearing!

big idea: ALLIANCE STRENGTH α ATTENTION TO SOFT SKILLS.

Who's running the organization?

Customers!

E(C)

Empowerment (customers) = Information + access + decision making + choice + customization + perception of control/ownership

The word "empowerment" has been overused . . . and cheapened. I've stricken it from my vocabulary. But now, I'm resurrecting it . . . my way. That is . . . E(C).

In short, I contend that over the next 10 to 15 years the primary strategic battle, in virtually any industry you can name, will be the battle to see who can go the farthest in empowering customers.

Empowering customers means:

- Providing them with gobs of information.
- Providing intimate/immediate/all-the-time access to your innards.
- Allowing them to make decisions about the use of your resources.
- Giving them choices.
- Allowing them to customize products and services . . . provided by you . . . to meet their specific needs.
- Giving them the perception of control and ownership . . . over you.

IT IS A **V-E-R-Y** BIG DEAL.

Consider: Over the last half-dozen years, two extraordinary institutions (and competitors), FedEx and UPS, have spent billions upon billions of dollars on information systems. A little of that money has gone to speeding up package delivery . . . but not much. Most of the dough has gone to build systems that allow you and me access to the insides of the two shippers.

It's ironic. The reason we turned to FedEx and UPS in the first place was their reliability. We knew they would get it there, and get it there fast. And we knew they would get it there when they said they would get it there (which you couldn't always say about the U.S. Postal Service). Reliability was the name of the new game. Nonetheless, relatively expensive FedEx was thumping relatively inexpensive UPS badly a few years ago. FedEx allowed customers to track their packages from the moment they left home to the moment they arrived at the recipient's place.

Why in the hell should we care? With FedEx, we knew exactly when it was going to arrive. And it did. But that's ignoring the nature of the human beast: our unslakeable thirst for information/knowledge/perception of control. So normally skinflint UPS threw a few billion bucks into the fray to catch up, which it's now done. It is a battle royal—*the* battle royal—over E(C) . . . EMPOWERMENT (CUSTOMERS).

E(C) means, in this case, that I—a small business owner—am, literally, scheduling FedEx's flights. Of course, its collective "I's" that do that . . . but I do diddle directly with FedEx's innards, place the order on my own, with no clerks, no intermediaries, no FedEx decision makers involved.

- Disintermediation . . .
- Transparency . . .
- E(C).

It's eminently arguable that the *strongest force in the universe* is our need for perceived control . . . which adds up to an intriguing angle on the argument about E(C) . . . the race to empower the customer the fastest, the mostest.

More: Some recent experiments have begun with self-scanning at grocery stores. For some reason . . . FREAKING HUMAN BEINGS . . . we love to scan our own groceries. The force is so strong that in several places where the experiment is taking place, people choose to wait in the longest line for the privilege of . . . scanning their own groceries . . . and then bagging them themselves. WE WANT/NEED/DEMAND CONTROL (PERCEPTION OF).

HOLY SMOKE! Or . . . rather . . . HOLY E(C)!

B-I-G IDEA: Innovation = Organizations are Disappearing!

big idea: IT'S MILES BEYOND LISTENING TO THE CUSTOMER. IT'S PUTTING THE CUSTOMER IN THE DRIVER'S SEAT...AND HANDING HER/HIM THE KEYS TO Y-O-U-R CAR.

Who's running the organization?

organization?

Customers!!

"Anything that tightens your relationships with an existing customer increases the revenue you get from that customer."

—Michael Taylor,
Arthur D. Little

"The web allows you to have an iterative debate with your customers and your prospects . . . Make a website where the debate about the soul of the company is going on with employees as well as prospects. That is much more powerful than just 'I'm going to put my catalog on the Net,' or 'I'm going to sell my goods on the Net.'"

—Watts Wacker,
SRI Consulting

> "Changes in business processes will emphasize self-service. . . . Your costs as a business go down and the perceived service goes up because customers are conducting it themselves."
>
> —Raymond Lane,
> president, Oracle

EC (electronic commerce) is coming. What form? Jillions of forms! Jillions of failures! And some successes, too. And . . . along the way . . . total transformation.

Small headline *Rutland Herald* (8/24/97): "Microsoft Aims At Home Buyers on Internet." The National Association of Realtors, we learn, already has 900,000 properties on its Web site . . . and it gets 22 million (M-I-L-L-I-O-N) hits a month. Now . . . surprise . . . Microsoft wants in. And then there was the discussion I had with execs at World.hire. They (and their competitors), they figure, are going to re-invent the entire process of recruiting and hiring . . . into a customer-(applicant-) led business. Tighten those electronic links. NOW. Emphasize self-service. NOW. Start a deep dialogue. NOW. Experiment madly. NOW.

It/EC+E(C) is happening. NOW.

**B-I-G IDEA: Innovation = Organizations
are Disappearing!**
**big idea: SOMEHOW . . . SOMEDAY . . . (MUCH) SOONER . . .
OR (A LITTLE) LATER . . . (INTERMEDIARY-LESS) ELECTRONIC
COMMERCE WILL BE "IT."**

Who's running the organization?

Customers!!!

"How fast can we give it away?"

<u>Netscape</u>

<u>FedEx/UPS</u>

<u>Charles Schwab (et al.)</u>

<u>Healthcare</u>

<u>Yours truly</u>

Empowering customers redux: Who can give away the most . . . the fastest:

Example: Internet browsers.
Netscape has peanuts in revenue . . . and billions in market capitalization. How did Netscape do it? By giving away the latest version of everything it produces. Netscape gave away browsers by the jillion . . . and established, for a while, an arm lock on the Internet market. Microsoft returns fire . . . by "giving away" its browser . . . just as Netscape has started to charge for its.

Example: Brokerage firms.
Charles Schwab has, in effect, re-invented the brokerage business by working day and night to put itself out of business: allowing customers, on-line, via the telephone, etc., to make choices that formerly only brokers and certified financial advisors made.

Example: Patient-driven healthcare.
Regina Herzlinger, a senior professor at the Harvard Business School, has brought her several decades of healthcare research to bear in a marvelous book . . . *Market-Driven Healthcare.* One of the largest shifts on the healthcare landscape, she argues, is growing patient involvement in their own healthcare. For example, there are already thousands of busy healthcare sites on the Internet . . . informing patients in depth about their ailments and alternative treatment strategies. Herzlinger contends that those who are wisest in the healthcare business will care for their customers via the Big 2: (1) convenience and (2) mastery. Convenience meaning . . . cut the crap! Healthcare delivery should not be a hopelessly complicated process loaded with delays for patients. And mastery: Customers

want to take charge of their own lives. Thanks to the new information sources, it won't be unusual for the consumer/patient to know more about his or her specific disease than the generalist/internist in the white coat.

Another outcropping of the same phenomenon: Have you noticed the torrent of multi-page prescription drug ads in general-purpose consumer magazines? Same idea: Pharmaceutical makers want you to take charge of your disease . . . and demand directly that Old Doc give you the hottest new pills.

Hint: It's working. Hint: transparency/disintermediation/E(C) redux.

Example: Yours truly. In 1981 Bob Waterman and I developed a lengthy presentation around the material that was about to become *In Search of Excellence*. We bound the presentation . . . about two inches thick . . . added a bright orange cover . . . and started giving it away to friends and colleagues. As the publication date for *In Search of Excellence* approached, we continued to distribute the fat presentation books . . . at an accelerating pace. Our publisher was appalled. *Search*'s first printing was pegged at 10,000 . . . and we had already distributed 15,000 full-scale preview copies!

Hint: It worked.

Example: Yours truly (again). I'm working with a tiny textile start-up. The home-furnishings market is very fragmented. Very underbranded. We want to brand. Our marketing executive planned to take a couple of hundred catalogs ($20 each . . . production costs!) to an early trade show. I said no. Take a couple of thousand . . . AND GIVE THEM AWAY AS FAST AS YOU CAN. I was in pursuit of "BUZZ!" I.e.: Build Buzz! Cause a Stir! Brand! And the halo effect . . . just might make you rich!

Many economists—and yours truly—believe that this game is *the* game . . . for practically everyone. Economists call it increasing returns to scale. It means that the more you give away, the more dominant your position/share of mind becomes in the larger network . . . and the more you make . . . from the pennies you take from each transaction. It's a sophisticated version of the old saw that, "Giving (all the) credit to as many others as possible . . . and little/none to yourself . . . is a/the key to success."

The more people you give credit to, the bigger your network grows . . . the more help you get as you take on larger tasks. What a merry daisy chain!

Now, it's the essence of smart strategy to master the new hyper-crowded-with-products-and-services-and-messages economy.

B-I-G IDEA: Innovation = Organizations are Disappearing!

big idea: E(C)/HOW FAST CAN WE GIVE "IT" AWAY?

Where has all the friction gone?

INTERACTION REVOLUTION

Vertical integration ↓/
horizontal linkage ↑/ scale ↓/
"network scale" ↑/network forms ↑/
intermediaries ↓/
direct sales + distribution ↑/
interaction cost ↓/
customization + global reach ↑/
market fitness tests ↑.

Researchers at McKinsey call it the Interaction Revolution. Sounds pretty dull . . .but it boils down to the main point of this chapter . . . and the stakes are $$$$ . . . by the T-R-I-L-L-I-O-N.

An entire "school" of economics focuses on transaction costs . . . i.e., the price and implications of friction in the economy. The new technologies are eliminating a lot of that friction (that is, passing papers . . . slowly . . . inside and outside the corporation). And it is changing the essence of the global economy. To wit:

- Vertical integration is declining. "Owning it" to take advantage of it (the experts are on "the 19th") is increasingly unnecessary . . . and downright foolish.
- Horizontal linkage is surging . . . i.e., working side by side with partners of all sizes and shapes: e.g., that new VW factory in Brazil.
- Scale is losing its grip . . . that is, "old" scale . . . which meant encasing all necessary resources inside our walls/tower.
- "Network scale" and network forms of organization are taking off. The network can be H-U-G-E . . . though the elements (old orgs) can be rather small: i.e., very big collections of very little specialist practitioners.
- Intermediaries are . . . you've heard it from me (and others) here . . . D-O-O-M-E-D.
- Direct sales and distribution are on the (rapid) rise. Take it straight to the customer—e.g., Campbell in soup—is coming . . . fast . . . everywhere.
- Interaction costs are plummeting. That's the B-I-G D-R-I-V-E-R. It used to cost hundreds of bucks (and take days) to process the simplest transaction. Now . . . in Malaysia or Australia . . . the grocery store's automated credit card approval system clears my

California bank-based Visa transaction in two or three seconds. And each time I put a credit card directly into a gas pump at a service station, it adds another two minutes to my productive life. Etc. Etc. Etc.

- Customization and global reach are becoming commonplace. Jane Peanuts, the one-woman consultancy, can today . . . easily . . . be a global player . . . from her loft in San Francisco . . . or farm in Tinmouth, Vermont. And old Burger King's "Have It Your Way" slogan (though mostly phony baloney in BK's case) is becoming the battle cry of most every firm . . . Be Your Own Rock (Prudential) . . . Rule Your Kingdom (Dreyfus) . . . etc.

- Market fitness tests are becoming the norm . . . fast . . . for every internal service (HR, accounting) and every one of us (IF YOU CAN'T SAY WHY YOU MAKE YOUR COMPANY A BETTER PLACE, YOU'RE OUT). I.e., the Market (capital "M") will decide!

"Interaction Revolution" may well be a dreary term. Look inside, however, and one is reminded of the prescient epigraph to this book: IT'S THE END OF THE WORLD AS WE KNOW IT.

B-I-G IDEA: Innovation = Organizations are Disappearing!

big idea: FRICTION ↓ TRANSACTION COSTS ↓ = ORGANIZATIONS (AS WE KNOW THEM) COLLAPSING.

Where has all the friction gone?

TOP ↓↑   (smaller, but: vision/coher-
ence/character)

OLD MIDDLE ↓ (as we knew it: cops
checkers)

NEW MIDDLE ↑   (V.A. projects/intel-
lectual capital)

BOTTOM ↑   (aided by software for
info + decision making)

OUTSIDE ↑   (power to the customer)

Bottom line. New Corp. Frictionless (by and large):

At the top. The top of the pyramid (a.k.a. headquarters) is much smaller ($\downarrow$) ... but much more important ($\uparrow$); that is, the new top must keep a far-flung/ever-changing/ephemeral network "organization" more or less together. It is responsible for (network) coherence and the character/vision of these odd, new fangled organizational creations.

Old middle. Simple: Old middle/old-middle-as-checker/old-middle-as-cop/old-middle-as-hoarder-of-information is ... DEAD ... a cooked goose ($\downarrow$).

New Middle. The new middle—albeit drastically shrunken—is more important than ever ($\uparrow$) ... in its PSF 1.0 (Chapter 6)/value-adding/transformational projects role.

At the bottom. The new bottom is much more powerful than before: ($\uparrow$) front-line-employee-as-businessperson (Chapter 4)/front-line employee abetted by state-of-the-art-software-based decision-making aids (Chapter 6).

Outside. E(C). Transparency. Self-service. The outside (e.g., customers) moves inside ... and becomes much more present/powerful ($\uparrow$).

Add it up and we have ... well ... a brand-new/post-industrial organization species ... that barely resembles its predecessors.

B-I-G IDEA:

Organizations are Disappearing!

big idea: NEW TOP/NEW MIDDLE/NEW BOTTOM/

NEW OUTSIDE = NEW CORP.

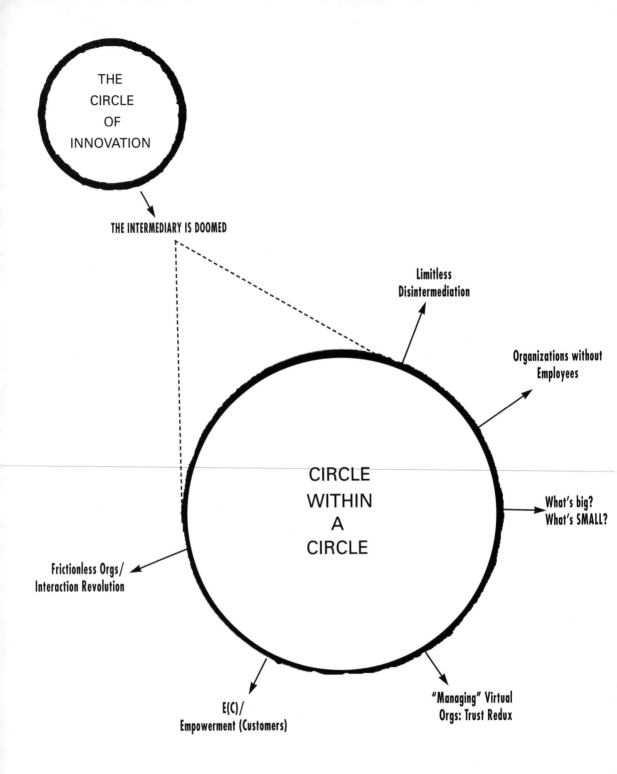

THE
CIRCLE
OF
INNOVATION

THE INTERMEDIARY IS DOOMED

Limitless
Disintermediation

Organizations without
Employees

CIRCLE
WITHIN
A
CIRCLE

What's big?
What's SMALL?

Frictionless Orgs/
Interaction Revolution

E(C)/
Empowerment (Customers)

"Managing" Virtual
Orgs: Trust Redux

The Intermediary is Doomed
Disintermediation (Infinite)
Circumvention Mechanisms
$10,000-loan-in-10 minutes/
Soup-by-UPS
Organizations without borders
Organizations without employees
Plant-as-hotel-
for-sub-systems-vendors
Small = BIG
Strategic Alliance Effectiveness = Trust + Time Invested
Transparency (total)
E(C)/Empowerment (Customers)
Self-service revolution
Friction-free "Interaction Revolution"

In this chapter the reintegration process takes off from PSF 1.0 (Chapter 6) and examines the enterprise as a whole . . . or "new whole"/"network whole"/"disembodied whole." We considered organizations without workers . . . organizations transparent to every member of the (external) value-adding family. The friction-free game is about uniting—fast—the best talent anywhere to take advantage of fleeting market opportunities.

The System is the Solution.

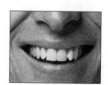

On the one hand . . . it's the age of information.
On the other . . . information is worthless.
"Information," writes poet and social commentator
Donald Hall, "is the enemy of intelligence."
<u>Enemy</u>. Strong word.
Deserved!
"The" answer? How about . . . systems?
Or . . . rather . . . BEAUTIFUL SYSTEMS?

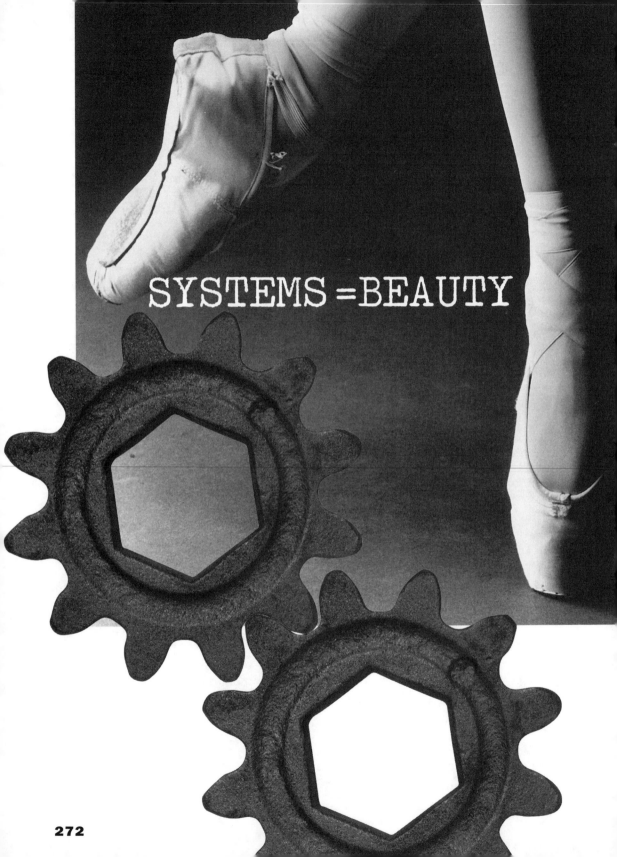

SYSTEMS = BEAUTY

Wiring
Plumbing*
Underpark**
Highways (and Byways)
The Way We Do Things
The "ord" in "chaordic"***

I am not a closet anarchist. I carry three wind-up alarm clocks on the road . . . and check my watch setting daily with the U.S. Naval Observatory master atomic clock (202-762-1401—try it).

I do believe in the orderly side of things:

- Systems = wiring
- Systems = plumbing
- Systems = Disney's underpark
- Etc.

Fact is . . . systems are (far) more important than ever before. We are routinely accomplishing large projects . . . working with hundreds of people . . . from hither and thither . . . many (most?) of whom we've never met.

The ethereal organization/disembodied organization/disintermediated organization/transparent organization (Chapter 7) demands great systems. And therein lies the rub. Most systems are jury-rigged, bogged down in detail (even post-reengineering). So we need some new ways of thinking about systems. My suggestion: What about . . . BEAUTIFUL systems? Yes . . . systems . . . AND . . . beauty . . . can . . . and should . . . and must . . . go together . . . if we are to capitalize upon these New Corp./new weird organizations (Chapter 7 redux).

Systems work is not a cipher's work. It's . . . well . . . artists' work.

Read on . . .

---

* Silicon Valley's fastest growing big company in 1997: Cisco Systems. Its product line? Plumbing for the Internet . . . which is what Cisco proudly calls it.
** From Disney . . . the park beneath the park . . . where the whole thing is made to work.
*** Dee Hock, Visa founder. Great organizations = Chaos + Order = Chaordic.

Systems Engineering Department, a.k.a. Department of Beauty

There's no reason why

EACH A-N-D EVERY form,

policy, and procedure

can't be a work of . . .

art/beauty/grace/

clarity/simplicity!

Reengineering-guru Mike Hammer broke into view, in 1990, with a masterful *Harvard Business Review* article, "Reengineering Work: Don't Automate, Obliterate." He said that the first 30 years of the information technology age amounted to automating yesterday's clunky, bureaucratic systems.

Hammer and Jim Champy's business process reengineering changed all that. It *was* a revolution. Done poorly a lot of the time? Of course! But no less revolutionary because of the mistakes that were made . . . and the frequent bastardization of the concept as a mindless excuse for mindless layoffs.

The core idea: Formerly warring departments ("functional stove pipes," as quality-guru Bill Creech calls them) must be on the same side, reorganized around essential processes that cut across—demolish—vertical barriers and boundaries.

That's all well and good, but now the next-step virtual organization revolution (yet another damned, real revolution!) is sweeping the world . . . LITERALLY . . . THE WORLD.

So, we need to go further, to really look at the essence of the new plumbing: systems that transform enterprise. Our (big) problem: Think "systems" and what words come to mind? "Buttoned down." "Details." "Dry." "Meticulousness." I don't have any problem with those words . . . .

Or maybe I do.

Sure, details are essential. But ponder systems . . . and do you hear people speak of . . . art . . . beauty . . . grace? I bet not. And they're making a B-I-G mistake. Systems . . . GREAT SYSTEMS . . . are about . . . ART . . . BEAUTY . . . GRACE . . . CLARITY . . . PARSIMONY.

I'm not pulling this out of the air. The father of modern operations research (i.e., systems), Dr. C. West Churchman, claimed that superior systems did more than meet efficiency criteria. They were marked by integrity and an aesthetic sense.

Nice!

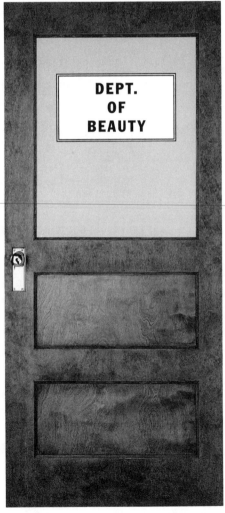

What I'm trying to do is—unabashedly—alter the language. Get all discussions about systems (which are important/imperative/strategic!) to focus, first and foremost, on . . . art . . . beauty . . . grace . . . clarity . . . parsimony.

We (companies/units) are . . . TO A SURPRISING DEGREE . . . known by our systems . . . our forms, our policies, our procedures. There's no reason why EACH A-N-D EVERY ONE can't be a work of . . . art/beauty/grace/clarity/parsimony. Take the form/procedure you're working with right now. Cut it by 90 percent. Fine. But does it read "human"? I.e.: Chatty? Friendly? Graceful? Artistic? If not . . . SCRAP IT . . . N-O-W! (Seriously.)

Systems. Little (or nothing) is more important. So: Shutter the door of the Systems Engineering Department! (NOW!) Off you go to the sign shop! (NOW!) The new title for this essential function: DEPARTMENT OF BEAUTY. If you think I am being the slightest bit facetious . . . you're passing up an (E-N-O-R-M-O-U-S) opportunity.

B-I-G IDEA:

Innovation=Beautiful Systems.

big idea: DEPARTMENT OF BEAUTY.

Southwest Airlines
(a.k.a. Beauty, Inc.)

21,000 people totally/passionately/ b-e-a-u-t-i-f-u-l-l-y focused on the well-being of 25 million passengers.

Southwest is a "systems" company. It's TOTALLY focused on moving large numbers of people efficiently from one place to another. And, every little/big bit counts: Southwest has only one kind of aircraft . . . the 737. Maintaining only one kind of aircraft MAKES LIFE A HELL OF A LOT EASIER . . . FASTER . . . SIMPLER . . . MORE RELIABLE. And: Southwest won't do "interline" baggage transfer. And: Southwest doesn't feed you. And: Southwest doesn't offer seat assignments. And . . . and . . . and: And it adds up to 21,000 people (employees) totally/passionately/B-E-A-U-T-I-F-U-L-L-Y focused on moving 25 million passengers . . . from one place to a nearby place . . . with no muss . . . no fuss . . . AND . . .

A LITTLE BIT OF FUN.

Southwest vociferously denies it is a "no-frills" airline. I heartily agree. First, the biggest "frill" of all for the (very) frequent flyer is awesome (beautiful?) reliability. Plus Southwest grooves on soul . . . calls itself Love Airlines (that is . . . LUV . . . the stock-ticker symbol) . . . and . . . "seeks to amuse, surprise, entertain," in the words of Chairman Herb Kelleher. I.e., Southwest *is* systems. Southwest's systems have . . . beauty . . . AND . . . grace.

B-I-G IDEA:

Innovation=Beautiful Systems.

big idea: 21,000 GRACEFUL PEOPLE = BEAUTY AT 21,000 FEET = POSSIBLE = SOUTHWEST AIRLINES.

Marriott
(a.k.a. Beauty, Inc.)

10 Precious Minutes!

The company's market research is clear: A guest's experience at Marriott (and probably any other service establishment) is overwhelmingly influenced by the first few—10, to be exact—minutes in the joint. So Marriott has gone to work . . . SYSTEMATICALLY . . . to improve those initial 10 minutes.

It creates a listing of the day's guests in the order of expected arrival: Those expected to arrive first have their rooms cleaned first. A simple . . . obvious . . . AND POWERFUL . . . idea.

Marriott is also combining the tasks of doorman, bellhop, and desk clerk into a single position—guest service agent (GSA). A guest is greeted at the door . . . checked in . . . and taken to his or her room by the same person. Obvious? Of course! Brilliant? You bet! Does it work? Absolutely! Call it . . . B-E-A-U-T-Y. Call it . . . P-A-R-S-I-M-O-N-Y.

CarMax
(a.k.a. Beauty, Inc.)

```
A loaf of bread.
A quart of milk.
A pound of hamburger.
A car.
```

If the system is the solution . . . it ought to be a parsimonious/focused system. Richard Sharp, boss of Circuit City . . . and so boss of CarMax, says that buying a car "shouldn't be any more trouble than buying groceries" and should take "no longer than a lunch hour."

I agree. Do you?

Sound silly? Sound absurd? Think about it . . . PLEASE . . . I BEG YOU.

P.S. CarMax isn't there . . . yet. But its own approach to BEAUTY—e.g., no dickering, low mileage used cars, and insurance—has earned it a 98-percent customer satisfaction score . . . about 30 to 35 (BIG) points above the typical car dealer's.

> **B-I-G IDEA:**
>
> **Innovation=Beautiful Systems.**
> **big idea: PARSIMONIOUS SYSTEMS**
> **(A.K.A. CUT . . . A-L-L . . .THE CRAP).**

Susan Sargent Designs (a.k.a. Beauty, Inc.)

I recently co-founded a textile firm. We're trying to do a lot of things right. VERY RIGHT. One big item is . . . SYSTEMS/POLICIES/PROCEDURES. That is . . . I THINK THAT SYSTEMS/POLICIES/PROCEDURES can be HUMANE/FRIENDLY/ENTIC-ING . . . and . . . a (BIG) plus.

I got a draft of an advertising policy from a member of the firm. It was punishing in its tone. That is . . . the subtext seemed to suggest that our average customer was a crook . . . who needed to be kept on a tight leash.

I disagree.

So I insisted on a complete rewrite.

I wanted the language to be friendly. I wanted it to explain *why* we were doing what we were doing. I wanted it to have fewer technical clauses and sub-clauses and sub-sub-clauses (UNREADABLE BULLSHIT). If getting rid of a little of the fine print means that the 1 percent (or less!) of bad guys may screw us now and then . . . SO BE IT. I'm interested in our real customers. And interested in their repeat business. I'M INTERESTED IN MAKING FRIENDS . . . FOR LIFE!

Our customers aren't crooks. Are yours? Look at your policies. Of course, you don't think they're "crooks." But I'll bet your policies reek of labeling them as crooks. Do you disagree? Read v-e-r-y carefully before answering.

At Susan Sargent Designs we sell our products almost exclusively through reps. While they are open with us, we still want to establish direct relationships with the

PLEASE
Complain
Thanks for your order!
We want everything to go
PERFECTLY!
If the order was late. Or wrong.
Or if any of the goods are damaged
in the slightest.
Or if you're just having a lousy day
and want to unload on someone...
Call our customer care hotline.
1-800-245-4767
SUSAN S SARGENT

retailers to whom our goods are going. Thus, among other things, we decided to put a prominent card in each shipment (rugs, bedding, pillows, etc.) to a retailer.

I went to our director of operations and said, "Please design a card that begs people to communicate with us. And . . . PLEASE . . . use plain English and make it amusing and memorable."

The result, I think, speaks for itself. (I went into convulsions over . . . "Or if you're just having a lousy day and want to unload on someone . . . call our customer care hotline.")

B-I-G IDEA:

Innovation=Beautiful Systems.

big idea: GRACEFUL LANGUAGE.

Burger King (a.k.a. Beauty, Inc.)

What gets measured gets done.
What gets paid for gets done more.

As Burger King CEO, Barry Gibbons crafted a major turnaround versus perennial champ McDonald's! Focusing on service quality is the key, according to Gibbons. And how do you get very busy people focused ...CLEARLY... on service quality? By following the saw, "What gets measured gets done." And the even sharper saw, "What gets paid for gets done more."

Gibbons got it. "Raise awareness by the only method that is effective: Build personal quality goals into personal objectives. If corporate quality goals are not met, no bonus of any kind gets paid. To anybody. P-E-R-I-O-D."

Reread those words. If corporate quality goals are not met ... NO bonus ... of ANY kind ... gets paid ... to ANYBODY ... P-E-R-I-O-D.

Lesson: Focus. Clarity. Parsimony ... and ... yes ... BEAUTY.

Your first step
(a.k.a. Beauty, Inc.)

Practice using the words . . . BEAUTY . . .
GRACE . . . PARSIMONY . . . FOCUS.

Do it today. Do it alone or with colleagues. Select one form/document. E.g.:

- Airbill
- Invoice
- Returns Policy
- Sick Leave Policy

Rate the form (it's best to do this with 3 or 4 colleagues) . . . on a scale of 1 to 10 (1 = Bureaucratic Bullshit; 10 = Nirvana) . . . on each of 4 dimensions:

- Beauty
- Grace
- Parsimony
- Focus

Then repeat the process: e.g., weekly. Hint: I have done this . . . and it works. We (you!) *can* make precise judgments about . . . BEAUTY . . . GRACE . . . PARSIMONY . . . FOCUS. Truth is . . . the most powerful part of this (strategic) exercise is toying with the words (BEAUTY, GRACE, PARSIMONY, FOCUS) per se. It is awkward at first. (Good.) And gets much less awkward as you go along. Hint: The B/G/P/F (beauty/grace/parsimony/focus) Standard is Olympian! (Good.)

The Social Side of Systems (TAKE 1)

Time and time and time again—these days—we underestimate the SOCIAL SIDE: The computer, the network, the s-y-s-t-e-m will take care of it.

NOT SO!

"All depends," writes *Fast Company* founding editor Alan Webber, "on the quality of the conversations."

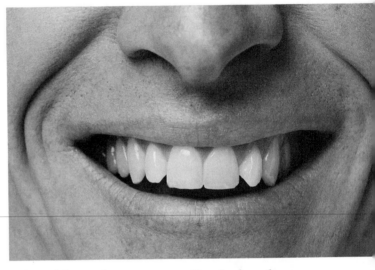

You can have the perfect e-mail system. The perfect groupware. Be wired up the gazoo. But it doesn't mean that the organization rapidly—and exhaustively and in a timely fashion—shares information.

The "quality of conversations"—a cultural/soft trait—is, in the end, the determinant of whether the technology pays off. OR NOT. Sun Microsystems' CIO Bill Raduchel is, not surprisingly, a big champion of the Net . . . who understands its (clear) limits. "The indispensable complementary technology to the Net," he said, "is the Boeing 747." That is . . . FACE-TO-FACE STILL COUNTS. A LOT!

The Institute for Research on Learning (IRL), based in Menlo Park, California, and a spinoff of Xerox's famed Palo Alto Research Center, exists to examine the quality

"All depends on the quality of the conversations."

—Alan Webber, founding editor, *Fast Company*

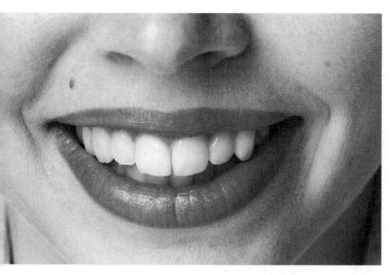

of conversations as well. IRL has discovered that most "learning" in organizations isn't attributable to formal structures . . . or formal electronic networks. Learning occurs (is spurred . . . or thwarted) via informal "passing of the word," in what IRL calls "communities of practice." IRL researchers have discovered, for example, that mindless reengineering in pursuit of extraordinary efficiencies can screw up an organization . . . IF IT INADVERTENTLY DESTROYS COMMUNITIES OF PRACTICE THAT WERE THE BASIS FOR COLLEGIAL LEARNING.

But it's even more subtle than that. Case in point: To increase efficiency in an air-traffic control center, workers were issued ear-covering devices to suppress sound. Productivity dropped instead of improving. Why? Workers in the control tower learned a lot—subconsciously—via being half tuned in to the buzz of nearby conversations. Cut the buzz off, IRL researchers observed, and effectiveness was impaired.

That's practical learning (albeit at a subconscious level). But there's also the social factor per se . . . that is, the glue of human networks. A new factory boss quickly realized how miserably hot the workplace was. To increase productivity, he installed air conditioning. And . . . PRODUCTIVITY DROPPED. What happened? When the air conditioners were on, the noise level was too high for social chitchat. Workers performed better when they were chatting up one another . . . sweating or not . . . as they ran their machines.

It's even more than the human condition. Study after study suggests that apes spend about one-third of their time on "social grooming." That is, ape-chitchat and ape-gossip. Studies of humans turn out about the same. This "unproductive" time is, in fact, extraordinarily productive. It creates the basis from which the "practical" work of being a useful ape—or effective human being—proceeds. Cut out the social chatter . . . and watch efficiency and effectiveness plunge. Hint: This helps explain why open chat rooms remain, by far, the most popular on-line sites.

> **B-I-G IDEA:**
>
> **Innovation = Beautiful Systems.**
>
> **big idea: SYSTEMS "STUFF" = PEOPLE "STUFF" = THE R-E-A-L "HARD" STUFF.**

The Social Side of Systems (TAKE 2)

----

5 percent technology
95 percent psychology and attitude

It is THE great paradox—or perhaps irony is the better word. This is the age of intranets ... the Internet ... virtual organizations ... wired-up organizations. And yet...

THE "MISSING 95 PERCENT" IS SOCIOLOGY ... PSYCHOLOGY ... ANTHROPOLOGY. That is, the information technology—no matter how powerful—is "merely" an ENABLER. You can wire yourself up until you are blue in the face (and broke) ... but in the end it's a people game.

People must willingly contribute knowledge. Drop what they're doing (amidst their increasingly busy schedules) to share knowledge. Research done at Bell Labs shows that any damn fool can send out an e-mail query to 100,000 people. But the senders who get lots of responses are not necessarily the high IQ gang ... instead they're the high E(Emotional)Q gang ... those with the best human/social skills.

Example: VeriFone. VeriFone is a technology company. VeriFone is a systems company. VeriFone is one of my favorite companies. VeriFone is a BEAUTIFUL company. CEO Hatim Tyabji is an avowed technologist. Yet he insists the key to success is "5 percent technology, 95 percent psychology and attitude." That is, a company can spend a king's ransom on 25,000 Lotus Notes licenses . . . but that still doesn't mean there will be any form of automatic sharing of information. (Oh . . . the head nods I get when I make this comment.)

Sharing. Self-organizing. Those are the keys. And they're no easy things to pull off. Tyabji insists on widespread sharing. He spends 90 percent of his life on the road . . . acting as a "beacon" to preach the gospel/"culture of urgency and sharing."

> Hoarding has been the nature of the (fatted) beast. The way a staff professional/middle manager kept her/his position was (is!) to be the sole repository of some set of information.

And still it's not easy! He has significant turnover amongst folks he has painstakingly recruited. The problem: Many of them come from traditional bureaucracies, where hoarding information/knowledge was the norm . . . sharing goes against the grain. They just can't cotton to it. Once again—ho hum. NOT. We are flying into the face of over 200 years worth of de facto organizational doctrine.

What has been the quintessential signature of the staff professional/middle manager? You've got a particularly complex purchasing problem, dealing with some thorny international issues. Where do you go? "To old Dick, up on the 23rd floor." You call Dick. (Or, rather, you call his secretary.) Get an appointment. Five days hence. At 4:15 p.m.

You arrive a few minutes early, and whether Dick is playing bingo or busy, you're kept waiting for 15 minutes, so that he can demonstrate his busyness/importance. (Dilbert would understand!) At 4:30 you're ushered into the Great Man's presence. (Don't forget to bring the kneepads!) He offers you a few driblets of precious info, enough to move you along, but not enough to deplete his reservoir of Dick-alone-has-the-secrets-to-the-issues-that-you-are-interested-in.

I exaggerate. But not by that much, as the reactions from my seminar audiences to this vignette repeatedly suggest. Hoarding has been the nature of the (fatted) beast. The way a staff professional/middle manager kept her/his position was (is!) to be the sole repository of some set of information. Playing the role of the oracle—and keeping the game going for decades in some cases—is the overarching logic in Average Corp. Now Tyabji tells us we must throw away all the rules . . . and play the game . . . HARD . . . by precisely the opposite rules: SHARE . . . SHARE . . . SHARE. GIVE IT AWAY . . . GIVE IT AWAY. FAST . . . FASTER . . . FASTEST.

No easy feat!

> **B-I-G IDEA:**
> **Innovation = Beautiful Systems.**
> **big idea:** WANT HELP WITH YOUR "SHARING"
> NETWORK . . . CALL A SHRINK, NOT A TECHIE.

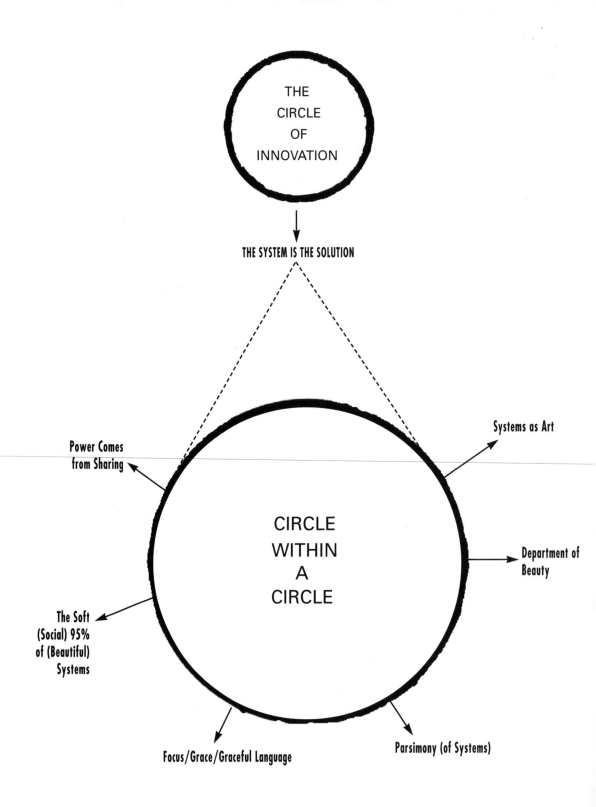

THE
CIRCLE
OF
INNOVATION

THE SYSTEM IS THE SOLUTION

Power Comes
from Sharing

Systems as Art

CIRCLE
WITHIN
A
CIRCLE

Department of
Beauty

The Soft
(Social) 95%
of (Beautiful)
Systems

Focus/Grace/Graceful Language

Parsimony (of Systems)

SEMANTICS ALERT No. 8

Systems = BEAUTY

Department of BEAUTY

Systems = Grace, BEAUTY, Clarity, Focus, Parsimony

Graceful language

Social Side of Systems

Quality of Conversations

Communities of Practice

Systems Success = 95 percent "soft" stuff

The more ephemeral the disembodied new organization, the more important the new plumbing: i.e., it is the new world of systems . . . but systems here are redefined as sources of . . . beauty/parsimony/grace/focus. It's a big part of the answer to "what comes after the dust settles from a major reengineering exercise."

Create Waves of Lust.

Commoditization ISN'T inevitable.*

*It damn well better not be.

The blight of COMMODITIZATION

"There's an absolute dearth of new and exciting fashion-forward products . . . ."

—David Glass, CEO, Wal-Mart

"The Sameness of Things"

—Headline, special issue of *The New York Times Magazine*

"While everything may be better, it is also increasingly the same."

—Paul Goldberger,
chief cultural correspondent,
The New York Times

"Quality as defined by few defects is becoming the price of entry for automotive marketers rather than a competitive advantage."

—J.D. Power and Associates, auto pollster

We've made great quality a religion. (Great. Overdue.) And we've reengineered almost everything. (Great.) We've worked hard on making the customer king. (Great.) We've installed the virtual organization. (Great.) And we've created the learning organization. (Great redux.)

We've empowered anybody . . . and damn near everybody. (Way to go.) We've dramatically shortened product development cycles. (Hooray. And overdue.) And we've adopted quick response practices. (Finally.)

And yet . . . .

I get call after call . . . after call . . . from managers of all kinds of companies . . . from retailers, office-furniture makers, consumer-goods manufacturers, small banks and large banks . . . from Big Six accountancies, insurance companies, software developers, computer manufacturers, telecommunications giants . . . and from engineering-services firms.

All of them have the same complaint. In almost exactly the same words (it's eerie, to tell the truth): "We're faced with an explosion of new competitors, from all over. With an explosion of new products. And they all have fine quality. Customers are getting more and more value conscious. Distributors are ruthlessly exercising their bulging muscles. My margins are eroding. My product/service is becoming commoditized." And they're right. We are experiencing a Blight of Sameness. Good stuff. Coming out fast. And it all looks/feels/tastes/computes . . . about the same.

The problem: The competitiveness wars are still picking up steam. (Reread the forward to this book . . . KLM 0807 . . . to Kuala Lumpur.) And good quality now comes as readily from Malaysia and Brazil and much of China . . . as it does from San Jose (California and Costa Rica) and Tokyo-Osaka and Frankfurt-Stuttgart. Growing look-alikeism (*good* look alikes!) is the kiss of death . . . for the high-wage nation. Hence . . . recall . . . the basic logic behind this entire book/Circle of Innovation: PURSUIT OF THE NEXT ACT. Or: DEATH TO THE BLIGHT OF SAMENESS!

The blight of COMMODITIZATION HITS HOLLYWOOD

(and it's headed for Sundance).

"The mainstream is just ever more costly, more formulaic, more cluttered with special effects."

—Robert Redford,
actor, director, and Sundance founder

The blight of commoditization . . . in MOVIEWORLD. Bob Redford knows. And he gets it exactly right: "The mainstream is just more costly, more formulaic, more cluttered with special effects."

Amen! Which is exactly why more and more "mainstream" agents are coming to Redford's Sundance Film Festival. It's where an astonishingly high share of weird/wacky/pioneering/adventurous work has first been shown—e.g., Steven Soderbergh's *Sex, Lies, and Videotape* in 1989. Tony Vitale's *Kiss Me, Guido*, featured this year at Sundance, is about a straight guy from the Bronx who comes to room with a gay man in New York's Greenwich Village; it is expected to be a fiscally viable film. Only the kooks used to attend. Now the "big guys" come . . . looking for something . . . anything . . . i-n-t-e-r-e-s-t-i-n-g. Which . . . in turn . . . and ironically . . . is moving Sundance into the mainstream . . . and its own
. . . PATH TO SAMENESS.

Look out, Bob!

B-I-G IDEA:

Commoditization Isn't Inevitable.

big idea: TODAY'S "HOT" = TOMORROW'S

(TONIGHT'S) COPYCAT TARGET.

The blight of COMMODITIZATION HITS CONSUMER ELECTRONICS
(and Sharper Image is hitting back).

"I'd rather have the customer come in and say, 'Wow, I've never seen that before,' rather than, 'Wow, look how they've changed that.'"

—Barry Gilbert, COO, Sharper Image

Sharper Image COO Barry Gilbert distinguishes between wow . . . and WOW! On his list, "never seen that before" readily tops "look how they've changed that." These are V-E-R-Y wise words. Listening?

> **B-I-G IDEA:**
> **Commoditization Isn't Inevitable.**
> **big idea: THERE'S wow . . . AND THEN THERE'S WOW!**

The blight of COMMODITIZATION HITS GROCERY STORES

(and Procter & Gamble is hitting back).

"Curb the flavors of the month approach to product development."

—John Pepper, chairman and CEO, Procter & Gamble

Procter & Gamble's CEO John Pepper spotted the Blight of Commoditization in the grocery store. He now gets what you and I have known for years: that the grocery store—despite a 10-fold increase in the rate of "new" products introduced in the last decade—is home to a Sea of Sameness. Worse yet, Pepper admits that even P&G has energetically participated in the me-tooing of the marketplace. And he's determined to put the consumer-goods giant back on a true innovation track.

Pepper wants fewer line extensions, fewer "flavors of the month." Instead . . . he's putting a greater emphasis on the creation of new products with real distinction. Pepper reviewed his proud company's history. Real growth spurts (and bucks!) came from a few products that had a "genuine technological advantage," Pepper says. To wit: Tide . . . Pampers . . . Crest.

Good call, Mr. Pepper. (And it's high time!)

The blight of COMMODITIZATION HITS FAST FOOD

(and Burger King is hitting back).

Ho F----ing Hum

Nightmare No. 1 . . .
"When we did it 'right,' it was still pretty ordinary."

—Barry Gibbons, former CEO, Burger King

When I was a kid, McDonald's was . . . VERY . . . special. Now it's not. (At least in the U.S. of A.) Same store sales are stagnant. (Kind word.) The 55-cent discount deal was a flop. (They can't give the stuff away.) Arch Deluxe . . . aimed at re-reaching out to old McDonald's clientele—e.g., me—was a fiasco.

Well . . . tough as it is for Mickey D. . . . it was worse . . . a handful of years ago . . .

for Burger King. And then along came Barry . . . .

Barry Gibbons is the widely acclaimed "turnaround CEO" who brought Burger King back against McDonald's. (He's now working on various leisure and entertainment ventures.) In his charming memoir about the experience (ordeal), *This Indecision Is Final,* he describes a seminal moment: Early in his tenure, Gibbons was standing offstage prior to a critical meeting with restless franchisees. His first task was to introduce a renowned speaker on customer service. They chatted. The speaker allowed as how, in preparation for the talk, he had visited several Burger Kings.

Gibbons froze. He knew horror stories would undoubtedly be forthcoming. In public. This wasn't the tone he had wanted to set. This was to be a pump-up meeting, for God's sake! Then blessed relief. "I didn't find any problems," the speaker told him. And then it happened . . . .

The speaker continued: "Ho F----ing Hum."

As he reflected, later, on what he dubbed the H.F.H. effect, Gibbons said it may have been his most important learning experience as CEO: "When we did it 'right,' it was still pretty ordinary."

That began his Campaign to Wipe Out H.F.H. It was a great success!

THIS LITTLE ("little" . . . hell) VIGNETTE JUST KEEPS RATTLING AND RATTLING . . . AND RATTLING . . . AROUND IN MY MIND . . . . IT'S THE WORST THING I HAVE EVER HEARD. (I was tempted to call this book . . . "JUST SAY NO TO H.F.H." . . . except that's the title Gibbons has more or less chosen for his next book. More power to him. I hope it outsells mine!)

B-I-G IDEA:

Commoditization Isn't Inevitable.

big idea: ENEMY NO. 1: WHEN WE DO IT "RIGHT". . .

IT'S STILL PRETTY ORDINARY. (OK . . . H.F.H.)

The blight of COMMODITIZATION HITS THE QUALITY MOVEMENT (and it's a knockout punch).

"Quality is conformance to requirements, not goodness."

—Phil Crosby, quality guru

The Concrete Floater Plus!*

ISO 9000 Approved

*Endorsed by Friends of the Dead Poets' Society

"With ISO 9000 you can still have terrible processes and products. You can certify a manufacturer that makes life jackets from concrete, as long as those jackets are made according to the documented procedures and the company provides next of kin with instructions on how to complain about defects. That's absurd."

—Richard Buetow, director of corporate quality for business systems, Motorola

---

"Quality is conformance to requirements," asserts quality guru Phil Crosby, "not goodness."

NONSENSE! (I.e., UTTER nonsense!)

Of course, "conformance to requirements" is (very) important! Not a micrometer of doubt about it. But it's not the whole story. Not even much of the story.

"I know it when I see it." (Quality, that is.) AND I DO!

Quality—the kind that makes you say WOW! whether in a $50-million-a-year-information-systems outsourcing contract, in a jet engine by General Electric, or at a 20-table Italian restaurant in Auckland, New Zealand—is about something that goes far beyond "conformance to requirements." It is about . . . yes . . . GOODNESS! (DAMN IT!)

B-I-G IDEA:
Commoditization Isn't Inevitable.

big idea:
BY-THE-NUMBERS QUALITY IS THE LEAST OF IT!

Just say no to

COMMODITY

This is . . . THE WHOLE DAMNED POINT . . . of this book. "Commoditization" will not do. I.e.: INNOVATE OR DIE. DE-COMMODITIZE OR DIE.

L-I-S-T-E-N UP!!

P-L-E-A-S-E.

B-I-G IDEA:

Commoditization Isn't Inevitable.

big idea:

SHOUT "NO! NO! NO!" TO COMMODITIZATION.

Say
yes
to
WOW!

WOW! is the answer.

B-I-G IDEA:

Commoditization Isn't Inevitable.

big idea:

WOW ! !

The Ritz-Carlton says yes to WOW!

"The Ritz-Carlton experience enlivens the senses, instills well-being, and fulfills even the unexpressed wishes and needs of our guests."

—from The Ritz-Carlton credo

What's the next act? World-class quality alone won't do it. Reengineering alone won't do it. Rapid product development alone won't do it. The next act ....

How about: "Fulfills even the unexpressed wishes and needs" ... "enlivens the senses."

It's not that Ritz-Carlton tolerates pretzel crumbs under the bed. It doesn't. But pretzel crumb-less beds, like the TQM'd product, is not enough to stand out in a crowded, pretzel-crumb-free market. It takes something (VERY/INCREASINGLY) special ... to stand (WAY) out.

So ... can you imagine "enlivens the senses"/"fulfills even the unexpressed wishes ..." as a specific test/hurdle in your product development manual? CAN WE LEARN TO USE WORDS LIKE THIS? (WE MUST!) And not just for hotels. Or restaurants. What about those terms for a professional *accountancy*? A *steel*-services company? Makes (very good) sense to me!

And you??

"The Ritz-Carlton experience . . . conforms to requirements."

—Ritz per Phil Crosby?? (Mr. Anti-"Goodness")

And if Phil Crosby had been consulted on the Ritz-Carlton credo . . .
WHAT DO YOU THINK?

B-I-G IDEA:
Commoditization Isn't Inevitable.
big idea: EMBRACE THE STANDOUT (ODD?) LANGUAGE . . .
E.G., ENLIVENS THE SENSES. CAN YOU?

Virgin says yes to... WOW!
(So does... Southwest!)

"We didn't want to get in the transportation industry. We're still in the entertainment industry—at 25,000 feet."

—Richard Branson,
chairman and CEO, Virgin Group

"We defined a personality as well as a market niche. We seek to amuse, surprise, entertain."

—Herb Kelleher,
chairman and CEO, Southwest Airlines

Consider Virgin Air, the upstart gnat that gives British Air fits. Virgin's in-flight amenities include . . . magicians and masseuses (and not just for first-class travelers). It's . . . well . . . ENTERTAIN-MENT . . . at 25,000 feet.

Or take . . . SOUTHWEST.

On-time record: stunning. Lost baggage: negli-gible. Safety record: the very best. Customer com-plaints: the fewest.

All that's great (!) . . . but it's far from the whole SWA story. Southwest's flight attendants may well begin the standard safety announcement by saying, "THERE MAY BE 50 WAYS TO LEAVE YOUR LOVER . . . BUT THERE ARE ONLY SIX EXITS FROM THIS AIRCRAFT." SWA has made flying . . . FUN AGAIN . . . even for the (v-e-r-y jaded) likes of me.

It's those special touches that take Southwest and Virgin Air over the top.

AMEN! (Or . . . rather . . . WOW!)

B-I-G IDEA:

Commoditization Isn't Inevitable.

big idea:

QUALITY = GOODNESS (+ ENTERTAINMENT) (+ FUN).

Domain says yes to WOW!

"We do not sell 'furniture' at Domain. We sell dreams."

—Judy George,
chairwoman and CEO,
Domain Home Fashions

Sell dreams . . . not furniture. And, indeed, Judy George does just that in her scintillating, fast-growing, home-furnishings chain, Domain Home Fashions.

But what about her language?

I was addressing a group of furniture makers and retailers. There was a strong contingent—surprise!—of old white males/OWMs. (It's an old industry, particularly on the production side.)

Their reaction to my Judy George line? Tittering. Worse still, wondering why they'd wasted their time listening to me fawn over such flowery language.

So I attacked the problem head on. "Okay," I said, "I know what you're thinking. You're thinking the only time 'dreams' have anything to do with furniture is when you're selling a bed. Is this guy smoking funny stuff . . . and inhaling? Real people—g-u-y-s—don't talk like that.

"Well, I beg to differ.

"First, Judy George is as real as they come. Much more important: She believes . . . and lives . . . exactly those words. They have been her key to success. I think the problem with the furniture industry is that it sells far too much 'furniture' and nowhere near enough 'dreams.'" (And besides, as I'll explain later, "guys" buy d-a-m-n little of the product . . . .)

> "I think the problem with the furniture industry is that it sells far too much 'furniture' and nowhere near enough 'dreams.'"

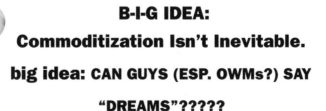

B-I-G IDEA:

Commoditization Isn't Inevitable.

big idea: CAN GUYS (ESP. OWMs?) SAY

"DREAMS"?????

INTEL says yes to WOW!
(and then some!)

"We need to create waves . . . of lust for our product."

—Andy Grove, chairman and CEO, Intel

This is Andy Grove. Talking to customers? Nope! TALKING TO SECURITIES ANALYSTS. And, yes, using those words: WAVES OF LUST. I love it!

Intel is the prototypical engineering firm . . . and yet Grove and company understand lust . . . intimately. Can you use words like "lust" in your organization? If you can't . . . you've got a B-I-G problem . . . as Andy . . . and I . . . see it.

B-I-G IDEA:
Commoditization Isn't Inevitable.
big idea: L-U-S-T!

Jerry Garcia says yes to WOW!
(and then some!)

"You do not merely want to
be considered just the best
of the best. You want to be
considered the **only** ones
who do what you do."

—Jerry Garcia,
the late legendary musician/philosopher-king

What is genuine excellence? It's Michael Jordan. No one has . . .
EVER . . . played the game the way he does. He's taken it to a new
level. More than that: He has reinvented basketball.

It's my problem with benchmarking. Benchmark
against "the best." But that evades the biggest
issue: Those who really make a difference
create a . . . whole new way . . . of
doing business (basketball!) in
their part of the market. Invent
whole new markets. Best of the
best? That wasn't Netscape's
approach to the Internet. They
wanted to "be the only ones who
do what we do." Jerry Garcia
would have been proud!

This, of course, is the "analytic" point of
the book and my chief economic argument:
Innovation/Just Say No to Commodity/Just Say Yes to
Wow! But it's more personal than that: I cannot . . . for the
life of me . . . understand why one would get up in the
morning unless—à la Jerry Garcia—it was in an effort to "be
the only ones who do what we do."

"You do not merely want to be considered the best of the best. You want to be considered in conformance with requirements."

—Guess who?

One more (repetitive?) time: Perhaps this is the way Phil Crosby ("conformance to requirements . . . not goodness") would have put it. WHAT DO YOU THINK?

HINT: I THINK IT SUCKS.

> **B-I-G IDEA:**
> **Commoditization Isn't Inevitable.**
> **big idea:**
> **WINNERS = RE-INVENTORS = JERRY KNOWS.**

Feel WOW!
(and lust!)

```
MY LUST HIERARCHY:
Satisfy . . .
Conform to requirements . . .
Exceed expectations . . .
Delight . . .
WOW! . . .
Raving Fans . . .
Lust After . . .
ONLY ONES WHO DO WHAT YOU DO
```

Nothing is so dry as "satisfy the customer." Except: "conform to requirements." And I despise "exceed expectations" . . . it lacks any emotion. But I do like:

CUSTOMER DELIGHT . . . WOW! . . . RAVING FANS (Ken Blanchard and Sheldon Bowles wrote a book by that name) . . . LUST AFTER (Grove/Intel) . . . ONLY ONES WHO DO WHAT YOU DO (Jerry Garcia . . . himself).

Yes . . . THE LUST HIERARCHY! How do you stack up? (Remember: Words are important! If you're not discussing topics like "raving fans" . . . you're missing a b-i-g beat.)

B-I-G IDEA:

Commoditization Isn't Inevitable.

big idea: LEARN TO USE THE "W"-WORD (*WOW!*) AND
"L"-WORD (*LUST*) IN SERIOUS/SOBER/BUSINESS
DISCUSSIONS . . . OR . . . PERISH.

Get WOW!
(everywhere)

Rubbermaid
(most admired)

SWA
(!!)

Andersen
(windows at the Super Bowl)

Granite Rock Co.
(Baldrige + Ready Mix do mix)

Etc.

Once again, I'd ranted . . . and raved . . . on my favorite topic . . . NO SUCH THING AS A COMMODITY. The fellow came up at a break. He was in the fencing business. (Barriers . . . not swords.) "But surely, Tom, there are limits," he said. I.e., fencing?

My quick answer: NO!!

Upon reflection . . . I meant it. In 1994 and 1995 America's most admired corporation, according to *Fortune*, was . . . Rubbermaid. Brand recognition hangs in there with the Nikes and Levi Strausses of the world. Quality is great. Design awards are theirs by the bushel. They've even managed to establish Rubbermaid "boutiques" in mass merchants' stores. The product: often as not, a 97-cent rubber or plastic storage item. Others would call it a . . . COMMODITY. Not Rubbermaid! Not by a long shot.

Or take Southwest Airlines. (I do take them.) Sure . . . they are a "discounter." That is . . . their prices are low. But their service? NOBODY BEATS IT! Message: A low sticker price and sky-high service do go hand-in-glove . . . as does an astonishingly strong P&L/balance sheet . . . and "personality."

And . . . the humble window . . . not far from fencing. Andersen, the Minnesota-based window maker, has branded (!!!) windows. How do I know? All you have to do is watch the Super Bowl (along with everybody else in the world). Andersen, among others, typically advertises there. Window-as-commodity? Don't tell Andersen!

And then there's Granite Rock Co. (Oh yes!) Based in Watsonville, California, it was a 1992 winner of the small-company Malcolm Baldrige National Quality Award. Its business? Road rock. Ready Mix. That is, driving a cement truck . . . and providing a nationally recognized tippy-top-of-the-line service . . . does mix.

Fencing? Use your imagination, my friend! Andersen does! Southwest Airlines does! Rubbermaid does! And so does Granite Rock Co. What are you waiting for?

B-I-G IDEA:
Commoditization Isn't Inevitable.
big idea: N-O L-I-M-I-T-S (D-A-M-N I-T).

Be WOW!

Anything can be differentiated. (Witness Rubbermaid and Granite Rock.) Still, I do sympathize/empathize with those who attempt to decommoditize a 97-cent plastic product . . . or road rock.

But my sympathy and empathy run (TOTALLY) out when it comes to . . . professional services . . . of any sort. Oy vey! I've had Big Six accountants tell me that the audit is "becoming commoditized." I've had engineering-services professionals tell me that their business is being determined "entirely by price." I've had trainers lament that "leadership training" is now a commodity.

And . . . it makes me sick. Look . . . THE DELIVERY OF A PROFESSIONAL SERVICE IS ABSOLUTELY, POSITIVELY NOTHING MORE THAN THE DELIVERY OF YOU AND/OR ME!

Is the person you see when you look in the mirror at 6:00 a.m. a "commodity"? No! It's Tom Peters. It's Mary Jones. It's Jeff Smith. It's Jane Doe. It is a person. Singular. With character. Unique skills. The delivery of professional services is the delivery of . . . Jane Doe, Tom Peters, and so on.

If professional services become "commoditized," it means that you and I have become commoditized. I say again: The delivery of a professional service is the delivery of who you are, who I am.

P-E-R-I-O-D.

WANTED FOR COMMODITIZATION
(and early product rejection)

PD 564607 6830

B-I-G IDEA:
Commoditization Isn't Inevitable.

big idea: PROFESSIONAL SERVICE(S) = YOU
(AS A PERSON).

PROFESSIONAL SERVICE(S) = ME (AS A PERSON).

Follow WOW!
(Not the customer)

"The customer is a rear-view mirror, not a guide to the future."
—George Colony, Forrester Research

Chuck Williams is founder of the high-end cookware catalog and retail operation Williams-Sonoma. *Newsweek* says he and his company reinvented the kitchen. Williams explained his secret of success: "I just bought what I liked. I never bought anything I didn't like. Fortunately there have been a lot of people out there who like what I like."

Listening to customers . . . ALL-IMPORTANT. On the other hand . . . customers will, more or less, tell you only that they want what you've already got . . . in a different color, spiffed up a little bit, with this new feature or that.

Products and services that transform a small—or large—corner of the marketplace tend to be things that customers, with the exception perhaps of a few brave pioneers, couldn't imagine. An increasing part of your role—in a crowded marketplace/Sea of Sameness—is to push/lead your customers toward places where they did not know they wished to venture.

Simple (logical) truth: Virtually all products that have revolutionized the marketplace have been rejected by customers . . . often for years, even decades. Why: uncomfortable/scary!

Trust WOW!

EARLY CUSTOMER REJECTION:

Chrysler Minivans

Post-its

VCRs

Fax Machines

FedEx

CNN

Cellular Phones

Heart-assist Pumps

Etc.

Fortune ran an article on products rejected by customers at the get-go. The list included Chrysler minivans, Post-its, VCRs, fax machines, FedEx, CNN, cellular phones . . . and even heart-assist pumps!

Take the Post-it note. It took 12 years (!) for inventor Art Fry to transform his notion into a marketplace success. (Now 3M is booking in the neighborhood of $1 billion from Post-its and ancillaries.) That is, we were all pretty content with paper clips and scrap paper . . . and had no felt need to replace them. Post-its hardly looked like one of the world's great necessities . . . and that's putting it mildly . . . when they first (and second) popped out of the box. Now? Can't live without them. Right? (I can't.)

Or the fax machine. V-E-R-Y slow to take off. WHY? Obvious. (In retrospect.) There weren't any/many fax machines to send faxes to!

PRODUCTS THAT INVENT/REINVENT A MARKET ARE (ALMOST UNFAILINGLY) REJECTED AT THE START BY CUSTOMERS . . . A PAINFUL PROCESS THAT CAN TAKE YEARS TO WORK OUT.

Lesson: Would-be (serious) leaders must suffer significant pain. Some/many/most/almost all don't make it. But those who do survive the agony of early (and continuing) rejection end up being the . . . only ones . . . who transform the world.

> **B-I-G IDEA:**
> **Commoditization Isn't Inevitable.**
> **big idea: REALLY G-R-E-A-T STUFF = AWKWARD**
> **(FOR YEARS!).**

Find WOW!

"Most companies don't really believe they can make a better product."

—Ely Callaway, founder, Callaway Golf

Good God! Could this be true? In 1998 . . . 1999. . . 2000?
Ely Callaway's lines scare me to death . . . because I almost believe it.

**B-I-G IDEA:
Commoditization Isn't Inevitable.
big idea: YIKES . . . YOU GOTTA BELIEVE YOU CAN
BE SPECIAL . . . IN TODAY'S (ROWDY) WORLD/
MARKETPLACE. RIGHT?**

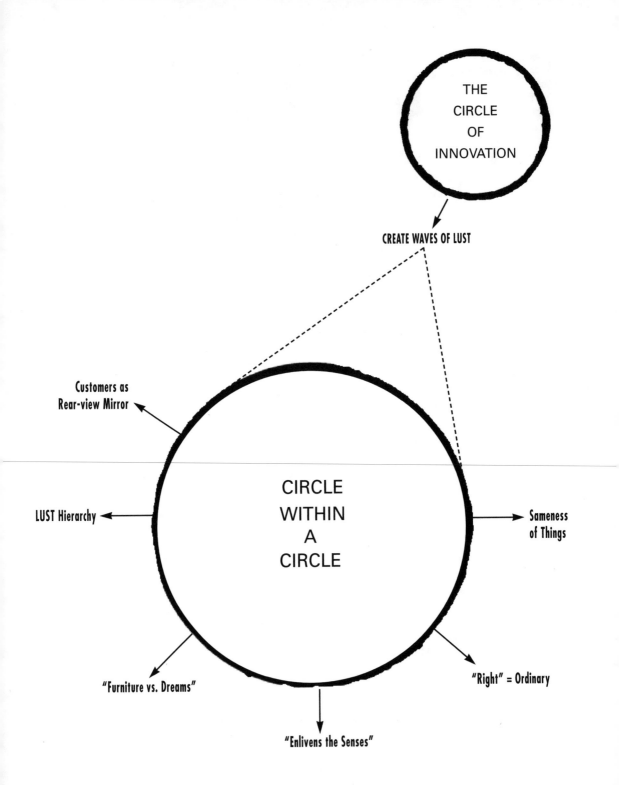

THE
CIRCLE
OF
INNOVATION

CREATE WAVES OF LUST

Customers as
Rear-view Mirror

CIRCLE
WITHIN
A
CIRCLE

LUST Hierarchy

Sameness
of Things

"Furniture vs. Dreams"

"Right" = Ordinary

"Enlivens the Senses"

SEMANTICS ALERT No. 9

Blight of Commoditization/Sea of Sameness
There's wow and WOW!
Stamp out FLAVOR OF THE MONTH
H.F.H. (Hmmm.)
Woe betide when "right" = ordinary
Conformance to Requirements vs. Goodness
Just Say No to Commodity
"enlivens the senses"/
"instills well being"/
"amuse . . . surprise . . . entertain"/
"dreams . . . not furniture"/
"waves of lust"/
"the only ones who do what we do"
LUST Hierarchy
Wowers of Ready Mix
Customer as rear-view mirror

Chapters 2 through 8 reinvent "organizations" and "workers" . . .
first deconstructing them (chapters 2 through 5) . . . then reconstitut-
ing them (chapters 6 through 8). ■ Toward what end? ■
The next six chapters attempt to answer that question . . . beginning
with this overview, which makes the case for moving (far)
beyond quality/TQM and even rapid product development to
seek new/bold/soft avenues leading toward exceptional (sustainable?) differentiation/decommoditization.

Tommy Hilfiger Knows.

Say (<u>SHOUT!</u>) YES to <u>BRAND</u>!

Stand (Brand) out

"The increasing difficulty in differentiating among products and the speed with which competitors take up innovations will . . . assist the rise and rise of the brand."

—Gillian Law and Nick Grant,
marketing experts, New Zealand

from the crowd!

Not long ago, just about everyone had given up brands for dead. It was ... THE AGE OF NARROWCASTING. Or ... ONE-TO-ONE-MARKETING. Every consumer would become a market-segment-of-one ... catered to with customized services and products ... sold to with customized advertising.

Fine. To a point.

I'm a fan of mass customization ... for example, catalogs from big catalogers tailored to my needs as discerned from past purchasing behavior. But when Williams-Sonoma sends me a tailored offering, I'm still mostly buying Chuck Williams' taste and the overall Williams-Sonoma brand. I trust him/it. In fact, with gajillions of catalogs assaulting my rural Vermont mailbox, the Williams-Sonoma brand—as Gillian Law and Nick Grant say—is more important than ever. Standing out from the (growing, stampeding, rambunctious) herd ... that's the message of this book, right? Of course, the product/service must be distinct ... WOW-ish/LUST-worthy as I keep saying. But, in an increasingly crowded market, product/service distinction alone is (increasingly) not enough. IF YOU BUILD IT (A G-R-E-A-T IT), THEY WILL NOT NECESSARILY COME. A/the answer: branding.

Stand (Brand) Outs!

AOL

Apple

Arthur Andersen

Blockbuster

Body Shop

Charles Schwab

CNN

EDS

Intel

MCI

MTV

Nike

Rubbermaid

Saturn

Snapple

Starbucks

Virgin

Etc.,Etc.,Etc.

The market is hopelessly crowded. As a result: BRANDING IS MORE—NOT LESS—IMPORTANT THAN EVER . . . if you want to stand out . . . even a little bit . . . in that insanely crowded/ever more crowded marketplace.

And it can be done! Today! In the most crowded markets!

Nike. Virgin. Body Shop. Saturn. (In three short years, Saturn became the second most valuable nameplate in the insanely competitive, $600 billion strong U.S. automotive marketplace.) CNN. MTV. AOL. MCI. Charles Schwab. Apple. (Sure, Apple's staggering . . . now. But the friendly Apple logo gouged a huge hole in IBM's seemingly impregnable fortress.) Blockbuster. Snapple. (Snapple, too, is having big problems . . . but it damn well wedged its way onto the shelves . . . in spite of the "impossible" task of bumping Pepsi and Coke.) Intel. ("Intel Inside" has paid off in spades for a super high-tech doodad that no one sees—i.e., it's "inside" someone else's box.) Starbucks. Rubbermaid. (Yes . . . Rubbermaid's been around for a while. Hardly new. On the other hand, in the last 15 years it has worked like hell at branding-the-bejesus-out-of-the-mundane. And has it ever worked! Most admired corporation in the United States in 1994! Most admired corporation in the United States 1995! Brand recognition scores that rank right up there with Coke and Walt Disney. With 97-cent plastic and rubber thingeys!)

Accountants were allowed to advertise, starting a few years ago. Nobody's done it better than . . . ARTHUR ANDERSEN. Now, other professional service firms are getting into the act . . . BRANDING THEMSELVES.

Take Electronic Data Systems/EDS: Its first global ad campaign was launched October of 1996. EDS projected an $80-million media buy in the first year.

No room for new brands? Exactly wrong! It's the age of message glut . . . and never has there been more room for/need for new brands/aggressive branding. Lobbing it out there . . . even if it's terrific and perfectly homed in on a particular consumer . . . ain't going to get you very far. (Sorry.)

Brand! Brand!! Brand!!! That's the message . . . for the late 90s and beyond.

 B-I-G IDEA: Innovation = Branding Mania.

big idea: IT CAN BE DONE . . . IN THE MOST CROWDED MARKETS.

Martha Stewart Stands (Brands) Out!

Today: Canapés with crème fraîche!

Tomorrow: The world!

"It's a really good thing."

I believe in being special. (No surprise!) And I believe that special is often inversely correlated with size. That is, the ability to stand out is more readily achievable by the clever mom-and-pop than by the giant.

And . . . I increasingly believe . . . this goes for branding as well.

Too many (most) people equate branding with Marlboro or Walt Disney. To be sure, Marlboro, Disney, Nike, Saturn et al. have done one hell of a job with branding. But not so many years ago, Martha Stewart was just piddling along as a caterer in a high-net-worth Connecticut town.

Then she began to brand herself. (Did she ever!) So, too, Dennis Rodman, he of the Chicago Bulls and technicolor hair.

Branding means nothing more (and nothing less!) than creating a distinct personality . . . and telling the world about it . . . by hook or by crook.

A textile startup I'm working with has only a handful of employees . . . and modest sales at this stage. But we are hell-bent and intent upon branding in our underbranded niche . . . nationally at first, globally eventually. That means spending like half-drunken sailors on, say, marketing materials. Spending "wildly" (though with precision) on advertising. Making sure that every bit of our message focuses on the designer/a consistent theme/a distinct look. Every piece of ancillary material is aimed at enhancing our image. No, we haven't pulled it off yet. But many in the industry would say that we have traveled an amazingly long distance in a very short time.

I believe it can be done! I believe it's *the* lost opportunity not to try! Hey, to some extent, I'm a brand myself! And I've done it, by and large, by myself . . . by aping the successes of the Oprahs, the Dennis Rodmans, the Martha Stewarts, the Anita Roddicks, the Richard Bransons, and other instinctive I-AM-MY-BRAND types.

> Branding means nothing more (and nothing less!) than creating a distinct personality . . . and telling the world about it . . . by hook or by crook.

Tommy Hilfiger Stands (Brands) Out!

"Brand power . . . how did Tommy Hilfiger do it? With a little money, a lot of chutzpah, and an almost magical touch for promotion."
—*Individual Investor*

Tommy Hilfiger has done it . . . from scratch. One of his secrets is "an almost magical touch for promotion." Another is his attention to detail. Look at most any Hilfiger garment, and you'll find that one button hole is ringed with bright green embroidery.

Anita Roddick of The Body Shop understands. So do Tiger Woods . . . and his dad. And . . . heaven knows . . . Howard Stern. And . . . in his own odd, nerdy way . . . B-I-L-L G-A-T-E-S.

Branding? Possible! From the start!! If that's your mindset. (Just ask Tommy and Tiger and Billy G. . . .)

 B-I-G IDEA: Innovation = Branding Mania.
big idea: START BRANDING . . . ON DAY ONE.

Virgin
Stands (Brands) Out!

"Quite a lot of companies don't build their brands. As the chairman, I'm trying to promote the Virgin name and spread the word."

—Richard Branson,
chairman and CEO, Virgin Group

Richard Branson is a shameless promoter! Make that . . . A VERY PURPOSEFUL . . . promoter. He is (seen) everywhere! He lives life on the wild side! He takes on Goliaths (British Airways) with glee! He's the billionaire underdog! He's the globe-circling, life-jeopardizing balloonist! He's . . . BRANSON! He's a brand builder. Branson talks brand. Branson lives brand. Brand = Branson = Virgin.

B-I-G IDEA: Innovation = Branding Mania.

big idea: LOVE YOUR BRAND. LIVE YOUR BRAND.

EnergyOne Stands (Brands) Out!

"I want to make the invisible
visible."

—Bill Burgess,
senior vice president,
marketing, UtiliCorp

"Soon, you'll buy your energy in
a box off-the-shelf at Wal-Mart."

—Richard C. Green, Jr.,
CEO and chairman, UtiliCorp

"I want to do to the electron
what Kellogg's did to the
corn flake."

—Richard C. Green, Jr.,
CEO and chairman, UtiliCorp

REVOLUTION is coming . . . to the huge electrical-utilities industy. And nobody is further in front of the curve than relatively unknown UtiliCorp of Kansas City, Missouri, and its chiefs . . . Richard Green and Bill Burgess.

Burgess and Green are on a holy mission. And, so far, they seem to be pulling it off. That is . . . THEY ARE BRANDING ELECTRICITY. Burgess and Green think it can be done. Green and Burgess know it can be done. The question is only one: Who will do it? They are determined that it will be them/UtiliCorp/UtiliCorp's brand signature . . . EnergyOne.

I wouldn't bet against them.

Branding . . . is No. 1 . . . according to Burgess . . . and Green . . . and me.

B-I-G IDEA: Innovation = Branding Mania.

big idea: ANYTHING (!) CAN BE BRANDED (!)

Southern Co.
Stands (Brands) Out!

"When you think about a power company, who do you think about? You don't think about anybody!"

—Bill Dahlberg, CEO, The Southern Co.

Bill Dahlberg. Utility executive. Marketing meeting. (Hmmm!) Atlanta. 1/97. He's dressed in his signature . . . BLACK BATMAN CAPE. (Yes . . . I said utility executive . . . not the dark knight.) He's ranting . . . and raving . . . about branding . . . long before utility deregulation comes to pass. But when it does, you and I are gonna remember . . . The Southern Co.

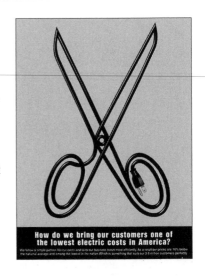

How do we bring our customers one of the lowest electric costs in America?

We follow a simple pattern. We cut costs and tailor our business to run more efficiently. As a result our prices are 15% below the national average and among the lowest in the nation. Which is something that suits our 3.6 million customers perfectly.

B-I-G IDEA: Innovation = Branding Mania.

big idea: BRAND TO BEAT THE HERD TO THE WATERING HOLE.

How do you
Stand(Brand)Out!

Sell MSEs . . .
Memorable Sensory Experiences

In their exciting and original book, *Marketing Aesthetics,* Bernd Schmitt and Alex Simonson got at the heart of effective branding . . . that is, creating a . . . memorable sensory experience.

"We coined the phrase 'marketing aesthetics,'" they write, "to refer to the marketing of sensory experiences in corporate or brand output that contributes to the organization's or brand's identity. Today's environments 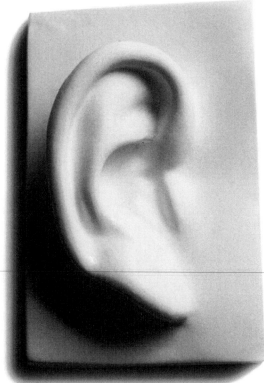 are multimedia, multichannel, multisensory, and digital. Communications, transportation and products and services are becoming global. Worldwide, more people than ever are living in cities, and consumer lifestyles and preferences—especially among young people—are intense, short-lived, and ever-changing . . . .

"In this world of heavy communications flow through interactive and sensory-laden multimedia, product attributes and benefits, brand names and brand associations are no longer sufficient to catch attention, to draw consumers. Businesses that engage consumers are those that afford them a memorable sensory experience that ties in with the positioning of the company, product, or service."

The operative word: EXPERIENCE. It's the Starbucks EXPERIENCE . . . the Nike EXPERIENCE . . . the Caterpillar EXPERIENCE . . . the Levi's EXPERIENCE . . . the Absolut EXPERIENCE. And that experience, Schmitt and Simonson argue, can be managed (VERY) specifically.

It begins with the word(s) . . . MARKETING AESTHETICS. That is:

"managing aesthetic experiences" . . . "aesthetics strategy" . . . "marketing of sensory experiences . . . that contribute to the organization's or brand's identity" . . . "mapping strategic vision to sensory stimuli." Taking these ideas per se (VERY) seriously is the whole point.

The book itself devotes entire chapters to . . . look . . . feel . . . taste . . . touch . . . sound . . . smell . . . texture . . . color . . . typeface (on logos, letterheads, etc.). And . . . it adds up to . . . ? E-X-P-E-R-I-E-N-C-E!

There's a lot more to it than this brief summary. (I.e., read the damn book!) My objective here is to titillate and . . . STRONGLY SUGGEST . . . that this is (VERY) important/strategic stuff. And . . . that it's wildly under-attended to. And: It applies to the independent contractor, the seven-person training department, the 22-table restaurant . . . as well as to our friends at Caterpillar or Starbucks or Nike or Levi Strauss . . . or Absolut.

B-I-G IDEA: Innovation = Branding Mania.

big idea: BRAND IMAGE/MEMORY = AESTHETIC

EXPERIENCE = MANAGEABLE.

How do you Stand(Brand)Out?

Develop a
Brand(ing)
obsession!

How do you get great quality? Motorola knows. Milliken & Co. knows. Obsess on it. Spend (lots of) time on it. Alter—usually dramatically—every system in every department in the organization to reflect quality-above-all-else. That is, as I've said so many times before . . . ATTENTION IS ALL THERE IS!

So, too, branding. Read the best books on branding (start with David Aaker's *Building Strong Brands* and *Managing Brand Equity: Capitalizing on the Value of a Brand Name*), and you will come across lots of tips. But there's really only one tip worth the name: Pay attention to it! Manage it! Treat it as an obsession! Talk it up . . . at any and every occasion, no matter how trivial.

Herb Kelleher? Master brander. How? Not a moment—literally, it seems—goes by when he isn't living the Southwest brand. So, too, Rich Teerlink (Harley-Davidson) and Larry Ellison (Oracle) and Andy Grove (why do you think technologist Grove is always so available to the media?).

An obsession with branding isn't simply a "marketing department" issue. It's an accounts receivable issue. A purchasing issue. An information systems issue. Heaven knows, a human resources issue. Every decision . . . every system . . . should reflect, visibly, the specific attention to (obsession with) BRANDING (voice, etc.).

An obsession with branding is also about leverage. Just look at where Nike and Disney have gone. The essence of branding is extending the name. TO A POINT. At some stage, that extension can become dilution. How much is enough? Nobody knows for sure. It's pure art. Leverage is good. Too much leverage is bad.

> **B-I-G IDEA: Innovation = Branding Mania.**
> **big idea: BRANDING AIN'T AN ACCIDENTAL AVOCATION.**

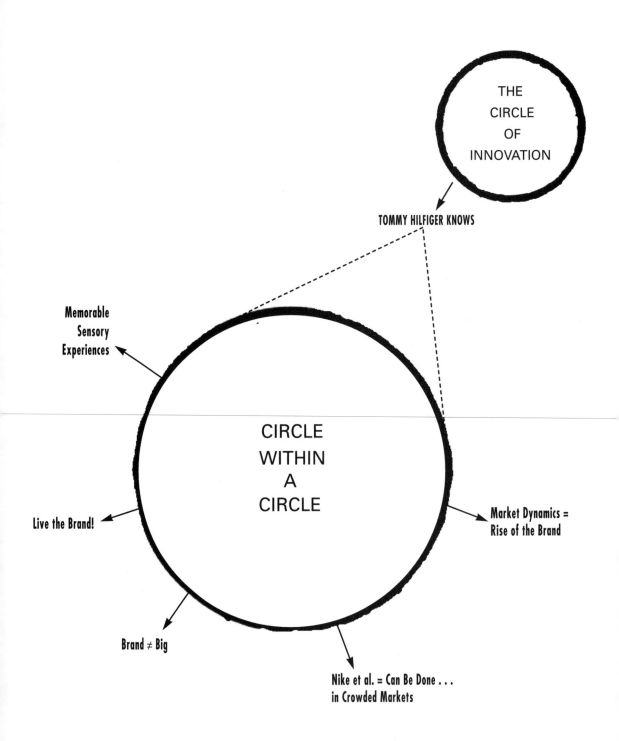

THE
CIRCLE
OF
INNOVATION

TOMMY HILFIGER KNOWS

Memorable
Sensory
Experiences

CIRCLE
WITHIN
A
CIRCLE

Live the Brand!

Market Dynamics =
Rise of the Brand

Brand ≠ Big

Nike et al. = Can Be Done . . .
in Crowded Markets

SEMANTICS ALERT No. 10

Age of THE BRAND

Branding = Possible in Crowded Markets

Martha and Tommy and Richard Know

Brand ≠ Big

Memorable Sensory Experiences

Marketing Aesthetics

Living THE BRAND

The move beyond "inevitable" commoditization is fleshed out in five chapters, beginning with this one. Consider each chapter a key tactic for implementing immodest differentiation/decommoditization.

Step No. 1: Brand the devil out of "it." Even the smallest firms can learn from Intel and Nike and Martha Stewart and Tommy Hilfiger that brand loyalty is not dead. It is more alive and more important than ever.

Become a Connoisseur of Talent.

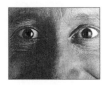

WOW needs WOW.

WOW-ers will WOW.

Who are the WOW-ERS?

Steve Jobs knows.

"Expose yourself to the best things humans have done and then try to bring those things into what you are doing."

—Steve Jobs,
Apple/NeXT/Pixar and philosopher king,
on developing "insanely great" new products

Sometimes Steve Jobs wins (Apple, Pixar.) Sometimes he loses. (NeXT.) But it's never for lack of trying . . . or imagination. Every product . . . any product . . . Jobs says . . . can be great . . . in fact "insanely great." Requirement No. 1: Great (read interesting) people. For his product-development teams Jobs hires individuals with "intriguing backgrounds" and "extraordinary taste"—for example, artists, poets, and historians. Their magic, according to Jobs: They have exposed themselves to "the best things humans have done and then brought those things into their projects." Jobs' original Macintosh team, for instance, was a marvelous mix of artists and engineers. Their aesthetic interests were as strong as their techie interests—hence, the still standard-setting user-friendly Apple operating system. Hired any poets, artists, or historians lately? (Hint: I'm . . . damned . . . serious.)

Who are the WOW-ERS?

Jack Mingo, Patricia Pitcher, and a therapist in Santa Cruz know.

"It's the cracked ones that let the light into the world."

—Therapist's bumper sticker, Santa Cruz, California

"You say you don't want emotional, volatile, and unpredictable, just imaginative? Sorry, they only come in a package ... I can offer you a dedicated, loyal, honest, realistic, knowledgeable package, but the imagination bit will be rather limited."

—Patricia Pitcher,
author, *The Drama of Leadership*

"Our most beloved products were developed by hunch, guesswork, and fanaticism, by creators who were eccentric—or even stark raving mad."

—Jack Mingo,
author, *How the Cadillac Got Its Fins*

Jack Mingo's book, *How the Cadillac Got Its Fins,* is entertaining. AND IT CONTAINS A . . . VERY . . . SOBERING MESSAGE. That is, really neat stuff seldom comes from "the suits" (especially if those suits are charcoal grey or black). To do something out-of-step requires . . . surprise (!) . . . an out-of-step person . . . in an environment that nourishes the out-of-step.

That's not to say the average out-of-step person is an automatic source of successful products or services. Most out-of-step people are . . . simply . . . out of step. And they fail. On the other hand . . . all the world's successes are due to the determined efforts—politics or products—of those fanatical/crazy few. I.e.: IT'S THE CRACKED ONES THAT LET THE LIGHT INTO THE WORLD . . . INCLUDING THE WORLD OF BUSINESS.

B-I-G IDEA:

Innovation = Talent-Based Enterprise.

big idea: ALL (GREAT) SUCCESSES COME FROM COCKEYED VIEWS OF THE WORLD.

Who are the WOW-ERS?

Alan Webber knows.

"Experience is out. Inexperience is in. It may make a lot of middle-aged business-men very uncomfortable, but it's a fact of life."

—Alan Webber,
founding editor, *Fast Company*

If you ask me (and by reading this, you implicitly have), *Fast Company* has no peers among magazines chronicling the new-organizational-world order. Savvy founding editor Alan Webber puts it this way: "Experience is out. Inexperience is in. It may make a lot of middle-aged businessmen very uncomfortable, but it's a fact of life."

Reluctantly, I must add my own . . . AMEN!! Of course, there's a role for experience. But there is—increasingly—a role for beautiful naïveté. "Industry" definitions are changing. Corporations are dropping off the likes of the Fortune 500 list in record numbers. Upstarts are doing them in . . . time and time . . . and time . . . again.

Perhaps you don't buy the above. Okay! But . . . at least . . . promise me one thing . . . THINK ABOUT IT . . . SERIOUSLY . . . SOON.

Tony Hsieh, Ali Partovi, Susan Cooney, and Sanjay Madan know.

Does this look like your top-management team? No? Maybe you (your company) have a problem. Meet Tony, Ali, Susan, and Sanjay . . . founders of LinkExchange . . . a top Web provider of advertising services.

Is this (are they) the look of the future? Nope. Make that the look of . . . t-o-d-a-y.

B-I-G IDEA:

Innovation = Talent-Based Enterprise.

big idea: YE GADS . . . EXPERIENCE-AS-MILLSTONE?

COULD BE. (PROBABLY IS?)

Bernard Arnault
is crazy for **crazies.**

"I'm not interested in anything else but the youngest, the brightest, and the very, very talented."

—Bernard Arnault,
chairman, LVMH Moët Hennessy Louis Vuitton

Bernard Arnault is chairman of LVMH Moët Hennessy Louis Vuitton, and, according to *Women's Wear Daily*, the "Pope of Fashion." Last year, his upscale company raked in $649 million in profits on $5.4 billion in sales.

What does Arnault believe in: "the youngest, the brightest, and the very, very talented." For one (not particularly small) example: The new head of Givenchy, Alexander McQueen, is all of 28 years old. Is there a lesson/message here? (*Hint: I think there is.*)

> **B-I-G IDEA:**
>
> **Innovation = Talent-Based Enterprise.**
>
> **big idea: ANY 28-YEAR-OLDS RUNNING B-I-G CHUNKS OF YOUR COMPANY?**

Marcy Carsey is crazy for crazies.

"I love running a business because I love gathering people together to do good stuff . . . . I love the fact people come together and bring their skills and work together. And something from nothing comes out of it, and everybody, hopefully, goes home feeling good about that. It's hard, and it's a struggle sometimes, but you always keep your eye on the goal. What do you want to do? What is this all about? It's about living gracefully . . . . And it's about the end result, which is, sometimes, as often as we can make it, wonderful television. And that, to me, is fabulous! Working with people you like—it's wonderful!"

—Marcy Carsey,
founder, The Carsey-Werner Company

Marcy Carsey is producer of "Roseanne," "The Cosby Show," and other exceptional television series. She's routinely tagged as the best of television's independent producers. Terrific groups? A collection of terrific/kinky people. And then those wonderful terms . . . LIVING GRACEFULLY . . . DOING IT GRACEFULLY.

How about you? Living gracefully? Doing it gracefully? And creating extraordinary things . . . IS THAT A DESCRIPTION OF YOUR (6-PERSON ACCOUNTING) UNIT? If not . . . WHY NOT?

B-I-G IDEA:

Innovation = Talent-Based Enterprise.

big idea: "WORK" = GATHERING GREAT PEOPLE TO ACCOMPLISH GREAT STUFF = LIVING GRACEFULLY.

The Chicago Bulls are crazy for crazies.

- -

"He was respected, because he brought a reality change."

—Phil Jackson, comparing Dennis Rodman to the Sioux heyoka, the cross-dressing, backward-talking tribal clown

- -

Phil Jackson, coach of the Chicago Bulls, is, in my view the best leader in professional sports. He's one of the best leaders . . . anywhere. His key: reinvention . . . which means . . . shaking (good/great) things up . . . a lot.

Dennis Rodman, rebounder supreme, is surely a pain. That is, he's a bit crazy and offbeat. Well, to be fair, a little more than "a bit" offbeat.

But Jackson . . . in the best sense of the term . . . took advantage of that. He brought Dennis Rodman into his (Jackson's) tribe. And, as he said, Rodman brought along a "reality change."

"It's all so simple," said a character in James Clavell's novel *Shogun*, "just change your view of the world." The Bulls were an established team. A good/great team. Then they added Rodman. They reinvented themselves. They "changed their view of the world."

Bravo! (And oh so rare.) (And oh so . . . to be truthful . . . risky. But how else do you reinvent the world? I.e.: Risk-free reinvention = Oxymoron.)

Hire for attitude, train for skill.

"1. What you know changes,
   who you are doesn't.

"2. You can't find what
   you're not looking for.

"3. The best way to evaluate
   people is to watch them work.

"4. You can't hire people
   who don't apply."

—Peter Carbonera, *Fast Company*

Cheryl Womack runs a fast-growing insurance-products company, VCW. She says the secret to success is . . . HIRING. She looks for . . . "passion, flexibility, excitement." She can train insurance, she adds, but not passion/flexibility/excitement. Gary Withers, who founded Britain's peerless marketing-services firm, Imagination, says he seeks a "demonstrated appetite for adventure."

Peter Carbonera, writing in *Fast Company*, seems to agree. The title of his article says it (almost) all: "Hire for Attitude, Train for Skill." The person you are—he says in Law No. 1—basically doesn't change. But the "what you know" part can be abetted by both the classroom and on-the-job training. That is . . . HIRE FOR ATTITUDE, TRAIN FOR SKILL.

Next, Carbonera says, you can't find what you're not looking for. Back to the cases of Womack and Withers: If you're not explicitly looking for passion/flexibility/excitement/appetite for adventure . . . and don't put it . . . explicitly . . . at the top of your "look for"/ "must have" list . . . then . . . YOU AIN'T GOING TO GET IT.

The best way to evaluate people is to watch them work, Carbonera adds. This means actually observing them at work. Or engaging them in substantial simulations. We are what we do . . . not what we say we do. So focus on the "do" . . . if at all possible. (And with imagination, it is.)

Carbonera's final axiom: You can't hire people who don't apply. That is, it is ever so critical to search in odd places, nooks and crannies . . . to get the "passion, flexibility, excitement" . . . the "appetite for adventure" . . . or whatever. If you want passion, flexibility, excitement . . . why not . . . for example . . . PUT IT IN THE WANT AD? That is: WANTED: PASSION, FLEXIBILITY, EXCITEMENT. (I've tried something like this . . . IT WORKS.)

Hire for intelligence (all kinds), train for whatever.

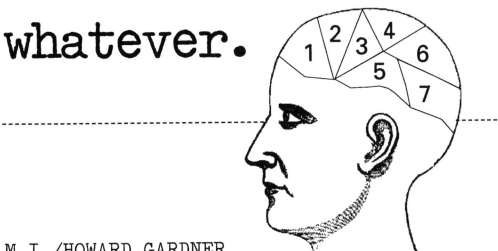

M.I./HOWARD GARDNER

Logical-mathematical intelligence ("logic smart")

Linguistic intelligence ("word smart")

Spatial intelligence ("picture smart")

Musical intelligence ("music smart")

Kinesthetic intelligence ("body smart")

Interpersonal intelligence ("people smart")

Intrapersonal intelligence ("self smart")

—Thomas Armstrong,
on Howard Gardner, in *7 Kinds of Smart*

Harvard professor of education Howard Gardner has pinpointed "Multiple Intelligences," based on decades of research. These include:

Logical-mathematical. This is the one that counts—almost exclusively—in the pantheon of student/employee evaluation. It's IQ.

Linguistic. The beautiful and powerful use of language to illuminate complex truths . . . or move masses. The writer Salman Rushdie. The speech giver Churchill. (And, yes, bad guys, too . . . e.g., Hitler.)

Spatial. Another . . . completely different . . . way to view the world . . . exemplars: Picasso et al.

Musical. Yet another wholly different way of imagining the world . . . epitomized by Leonard Bernstein or Igor Stravinsky.

Kinesthetic. Movement smart. E.g., the peerless Martha Graham. (Or Michael Jordan.)

Interpersonal. Relationships rule! Great sales people understand. And so does Bill Clinton (a peerless salesperson . . . love him or hate him!) . . . and Mohandas Gandhi.

Intrapersonal. Know thyself! Understand the importance of the inner workings of the mind/soul. Case in point: Freud.

***

Each of these intelligences is (very) different. And invaluable. The problem: The majority of our recruiting and selection and promotion processes focus on just one of the seven . . . logical-mathematical. What a mistake. What a waste! So . . . WHAT ARE YOU GOING TO DO ABOUT IT? (Be specific.)

B-I-G IDEA:
Innovation = Talent-Based Enterprise.
big idea: DON'T THROW AWAY 6/7 OF POTENTIAL STARS
. . . TAKE ADVANTAGE OF ALL 7 TYPES OF INTELLIGENCE.

Hire for talent, train for whatever.

ORGANIZING GENIUS

"The leaders of Great Groups love talent and know where to find it. . . . They revel in the talent of others."

—Warren Bennis and Patricia Ward Biederman

"Connoisseur of talent."

—description of Bob Taylor, Palo Alto Research Center (Xerox)

Okay. Okay. You've heard it a hundred times. Stand by for . . . No. 101. Every young, soon-to-be manager is told: "Your ability to achieve excellence is dependent upon your willingness to hire people who are better than you." Warren Bennis and Patricia Ward Biederman say that the leaders of Great Groups get this one. In spades! "The leaders of Great Groups," they write, "love talent and know where to find it. . . . They revel in the talent of others."

I LOVE IT: REVEL IN THE TALENT OF OTHERS.

It's the attribute of great football coaches . . . obviously. And the leadership of the likes of the Manhattan Project, one of Bennis and Biederman's Great Groups. But it also makes sense . . . PERFECT SENSE . . . for the leader of the seven-person training depart-ment! (And if you are the leader of a seven-person department, can you honestly claim that you "revel in the talent of others"?)

Computer pioneer Alan Kay uses similar language to describe the lead actor at Xerox's Palo Alto Research Center (PARC). He says Bob Taylor was a "connoisseur of talent." Again: I LOVE IT . . . CONNOISSEUR OF TALENT. (And you . . . ??)

How do you recruit such talent? One Great Group leader says the key is "fire in their eyes."

And a-g-a-i-n: I LOVE IT. Sure, the sheepskin may be Grade A, but the difference . . . the winning edge . . . is that **FIRE IN THEIR EYES** . . . and the willing-ness to acknowledge it/embrace it in the recruiting process.

***

P-L-E-A-S-E THINK ABOUT IT: CONNOISSEUR OF TALENT. (What else . . . in the Age of Talent-Based Enterprise?)

B-I-G IDEA:
Innovation = Talent-Based Enterprise.
big idea: TALENT-BASED ENTERPRISE DEMANDS AN OBSESSION WITH . . . TALENT.

Hire for diversity,

train for whatever.

"Where do good new ideas come from?"

"That's simple . . . from differences. Creativity comes from unlikely juxtapositions. The best way to maximize differences is to mix ages, cultures and disciplines.

—Nicholas Negroponte,
founder and director, MIT Media Lab

Diversity works. Diversity makes sense. Why? Well . . . for profit maximization reasons. That is . . . in the age of brainware/creativity . . . creativity comes from . . . DIVERSITY.

Negroponte, head of MIT's fabled Media Lab, gets it exactly right. (As far as I'm concerned . . . and as far as all sane students of creativity are concerned.)

Diversity = Mix = Creative = Source of all breakthrough products (as well as many/most painful failures . . . there's no free lunch).

Hire for diversity, train for diversity.

"There's always a force at work toward non-diversity . . . whom are you relying on to execute ideas, whom are you relying on to come up with ideas, whom are you relying on to feed off for yourself, to surround yourself with? There's always a push toward uniformity that we have to struggle against . . . . Most people's natural instinct is to hire people they are familiar with, that sound like them . . . . We have to fight against that all the time in ourselves, as well as in the people whom we hire, who are then going to be hiring other people. We try to reach for the broadest spectrum of points of view and personalities and backgrounds."

—Marcy Carsey, founder, The Carsey-Werner Company

May the force NOT be with you. That is, the force that Marcy Carsey says is "always . . . at work toward non-diversity." A lot of her success, she claims, is the blatant pursuit of diversity . . . for diversity's sake—i.e., reaching "for the broadest spectrum of points of view and personalities and backgrounds."

THAT'S WHY YOU PRACTICE DIVERSITY . . . FOR GOD'S SAKE. Get it!!!???

P-L-E-A-S-E!!

> **B-I-G IDEA:**
>
> **Innovation = Talent-Based Enterprise.**
>
> **big idea: DIVERSITY MAKES SENSE BECAUSE IT MAKES (ECONOMIC) SENSE.**

Talent renewal kit

1.0

What's your rate of depreciation?

I've devoted my professional life to humanizing enterprise. Yet this (critical) area is one where I'm willing to jump in bed with the accountants. To use their powerful language: You/I/We are . . . R-A-P-I-D-L-Y . . . DEPRECIATING ASSETS. I heard a university president say to engineering graduates that he hoped they had enjoyed their time at school . . . and he was sorry to inform them that the "half life" of what they had learned was about four years.

Same holds for the *purchasing* professional. The *human resources* professional. The *finance* professional. The *marketing* professional. The *advertising* professional. What is your/my rate of depreciation? I don't know! Call it 10 percent!? 20 percent!? 30 percent!? Whatever it is . . . IT AIN'T SMALL.

If you were in charge of a distribution facility or plant or computer system that was rotting at the rate of about one-third per year, you'd be scared to death. You would be doing something . . . SOMETHING BIG . . . about it . . . NOW.

Why is it, then, relative to the most important depreciating asset . . . you . . . and your unit/company . . . that we seem to do so relatively little?

The trick is obvious. I also call it NURI . . . or the New Universal Renewal Imperative. Back to the accountants. Requirement No. 1: a no-baloney INVESTMENT STRATEGY. First . . . it must be FORMAL. Even if it's "only" for private consumption . . . you need a PLAN. Call it a Renewal Investment Plan . . . or RIP. This is not a public "career planning" exercise. This is a private (or to be shared with a close advisor, spouse, significant other, group of intimates) and personal strategy for investment in renewal. Key words: private . . . personal . . . strategy . . . investment . . . renewal . . . now . . . big.

B-I-G IDEA:

Innovation = Talent-Based Enterprise.

big idea: FORMAL RENEWAL INVESTMENT PLAN. N-O-W.

Talent renewal kit

2.0

What's your audacity score?

Renewal ... IN A MADCAP WORLD ... is, to steal a line from Ford, everyone's Job No. 1. Is it selfish? Of course it is! But it's selfless, too! Why?

Because: UNIT VITALITY = THE SUM OF THE ENERGY AND COMMITMENT PUT INTO EXPLICIT RENEWAL INVESTMENT PLANS ... of the 6 (or 6,666) people who report to you.

Of course I believe in heavy investment in research and development. After all, I am an innovation freak. But corporate vitality is less a matter of high R&D spending than it is a matter of the commitment that *every* person in the organization makes ... in a *planned* fashion ... to personal *renewal* ... via those Renewal Investment Plans.

Moreover, you should think of each Renewal Investment Plan (everyone must have one, including this year's university graduate) in terms of its AUDACITY. Each RIP should be given a quantitative score. (I call it the Audacity Score.)

The senior folks in the enterprise are, of course, most responsible for "strategic" direction ... which means they are most responsible for the freshness of the enterprise. And therein lies a problem. (The problem?) Senior folks are busy as hell. They seldom seem to "get around to" taking that four-day Total Quality Management course . . . they leave it to the juniors. Moreover, the senior folks, particularly the very senior ones, ain't as young as they used to be. (Take it from one who isn't!) And with age . . . no matter what you do . . . comes inflexibility. Make no mistake about it: Just as you have to exercise four times as hard at 50 as you did at 25 to retain even a modicum of the shape you used to be in, so you must exercise the refreshment nodes in your brain four times as hard. That is, the Audacity Scores of the Personal Renewal Investment Plans of the Corporate Elders must be four times higher than those of their juniors. *(Hint: They seldom are.) (Hint: Understatement.)* Yes . . . I am serious (very serious!) about assigning quantitative Audacity Scores to each person's Renewal Investment Plan.

Here's my scoring system:

10 = Olympic reinventor

5 = Working hard at it

1 = I'm already overworked; leave me alone.

A Perfect 10 is the "Olympic" reinventor . . . bound and determined to turn her or his world upside down in the next 12 months . . . with (or without) the company's help. In the middle of the pack are the "working at it" bunch, committed to renewal, but not wildly imaginative: i.e., not paranoid like those perfect 10s. And then down at the bottom (fire them? . . . NO KIDDING!) are the "I'm already overworked . . . leave me alone" gang, who just "don't have the damn time" to put in on the renewal process: fair day's work for a fair day's pay, etc., etc., ad nauseum.

Audacity Scores for Renewal Investment Plans . . . TRY IT!!

B-I-G IDEA:

Innovation = Talent-Based Enterprise.

big idea: UNIT VITALITY = SUM OF AUDACITY SCORES OF EVERYONE'S RIPs (RENEWAL INVESTMENT PLANS).

Talent renewal kit

3.0

Notebooks!

One small . . . or not so small . . . step you can take TODAY . . . O-P-E-N Y-O-U-R
E-Y-E-S. I.e., START A NOTEBOOK.

My friend, the organizational learning guru Karl Weick, does it. Whenever he
hears something that tickles his fancy, he instinctively (mid-conversation at a cocktail
party) reaches into his sport coat pocket, pulls out a 3" x 5" card and writes it down.

And Richard Branson does it . . . BIG TIME. At last count, he was on Notebook
No. 227. The Virgin Group chief is an inveterate—
obsessive!—recorder of impressions and ideas. As I said
. . . you can start this . . . TODAY. And . . . it can
become the centerpiece of your renewal program.

Talent renewal kit

4.0

Invent oddball/change-of-pace projects.

Reorganize for reorganization's sake.

Go sideways!

Base formal evaluations on renewal success.

Move up . . . or move out.

Embrace inspired (NO CLONES!) recruiting.

Launch zany, spontaneous interventions.

De-couch potato!

Create zesty surroundings.

Encourage serious sabbaticals.

I had screamed . . . "WE'RE ALL R-A-P-I-D-L-Y DEPRECIATING ASSETS!!!" The president of the financial services company bought the act. And raised me: "So, Tom, what am I supposed to do? How do we 'put renewal on the agenda,' as you suggest?"

My reply (tidied up a little bit for print):

Invent oddball/change-of-pace projects. Creativity is about jolting us out of our comfort zones. In most organizations we complete project after project. The topics change a little. But it's basically (if you're perfectly honest with yourself) pretty much the same. But projects can be invented that are different—that offer that jolting change in pace. Years ago at McKinsey, I was going through a series of standard strategy projects. I was "offered" a chance to do something that felt like a step back: to work on an overall strategic examination of a Napa, California-based road-rock/asphalt outfit, called Basalt Rock Company.

I balked. But I wasn't given an option. Turned out to be about the best thing that happened to me in my first couple of years at McKinsey. That is, I had to remove myself entirely from my normal frame. The experience was so successful that I repeated the process— subsequently taking the initiative—of embracing off-the-beaten- path projects from time to time. I still do a version of it today: booking speeches where I have no expertise (no right to be invited!) . . . just so I will be forced . . . HARD . . . to do something . . . (very) different/(very) uncomfortable.

Reorganize for reorganization's sake. Change for change sake. "They" say it's a bad idea. "Spinning wheels." Etc. I'm not so sure. Years ago, when things were going well, Digital Equipment founder Ken Olsen used to reorganize from time to time . . . just to force senior executives to take on new tasks . . . and to work with a new set of people. He claimed it was a very useful practice. I wouldn't disagree.

(Of course you can go too far . . . e.g., if you irritate clients by such regular reorganization. On the other hand . . . RENEWAL IS JOB NO. 1 . . . and shaking up the org chart for the sake of shaking it up is not a bad idea from time to time . . . even if a little client confusion is included in the sticker price.)

Go sideways!   Even in 1997 we are still beset with "ladder-ism." As in "up the ladder." As in . . . if you ain't movin' up (the ladder) . . . you're movin' down (the ladder).

Mistake!

Some superbly managed companies, such as hi-tech materials maker Raychem, have long played the game differently. So does the average professional service firm. That is, "up"—new "up"?—is taking on an intriguing assignment . . . that may even amount to a "downward" move. But the only way you're going to learn something really new . . . and break your frame . . . is to be thrust into a (nearly) totally different environment.

Lateral need not mean sideways . . . or downward . . . pay. No reason not to give a top performer a pay hike (if you feel it's merited) along with a lateral/downward (per the org chart) move of a couple of years duration.

Base formal evaluations on renewal success.   Truism. And true. That is: WHAT GETS MEASURED GETS DONE. Wanna focus on quality? Put it in the measurement system! Put it in the performance evaluation system! List it among promotion criteria! And . . . surprise . . . the same thing is true for . . . renewal.

I've suggested we adopt the practice of "résumé-ing" . . . working with people to update their résumés every few months . . . as a spur to having something new + worth saying. (See Chapter 5.) I've also introduced the notion of Personal Brand Equity Evaluation . . . a bird with pretty much the same feathers. (Also Chapter 5.) The bottom line: These are ideas that focus on the measurement of renewal.

So . . . how about putting formal Renewal Investment Plans/Personal Brand Equity Evaluation/Résumé-ing into the formal evaluation process? Into the promotion process . . . formally? You want "more" renewal? Measure on renewal!/Reward on renewal!/Promote on renewal! It's just about that simple! And if you're really serious . . . as was the exec who asked me the question . . . put renewal evaluation per se at the tippy-top of the annual performance review!

Move up or move out. It's true for the Chicago Cubs. And the Chicago Bulls. And for Meryl Streep. And for Harrison Ford. And cameramen and camerawomen in Hollywood. And accountants at Arthur Andersen. And consultants at McKinsey. What's true? UP-OR-OUT.

It can be brutal. It need not be. It's the (new) idea that you're either getting better . . . or you're not worth retaining. Which must—tomorrow—permeate every firm of every size in every industry. Or else. It doesn't mean abdicating the responsibility for lots of coaching. (To the contrary.) Nor abdicating the responsibility for lots of training. (To the contrary.) But it does mean . . . in the end . . . a clear understanding . . . inculcated in the recruiting/hiring process . . . that the only way to "succeed (be retained!) around here" is to get better . . . all the time . . . forever.

Embrace inspired (NO CLONES!) recruiting. If you want people who are currently on the payroll to be hell-bent upon renewal . . . undertake an inspired (offbeat!) recruiting process . . . and keep inundating the joint with fascinating/potent talent.

Obviously this is the meat and the potatoes for the professional sports team. Drafting a hotshot wide receiver often as not lights a major conflagration under today's wide receiver . . . who can hardly afford to sit on his 2-million-dollar-a-year laurels. Well . . . the same thing holds true in the accounting department . . . or the purchasing department. Look for intriguing new people. They raise the bar. They change the shape of the bar. And keep the organization in a constant/energetic state of creative flux. (Yo . . . Dennis Rodman.)

Launch zany, spontaneous interventions. Weekly Operations Review meeting coming up at 2:00 p.m. today? Fine! And . . . it's June? Why not hold it in the park . . . a few blocks down the road? Just get news that you won a sizable contract? Ring the bell. (Surely you have one.) Gather the whole gang . . . trot down the four flights of stairs from your fourth-floor office . . . run around the block twice. And: Stop at Baskin Robbins and get ice cream cones for the group of 20. Talent renewal sounds like a Big League idea. It is. But the idea of renewal per se is also about constantly livening (and lightening) things up. Be on the lookout for opportunities to spontaneously intervene . . . to . . . once again . . . CHANGE THAT FRAME!

De-couch potato. I've got a few extra pounds. (And then a few more.) I was a lousy jock. So I'm not one of "those guys." But I am an outdoors/exercise freak. Financial services star Michael Bloomberg—and who would ever dare disagree with him—has free eats in his office space. So that people will stay close to home at noon.

Who would disagree with him?

ME!

We all need changes of perspective . . . regularly. Getting out and about . . . even to eat a high-cal lunch three blocks from the office . . . is important. We're learning that a little dose of morning sun goes a (very) long way. So, too, a walk around the block. (No, I'm not suggesting a brisk 5K run at lunch time . . . led by some fitness fanatic in the office . . . who wants you to be the same kind of dork he is.) We are also learning that any kind of exercise is of enormous value. So . . . since most of us work in Couch Potatoland these days . . . do something about it.

Create zesty surroundings. I admit it. I'M A SPACE FREAK! Some (most!/almost all!!) work spaces cool me down. Give me a (bad) case of the blahs. And some/few turn me on. A lot! Physical space is astonishingly important. And astonishingly under-attended to. Again: Some spaces are vigorous. Personal. Energetic. Innovative. And some/most/almost all . . . are not.

Join me: Become a space freak! (By the way . . . it's inexpensive.)

Encourage serious sabbaticals. At the very least . . . for God's sake . . . insist that people use their vacation time! And if they have, say, three weeks of vacation coming, insist that they take at least two of those weeks contiguously. That's the world of microsabbaticals. In short . . . if you take 15 working days vacation . . . two days at a time . . . you have in no way dealt with the New Universal Renewal Imperative.

Better yet . . . introduce a big-deal sabbatical program. You need not pay people to take long stretches of time off. But you need to create an environment where people understand that taking three or four months off (planned way ahead . . . so it doesn't screw up work patterns) is something that is . . . noble. Once again, we are faced with a great paradox: The times demand that we run around like chickens with our heads cut off. And the times also demand that we be refreshed and curious and creative . . . to an unprecedented degree. The two do not fit easily together. (Understatement!) Which means . . . THE POINT OF THIS EXERCISE . . . that we have to treat "talent renewal" as an important STRATEGIC idea.

Okay??

B-I-G IDEA:

Innovation = Talent-Based Enterprise.

big idea: TALENT RENEWAL CAN BE THOUGHT ABOUT (ACTED UPON) SYSTEMATICALLY AND STRATEGICALLY.

Talent renewal kit

"Our circuits are so overloaded by the technology that keeps us wired—the cell phones and modems and fax machines—that we've lost the capacity to daydream."

—James Atlas

Five minutes, four seconds. An Eternity of Excellence!

Madness is afoot!

On the other hand . . .

I was in my car the other day, listening to a CD. It included Pachelbel's Canon in D. I listened to it, for the umpteenth time, and was moved as always. Then a thought occurred. I played it again, this time observing the time code. Length: five minutes and four seconds.

Pachelbel is not Mozart or Beethoven. That is, not so prolific. We remember him . . . AND DO WE REMEMBER HIM . . . for five minutes and four seconds of work. Of brilliance! Of excellence! That is . . . his Canon.

It all boiled down to five minutes. And we remember it . . . centuries later (!!!).

Do you honestly think that what you're doing . . . right now . . . or in the course of your career . . . will be remembered a year from now? Twenty years from now?? One hundred years from now???

We hustle. We bustle. We race. We scream. We shout. We Thrive On Chaos!!! But in the end . . . WHAT THE HELL IS EXCELLENCE? Well, we do have to hustle and bustle. And everything is turned upside down. But we also ought to pause and think. And . . . DAYDREAM.

Oh . . . how I would love to be remembered . . . 100 years from now . . . for my five-minute-and-four-second contribution!

Think about it. Carefully. Please.

B-I-G IDEA:

Innovation = Talent-Based Enterprise.

big idea: DARE TO DAYDREAM.

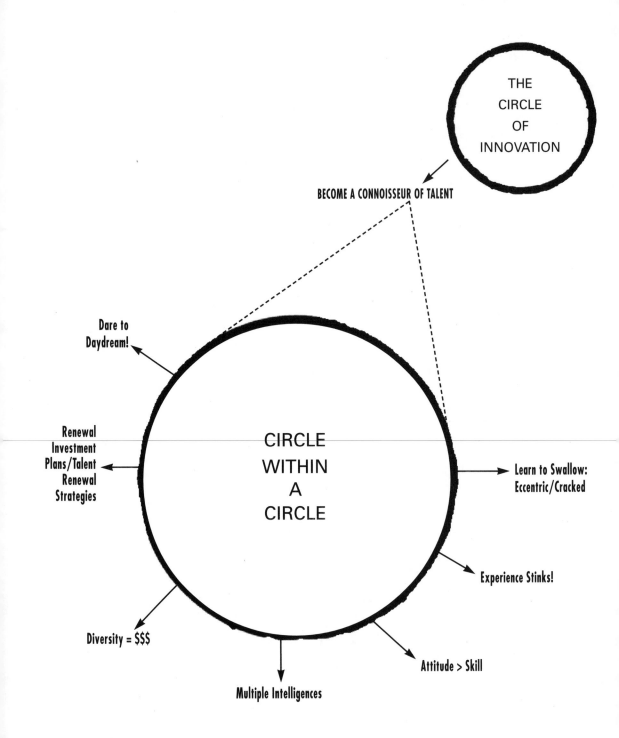

THE
CIRCLE
OF
INNOVATION

BECOME A CONNOISSEUR OF TALENT

Dare to
Daydream!

Renewal
Investment
Plans/Talent
Renewal
Strategies

CIRCLE
WITHIN
A
CIRCLE

Learn to Swallow:
Eccentric/Cracked

Experience Stinks!

Diversity = $$$

Attitude > Skill

Multiple Intelligences

SEMANTICS ALERT No. 11

TBE/Talent-Based Enterprise

WOW! (ideas) call for WOW! (people)

Crazy for Crazies

Cherish the . . . experience-impaired individual/the youngest/

the brightest/the very, very talented

Living gracefully (at work)

Welcome to the Purchasing Department . . . Dennis Rodman

Multiple Intelligences

Connoisseur of Talent

Diversity = $$$

RDA/Rapidly Depreciating Asset

RIP/Renewal Investment Plan

Audacity Scores (of RIPs)

Talent Renewal Strategies

Daydreaming Capacity/5:04

Another point of immodest decommoditization: a new look at "people stuff." This time the value-added-through-people lens is trained on diversity (diversity = creativity), creation of the TBE (Talent-Based Enterprise. . . . Hello, Hollywood) and personal/collective renewal . . . oh yes, and on the (new) power of inexperience!

CHAPTER 12

It's a Woman's World.

It is the (R-I-D-I-C-U-L-O-U-S-L-Y) rare corporation that takes

advantage of the WOMEN'S OPPORTUNITY. What a (COSTLY) mistake.

Women

10.2 million women (20 percent of
working wives) earn MORE than
their husbands.

Women purchase 51 percent of . . .
tires.

Consumer spending by women:
$3.3 trillion + purchasing agents
for government and industry > 50
percent U.S. Gross Domestic Product.

-----

rule!

Women = 43 percent of
Americans with assets
> $500,000

Percentage of choices to buy a product that
are made or decisively influenced by women*:

Home furnishings . . . 94%
Holidays . . . 92%
Homes . . . 91%
Bank Account (choice of new) . . . 89%
Medical Insurance . . . 88%

*Australian research

Three out of four healthcare
decisions are made by women;
two-thirds of healthcare
dollars are spent by women.

Women buy more . . . sports
shoes . . . than men.

AMERICAN
WOMEN ARE,
IN EFFECT,
THE
LARGEST
"NATIONAL"
ECONOMY
ON EARTH

Estimated size of software market . . .
girls age 7-12 . . . $4-6 billion/year.

Just a few not-so-little facts: Twenty-five years ago, about 400,000 American women owned businesses. Today, the total of women-owned businesses is nearing 8 m-i-l-l-i-o-n. These companies post $2.3 trillion in sales annually and employ over 18 million people. More than half the new jobs created in this country since 1992 are attributable to women-owned businesses.

Over 10 million women make more money than their spouses. And the number is rising . . . FAST.

And . . . women control over half the commercial and consumer consumption that contributes to American GDP. That means: American women . . . BY THEMSELVES . . . are in effect the LARGEST "NATIONAL" ECONOMY ON EARTH . . . larger than the entire (!) Japanese economy.

And . . . women fuelled the mutual fund boom. And . . . women are starting new investment clubs at a much faster rate than men.

Somethin's going on . . . eh??? (Call it "the women's thing.")

B-I-G IDEA:
Women Are Opportunity No. 1!
big idea: IT'S A B-I-G I-D-E-A.

Women rule!

So what's wrong with this picture?

---

65 percent of car-buying decisions
are made by <u>WOMEN</u>.

But only 7 percent of car <u>salesMEN</u> are
<u>WOMEN</u>.

The jock strap . . . invented 1874.

The jog bra . . . invented 1977.

(First-year sportsbra sales: 25 thousand

units; 1996: 42 million units.)

—*Women's Sports + Fitness*

It's just . . . SIMPLY . . . silly. The statistics, I mean. Why no sportsbra until 1977?
Why no (okay . . . so damn few) car salesWOMEN? God alone knows.

Women rule!

Women are smarter than men. Women are better managers than men.

The evidence is in—and it's compelling. Women are smarter than men. But let me be precise, because this statement is a controversial one. Women are smarter than men . . . on average. The bell-shaped distribution of intelligence (as measured by IQ) is more tightly concentrated for women, less tightly concentrated for men. That is, more men are "geniuses" . . . and (far) more are idiots!

American women are also, on average, better educated than men. Since the early 80s women have taken home over 50 percent of bachelor's and master's degrees. And: Yale Medical School's entering class for 1996 was 54 percent female.

Women are better managers than men . . . so say men as well as women. Definition of "better"? Better at relationships. (No surprise, eh?) And better at planning, goal setting, and follow-through. Obviously, it's not women's "soft" skills versus men's "hard" skills.

Some of the recent evidence comes from Lawrence A. Pfaff and Associates: Its two-year study included 941 managers (672 men, 269 women) from 204 organizations. The evaluation scheme is what's commonly called 360-degree feedback—that is, the managers were rated by subordinates, bosses, and peers. Some 20 categories were involved. In 15 of them, women were rated as better (with statistical significance) than men. Categories where women shone included "planning," "setting standards," and "decisiveness."

Women rule!

"Men and women . . . don't buy for the same reasons. He simply wants the transaction to take place. She's interested in creating a relationship!"

—Faith Popcorn, author, *Clicking*

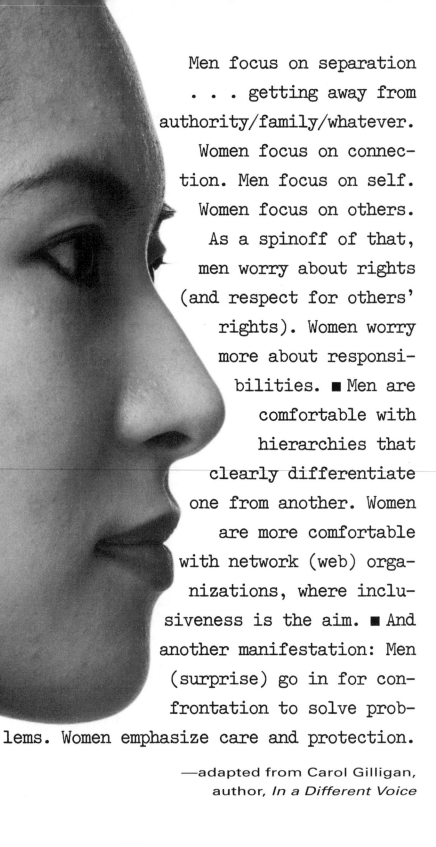

Men focus on separation . . . getting away from authority/family/whatever. Women focus on connection. Men focus on self. Women focus on others. As a spinoff of that, men worry about rights (and respect for others' rights). Women worry more about responsibilities. ■ Men are comfortable with hierarchies that clearly differentiate one from another. Women are more comfortable with network (web) organizations, where inclusiveness is the aim. ■ And another manifestation: Men (surprise) go in for confrontation to solve problems. Women emphasize care and protection.

—adapted from Carol Gilligan, author, *In a Different Voice*

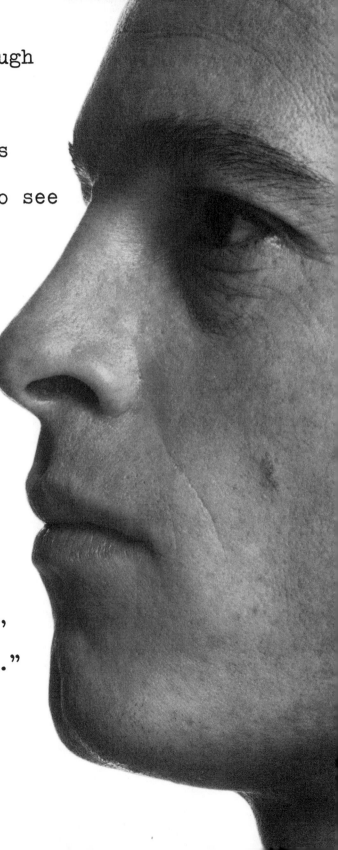

"Men will sit through the Olympics for almost anything, as long as they get to see some winners and losers. Women . . . want to know who the athletes are, how they got there, what sacrifices they've made. They want an attachment, a rooting interest."

—Dick Ebersol,
president, NBC Sports,
on his network's
(successful) approach to
the Atlanta Olympiad

Businesses must understand . . . first and foremost . . . THAT MEN AND WOMEN ARE DIFFERENT. To wit: He . . . simply wants the transaction to take place. She's interested in creating a relationship. (Faith Popcorn.)

Prior to the mid-1960s, women were considered distinct from men. Separate . . . and unequal. The feminist revolution of the late 60s, 70s, and 80s moved in the opposite direction. Not just toward "equal," but toward the diminishment of differences. Men were expected to behave like women. Women were expected to behave like men. Androgyny was in.

While equality was hardly reached, we have moved (substantially, many/most would say) in that direction. But equality doesn't mean that men and women are the same. Elissa Moses of The BrainWavesGroup, a market research firm in New York City, calls the women's movement (if that's still the right term) in the 1990s the pursuit of self-navigation. Equality? Yes! But with that equality comes the search for distinctions between the sexes.

> Women are looking for financial independence. Not wealth for wealth's sake, but "enough" money to have a room (or three!) of one's own.

So just what is self-navigation? The BrainWavesGroup's research offers some clues: Women are looking for financial independence. Not wealth for wealth's sake, but "enough" money to have a room (or three!) of one's own. Women are also demanding control over their lives and their working circumstances. Women go for "it" (wherever "it" may be), but they also stay open to possibilities and are flexible; not getting caught on old-fashioned career ladders leading to glass (or tungsten!) ceilings is part of what's driving women today. And speaking of careers . . . women continue to pursue balance. The search for pleasure and enjoyment, according to The BrainWavesGroup's research, is "a top priority" . . . for 88 percent of women.

The new woman? Responsible! She takes responsibility for herself. She takes responsibility for those around her. As always, but even more so, she lives multiple roles . . . and expresses multiple personalities: mom, provider, worker, boss, community leader, spouse, and so on.

Men claim they're busy as hell. That may be true . . . but women *are* busy as hell. "Time is of the essence," The BrainWavesGroup says, and the drive up the corporate ladder is more difficult given those multiple roles.

MEN AND WOMEN . . . ARE . . . DIFFERENT.

B-I-G IDEA:

Women Are Opportunity No. 1!

big idea: UNDERSTAND THE (BIG) DIFFERENCES.

Women rule!

As the data roll in . . .
I am stunned. Stunned at my
blindness. (At least I
belong to a big club.)
Stunned at the enormous
opportunity. That is
. . . this "Women's Thing"
is . . . unmistakably in my
opinion . . . ECONOMIC
OPPORTUNITY NO. 1 . . . for
the foreseeable future.

Where:

Healthcare

Financial services

Automobiles

Homes and home furnishings

Computers and software and

telecommunications

Sports and recreation

Business services

ANY DAMN PLACE YOU CAN THINK OF!!!

 B-I-G IDEA: Women Are Opportunity No. 1!
big idea: IT'S A B-I-G I-D-E-A.

Who gets it?

Amazon!

"One late Sunday afternoon, I started thinking about how I would feel, riding a Harley. I realized it was not at all the same as what I'd been reading about the Cult of Harley. When men ride Harleys, they join a tribe. They become part of The Legend. They become the Ultimate Bad Boys. Women riders flout the rules. They ride for self-expression. To defy expectations and filter out the losers. Women ride for the complete and very apparent *absence* of a male escort. Women ride to have personal control over their own pleasure."

—Lynda Pearson,
Co-founder, Creative Director, Amazon Advertising

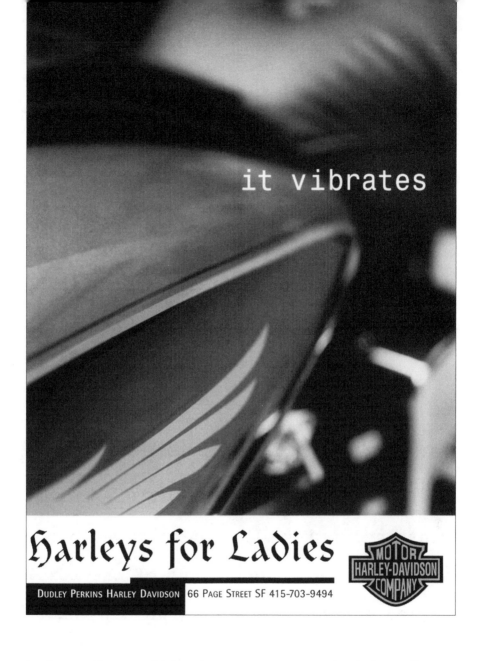

it vibrates

Harleys for Ladies

DUDLEY PERKINS HARLEY DAVIDSON | 66 PAGE STREET SF 415-703-9494

HARLEY-DAVIDSON MOTOR COMPANY

Harley-Davidson gets it! Or at least San Francisco Harley dealer Dudley Perkins does. A women-founded, women-run ad agency was asked for help. And now women customers are buying Harleys—for their own pleasure. Hats off to Dudley Perkins Harley-Davidson dealership . . . and the fab folks (women!) at San Francisco's Amazon Advertising!

Who gets it?

Sears!

"We had a company run by guys who thought they were in the 'dirty fingernails' business with autos and hardware. Unless we made the store and merchandise attractive to women, we weren't going to break out of the box we were in. It was a very big 'ah-ha!' discovery."

—Arthur Martinez,
chairman and CEO, Sears,
Roebuck and Co.

A very big "ah-ha!" YIPES!! Arthur Martinez has successfully reinvented Sears in the last few years. Much of the secret: catering to women. Women who buy apparel. (Yup.) And cosmetics. (Yup.) And . . . as "de facto purchasing agents for the household," per *Time* . . . women who buy . . . appliances . . . and electronics gear . . . and tools . . . and tires . . . and auto parts.

Fine! But . . . an "ah-ha"? Well . . . I guess it was! But I'm truly dismayed that this came as a surprise to Sears. In any event . . .

Sears gets it!

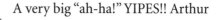

B-I-G IDEA:
Women Are Opportunity No. 1!
big idea: SEARS DISCOVERED WOMEN.
HAVE YOU?

Who gets it?

Ford!

As 1997 began, Ford aimed 60 percent of its magazine ads at men. And 40 percent at women. But women buy 65 percent of cars, Ford division boss Ross Roberts acknowledges. So . . . as of mid-1997 . . . Ford is aiming 60 percent of its mag ads at . . . WOMEN.

Ford has a long way to go. But that's a big/quick change!

B-I-G IDEA:

Women Are Opportunity No. 1!

big idea: FORD DISCOVERED WOMEN.

HAVE YOU?

Who gets it?
Westin!

1 percent to 50 percent . . . Ye gads!

Westin Hotels & Resorts, in a recent poll by J.D. Power & Associates, was tagged the top high-end hotel chain. One (big) reason: CEO Jurgen Bartels is focusing on women business travelers. Women were just 1 percent of business travelers in 1970. That number will be 50 percent by the turn of the century.

At Westin, new amenities were introduced, including full-length mirrors, hair dryers, irons, and ironing boards. Also, due to women's requests . . . more salads and low-fat meals were added to room-service and restaurant menus.

Of equal (greater!) importance, Westin is working on attitude change: I.e., show women guests respect! "A major complaint," *USA Today* reports, "was that [hotel] employees—especially in restaurants—catered to male business travelers. Bartels has instructed employees not to assume, for example, that the man is always paying the bill." It is such little things (little?? ENORMOUS!!) that can/will/are making the (BIG) difference. That is . . . Westin gets it.

B-I-G IDEA: Women Are Opportunity No. 1!
big idea: STATISTICS LIKE THIS . . . 49-FOLD INCREASE IN SHARE OF WOMEN ROAD WARRIORS . . . ARE COMMON.

Who doesn't get it?

The Auto Industry!

Salebreaker!

Open your ears (I recently did) and the stories just keep coming at you. During a break in one of my seminars, I was buttonholed by a female banking executive (E-X-E-C-U-T-I-V-E) who told me her version of this too-often-told tale.

She and her husband went into a car dealership. During the 20 minutes that they were there, she reports, the salesperson ignored her . . . "except at the very end, to explain a feature that would help me when I 'lost my key.'" He (salesMAN) missed something . . . the sale. (And I bet he was surprised!?)

> **B-I-G IDEA: Women Are Opportunity No. 1!**
> **big idea: WE INTERRUPT THIS BOOK WITH A NEWS**
> **BULLETIN: WOMEN BUY (LOTSA) CARS!**

WOMEN 1.0
Opportunity Kit

So what to do?
Forget the balloons!

"It" (seizing OPPORTUNITY NO. 1) is not a matter of launching . . . with a thousand balloons floating into the azure blue sky . . . a Women's Initiative.

Or if there is a "Women's Initiative," it had better be fundamental. That is, aimed at . . . ENTERPRISE REINVENTION. A total reconsideration of: (1) recruiting practices, (2) hiring sources, (3) reward systems, (4) promotions, (5) organizational structure, (6) business processes, (7) measurement, (8) overall business strategy, (9) company culture, (10) vision, and (11) leadership.

Try these six questions for starters:

1. **What share of your sales is attributable to women? What share of your segment's sales is attributable to women?** Begin with the obvious, which is what women are buying from you . . . now. And how does that compare with what's going on in your marketplace? Are you above average? Below average? WHY?

2. **How . . . specifically . . . do women's tastes influence product development, sales, marketing, logistics, and service in your**

company? Remember . . . WOMEN ARE DIFFERENT. Do product development, sales, marketing, logistics, and service reflect this . . . very specifically? Don't be hasty in answering! EXAMINE ALL PROCESSES V-E-R-Y CAREFULLY.

3. **What percent of senior people in product development and sales and service and marketing are women?** No . . . this is not the only issue. Not by a long shot! BUT IT ISN'T BAD FOR STARTERS! If you are trying to serve a different way of thinking (women's way) . . . then women in positions of formal/muckety-muck authority wouldn't be a bad idea. THINK ABOUT IT. CAREFULLY.

The big issue isn't women's satisfaction with your products and services. It's the women who are turned off to the point of not stopping by in the first place . . . to your company . . . or your industry.

4. **Is anyone in your segment doing a fabulous job (à la Sears) in catering to women-as-purchasers?** Are you benchmarking against best-in-serving women (regardless of the business/industry)? Benchmarking has its limitations. On the other hand, you've got to start somewhere. Study the best . . . and the worst. Then go beyond your marketplace: Can a car maker learn from Sears? OF COURSE!

5. **How big is the "women's opportunity" in your segment?** (ARE YOU SURE?) This may be the most important question here. The

big issue isn't women's satisfaction with your products and services. It's the women who are turned off to the point of not stopping by in the first place . . . to your company . . . or your industry.

6. **Do you have an explicit "women's strategy" that involves the market and the organizational capability associated with serving it imaginatively?** "Women's strategy" isn't enough. But . . . again . . . it's a start. However, any such strategy must include both sides of the coin: (1) the market opportunity *and* (2) the organizational capability associated with serving it imaginatively (e.g., percentage of women in senior positions . . . see question No. 3 above).

Hint: These are very hard questions to answer. Why? Most deal with things that aren't-happening-but-could-happen-if-we-did-it-right. DO NOT ACCEPT SUPERFICIAL ANSWERS TO ANY OF THESE QUESTIONS!

B-I-G IDEA:

Women Are Opportunity No. 1!

big idea: B-I-G OPPORTUNITY = B-I-G INTERNAL UPHEAVAL TO TAKE ADVANTAGE OF IT.

You Just Don't Understand.

—Deborah Tannen author, *You Just Don't Understand: Women and Men in Conversation*

"You just **can't** understand."

—Me

I recently went to a day-long meeting, where I was about the only man in attendance. The group included some of the most powerful women in the United States. At the end of the day, I was left with a tossing and turning mind . . . at the ripe old age of 54.

That is, I was born a male, white, Anglo-Saxon, Protestant. We are the ruling class . . . to this day. And there's not a damn thing I can do about that.

Which means I have a problem: I JUST CAN'T UNDERSTAND.

That is, as I listened to these very powerful women talk about the degree to which they had been slighted, particularly if they happened to be Asian-American women or African-American women, it dawned on me that for all my liberalness, I just didn't get it. I did not—and cannot—understand what it means to be systematically slighted and/or ignored.

There's an important message here. I can pretend to be very receptive to women's ideas. (I am . . . and I mean it.) But I'm not one of "them." I don't know (K-N-O-W) what it's like to be short-changed. Again and again . . . and yet again.

Which means that the only answer to dealing with these issues (OPPORTUNI-TIES!) is to have women in positions of great importance throughout the enterprise.

> **B-I-G IDEA: Women Are Opportunity No. 1!**
>
> **big idea: I NOT ONLY DON'T UNDERSTAND . . . I CAN'T UNDERSTAND. (BOYS: DON'T BULLSHIT YOURSELF ABOUT THIS.)**

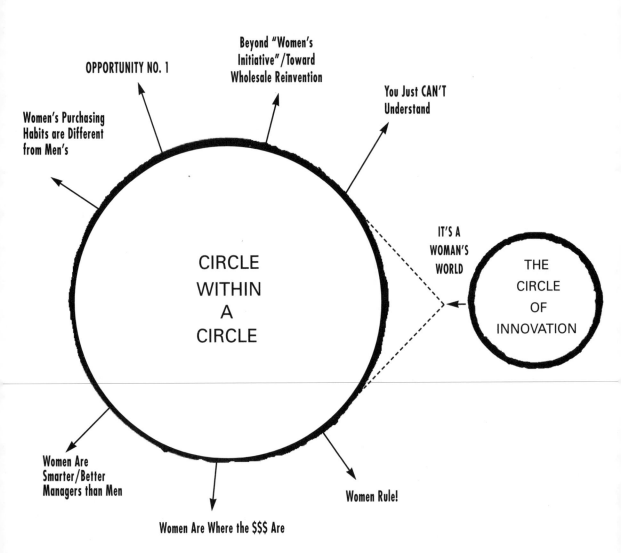

Women's Purchasing
Habits are Different
from Men's

OPPORTUNITY NO. 1

Beyond "Women's
Initiative"/Toward
Wholesale Reinvention

You Just CAN'T
Understand

IT'S A
WOMAN'S
WORLD

CIRCLE
WITHIN
A
CIRCLE

THE
CIRCLE
OF
INNOVATION

Women Are
Smarter/Better
Managers than Men

Women Are Where the $$$ Are

Women Rule!

SEMANTICS ALERT No. 12

THINK W-O-M-E-N

WOMEN OWN THE WORLD

Think . . . DIFFERENCE

OPPORTUNITY NO. 1

Women-and-cars

Women-as-road-warriors

Women-as-etc.

Only REINVENTION will do

Women 1.0/Opportunity Kit

You Just CAN'T Understand

FINAL NOTE

I am humbled.

I am blown away.

This idea is enormous (E-N-O-R-M-O-U-S).

It is simple.

It is subtle.

It is obvious.

It is the (economic) world's . . . BEST KEPT SECRET.

Still.

Katy, bar the door! This sterling differentiation/decommoditizing tactic is a/the blockbuster to end all blockbusters . . . i.e., "getting" women's collective/awesome/misunderstood/underappreciated purchasing power. Problem: You've got to undertake wholesale corporate reinvention to take advantage of this (stunning/mind-boggling) opportunity . . . i.e., OPPORTUNITY No. 1.

Little Things are the Only Things.

I don't understand why design remains a deep dark secret.

Sony gets it. Ditto Rubbermaid. Ditto John Deere.

They win (big) by design. So can you!

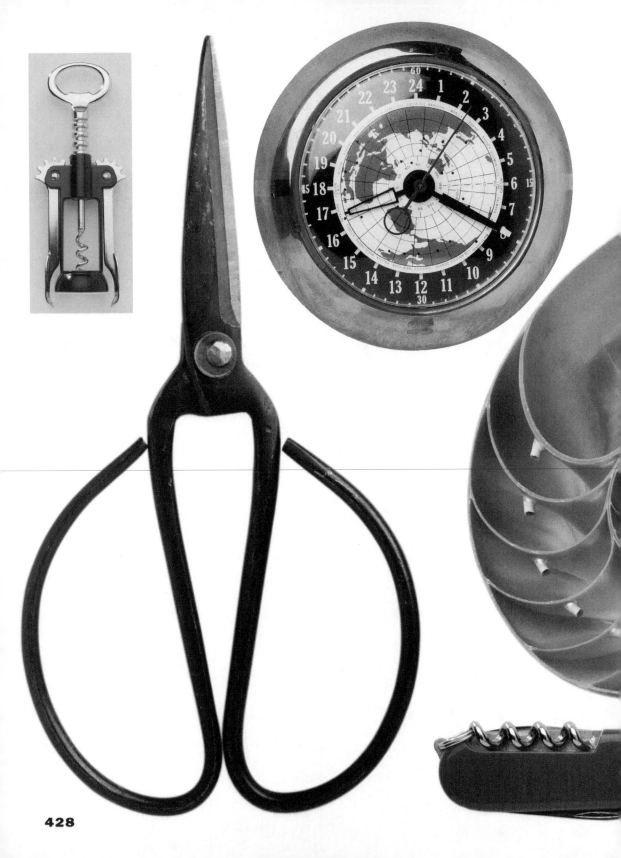

428

Design
is it!

"Fifteen years ago, companies competed on price. Today it's quality. Tomorrow it's design."

—Robert Hayes,
professor,
Harvard Business School

Bob Hayes is a man with a reputation for getting it right. Arguably he and Bill Abernathy triggered the American management renaissance, with their seminal 1980 *Harvard Business Review* article, "Managing Our Way to Economic Decline." They decried the fact that dispassionate analysis had driven out passionate attachment to the product itself.

Over the years, Hayes sharpened his message and became a leading spokesman in the quality revolution. But enough is never enough, and about a half dozen years ago Hayes began to pursue the possibility of a design advantage. As his extensive research accumulated, he arrived at a simple truth: Design is it.

B-I-G IDEA: Innovation = Design Is It!
big idea: ANOTHER (WILDLY) UNDER-HERALDED ADVANTAGE . . . DESIGN.

Design
hall of fame

Body Shop

Boots the Chemist

Braun

Dow

Chrysler

John Deere

Gillette

Herman Miller

Nike

Rubbermaid

Sony

Stanley

My Design Hall of Fame is made up of people and companies that take "it" seriously, of people and companies that put "it" at the v-e-r-y top of the strategic agenda, of people and companies with passionate attachments to the products and services they produce.

Body Shop.
It stands out in crowded retail markets, to a large degree because of its attention to design. The shops themselves are memorable and colorful . . . by design. The simple and instructive packaging is memorable . . . by design. And the shopping bags (I'm a shopping-bag fanatic . . . and you ought to be) are memorable and distinct . . . by design. Design is Body Shop's signature. Founder Anita Roddick gets it.

Boots the Chemist.
The huge British pharmacy and pharmaceutical products chain probably integrates design into corporate strategy and purpose as effectively as any company on earth. Boots' packaging stands (way) out from the herd. The Boots' shops are beautifully designed. Design considerations are intimately folded into every element of Boots' core business processes. Boots is a big winner . . . by design.

Braun.
A German-based subsidiary of Gillette, Braun has more of its products in the industrial design section of the Museum of Modern Art in New York than any other company. It hasn't happened by accident. Dieter Rams, Braun's chief designer, sits on Braun's managing board . . . and his word (vision!) carries enormous weight. Braun understands what the butter is on its bread . . . design . . . by design.

Chrysler. Lee Iacocca, father of the Mustang, was a design fanatic. Sometimes (perhaps even today) Chrysler's quality was/is not quite up to snuff. But there's the minivan. The Neon. Etc. Chrysler has exhibited more of an unabashed passion for design—and risky designs—than its peers. And it's paid off ... by design.

Dow. Actually, it's not Dow but a Dow product ... Ziplocs. I love 'em! I.e.: Can't live without 'em. That's design! That's special! And special for a buck! (Design = Tiffany. NOT.) That's a V-E-R-Y big WOW ... by design.

Gillette. The Braun magic has rubbed off—along with millions of bottom-line dollars—on Braun parent Gillette. Take for one (big/very big) example the Lady Sensor. Its look and mechanics are, well, revolutionary ... by design.

Herman Miller. The furniture business was a commodity business ... until 1945 when George Nelson arrived at Herman Miller. One of America's 20th-century hall of fame designers, he turned an entire industry upside down ... by design.

Nike. Nike is not about glitz. It's about mechanics and glitz. Founder Phil Knight was a track star on the

University of Oregon's fabled track team. Trackies have a passion for shoes. (No surprise.) It's just that Knight made his passion into all our passions. He pursued a better shoe . . . and also instinctively understood the role of aesthetics. In shoes. And . . . of course . . . the Swoosh logo. Knight's firm boasts a design shop of 350(!) . . . the largest in the United States. Nike/Knight outpaced the very (tough) competition . . . by design.

Rubbermaid. I do love Rubbermaid products. I love how they . . . work. I love how they . . . look. I love their . . . usability. Rubbermaid is a company of design fanatics. It starts—where else?—with CEO Wolf Schmitt. In all aspects of his life he has a passion/obsession for design. And very purposefully and methodically he's instilled that passion in Rubbermaid's 13,861 employees. Incidentally (not so incidentally) this is another great example of great design . . . for (in some cases) less than a buck. Talk about the "mass" market! (By design.)

Sony. Stay tuned . . . .

Stanley. I love . . . L-O-V-E . . . my Stanley hammers. And $2.6 billion in sales says I'm not alone. Like Nike, the functionality is . . . great. And so are the aesthetics . . . by design.

John Deere. Shit (excuse me, manure) and design do mix. Henry Dreyfus . . . say the name and every industrial designer in the world genuflects. He brought us Bell's Trimline phone. And Honeywell's award-winning thermostats. But he's best known for making John Deere's farm equipment a global winner . . . by design.

Henry Dreyfus. Say the name and every industrial designer in the world genu-flects . . . best known for making John Deere's farm equipment a global winner . . . by design.

B-I-G IDEA: Innovation = Design Is It!

big idea: DESIGN IS THE ADVANTAGE FOR A

SMALL . . . BUT V-E-R-Y IMPRESSIVE . . .

NUMBER OF COMPANIES.

Design
is differentiation!

"At Sony, we assume all products of our competitors will have basically the same technology, price, performance, and features. Design is the only thing that differentiates one product from another in the marketplace."

—Norio Ohga, chairman and CEO, Sony

In Sony's insanely fast-paced markets, price and performance are a wash. Even if it gets the lead, Sony can't hold on with technological wizardry alone. But it can and does hold on with design.

Design is Sony's ace in the hole.

Sony as technology company? Sure, but . . .

How about: Sony as d-e-s-i-g-n company? YES.

B-I-G IDEA: Innovation = Design Is It!

big idea: IT MAY LOOK LIKE TECHNOLOGY TO YOU . . .

BUT IT LOOKS LIKE D-E-S-I-G-N TO THEM.

Design

is design mindfulness!

---

20 Ways Design Gets Under Your Skin

(And Into Your Mind)

Design isn't just hiring a great designer. Design surely isn't merely "prettifying." Design—when it becomes a core competence—is about what I call . . . DESIGN MINDFULNESS. That is—like total quality management at its best—when design makes a difference, it is . . . a way of life.

When design is a way of life:

1 It's part of every new product/service development effort . . . from the start . . . not as an afterthought.

2 It's the subject of routine hallway chatter in the finance department as well as the marketing and research and development departments.

3 It's the executive team's unabashed obsession.

4 It permeates the reward systems (Ford may promote its chief designer to CEO).

5 It's embedded, à la Boots the Chemist in the U.K., in every core business process.

6 It's reflected on the organizational chart.

7 It's reflected in the informal power alignment.

8 It's reflected in who's chosen to serve on boards of directors.

9 You can see it, à la Steelcase, in the corporate headquarters . . . and every other facility.

10 You can see it in the delivery trucks . . . at Odwalla or Body Shop, for example.

11 You can find it in the packaging . . . at FedEx and throughout Japan.

12 You can observe it in point-of-purchase displays as well as in the product itself . . . Sony is terrific here.

13 You can carry it . . . in an FAO Schwarz or Banana Republic shopping bag.

14 You can sit on it . . . as in the fixturing in a Starbucks shop.

15 You can (lovingly) nail it . . . as with a Stanley hammer.

16 You can brag about it . . . as with Tiffany and Hermès.

17 You can smile about it . . . as with Swatch.

18 You can vacuum with it . . . as in Black & Decker.

19 You can hire it . . . as in . . . want great design, hire great designers (that's the Gap's new strategy).

20 In other words, "it" is part of e-v-e-r-y-t-h-i-n-g . . . the look/feel/taste/smell/color of your company's products, services, offices and other facilities, literature, ads, internal (and external) forms, policies (in human resources as well as engineering), and so on.

Design is the Big Enchilada . . . in fact the WHOLE Enchilada . . . at its (RARE) best.

B-I-G IDEA: Innovation = Design Is It!

big idea: DESIGN-AS-DISTINCT-ADVANTAGE =

DESIGN MINDFULNESS PERVADES ALL ASPECTS

OF THE ENTERPRISE.

Design mindfulness is risk seeking!

"We should do something when people say it is crazy. If people say something is 'good,' it means someone else is already doing it."

—Hajime Mitarai, president, Canon

DESIGN (design mindfulness) that transforms, that takes customers and companies to new places, is inherently risky. "Make something great," Nintendo's boss told one of his game designers. "Something great" is something unexpected . . . a surprise . . . and thus it's risky. "We are crazy," Canon president Hajime Mitarai told *Forbes*. "We should do something when people say it is crazy. If people say something is 'good,' it means someone else is already doing it."

To pursue the ultimate potential of design/design mindfulness is to routinely pursue the crazy, the surprising. Which is to routinely embrace risk . . . and the distinct possibility of rejection.

> **B-I-G IDEA: Innovation = Design Is It!**
> **big idea: GREAT DESIGN = THE RISK (& REWARDS) OF EMOTIONAL ATTACHMENT . . . OR REJECTION.**

Design mindfulness
is design for surprise!

"Our job is to give the client . . .
what he never dreamed he wanted."

—Dewys Lasdon, superstar designer

The shock of recognition. Leading the customer. I call it . . .
DESIGN FOR SURPRISE. (And it applies to accounting
departments . . . and purchasing departments . . . and IS
departments . . . and training departments . . . as well as to
industrial design/new products departments.)

DFS/Design For Surprise . . . does that describe YOU?
Does that describe the project you are working on . . . right
now? If not . . . you are missing one hell of an opportunity!

Superstar designer Dewys Lasdon says it exactly right: "Our job is
to give the client, on time and on cost, not what he wants, but what he never dreamed
he wanted; and when he gets it, he recognizes it as something he wanted all the time."

Shock of recognition . . . it is the ultimate goal of great design. It's a Rushmorean
standard . . . but the only standard, arguably, worth pursuing . . . in (again) a ludicrously crowded marketplace.

Design for surprise: Post-its. CNN. MTV. Lady Sensor. Macintosh. FedEx. Miata.
Lotus 1-2-3. Quicken. The Walkman. Virgin Air. Chronicle Books. Taurus' 1986 coffee-
cup holders. Ziplocs. Boeing 747. Velcro. Gore-Tex. J. Peterman. Star Wars. The Web!
S, M, L, XL, the book.

> Great design leads your customers.

Design mindfulness is little things!

"Over the years, I have fumbled my way through life, walking into doors, failing to figure out water faucets. . . . 'Just me,' I would mumble. But as I studied . . . the behavior of other people, I began to realize that I was not alone.

While we all blame ourselves, the real culprit, faulty design, goes undetected.

It's time for a change."

—Donald Norman,
author, *The Design of Everyday Things*

It's not me—it's the d e s i g n e r !

I just bought a fabulous pair of sweat pants in Australia. (I'm a sweat-pants freak.) But they're driving me crazy. The pockets are too shallow. My glasses keep falling out. I crushed a $250 pair in the driveway. I'm pissed. I'm pissed at myself for carrying my glasses in the pockets. W-r-o-n-g attitude: I should be (v-e-r-y) pissed at the designers who created short pockets!

It's not me—it's the d e s i g n e r !

Why can't I figure out my car-radio controls? Why can't I figure out *any* car-radio controls? Technical incompetence? No! There's no such thing as well-designed car-radio controls. The seek button? The scan button? Or any button, whatsoever, on a cold winter day when you have gloves on? IT ALL SUCKS!

It's not me—it's the d e s i g n e r !

Ditto refrigerator temperature controls. Everything is either covered with ice. Or covered with condensation. Can't find the controls. Are they behind the milk? Or in with the eggs? Which way is colder? Which way is warmer? What a klutz I am! (Redux.) NO! What a dork the designer is. (Redux!)

It's not me—it's the d e s i g n e r !

ALL SOFTWARE SUCKS! Sure, the best of it (software) is helpful . . . VERY HELPFUL. But "user friendly"? Give me a break. I've never gone more than 10 minutes . . . WITH ANY SOFTWARE PROGRAM . . . without running into a prob-lem. User friendly, my ass!!!

It's not me—it's the d e s i g n e r !

Speaking for us 45-year-

old-plus types whose eyes are going, have you E-V-E-R come across a hotel shampoo bottle . . . WHERE YOU CAN READ THE WORD "SHAMPOO"? I haven't! God I hate getting old! NO! God . . . I H-A-T-E designers. Now that's more like it!

It's not me—it's the d e s i g n e r !

And then there's the "touch" lamp switch. Touch any part of the lamp and turn the light on. Neat! Except . . . the damn lamp randomly goes on in the middle of the night and stays on for no discernible reason. May the designer twist in hell . . . in a special compartment situated right next to the designer who decided to place the switch on a very expensive lamp I recently bought too close to the bulb. The switch is made of metal . . . and it invariably burns my hand when I go to turn it off.

When you start blaming designers instead of yourself when something doesn't work, you've made the first (big) step down the path to . . . DESIGN MINDFULNESS. Let yourself get pissed . . . and then translate that anger into your own work . . . ensuring that the things you design (e.g., forms and procedures) don't lead to an angry reaction on the part of many of your customers (internal or external). That's the ticket!

You get the picture. Design can be a phenomenal advantage . . . IF WE ARE PERPETUALLY TUNED INTO IT . . . PARTICULARLY IN ITS MOST "MINOR" MANIFESTATIONS.

Design is pervasive.

Design is opportunity.

DESIGN IS GIANT OPPORTUNITY.

So . . . . ???

B-I-G IDEA: Innovation = Design Is It!

big idea: BLAME PRODUCT GLITCHES ON THE DESIGNER . . . NOT YOURSELF . . . THEN REMEMBER THAT YOU'RE A DESIGNER (!) IN EVERYDAY WORK LIFE.

Design 1.0 opportunity kit

Take your first steps toward design mindfulness.

The issue is design sensitization. Learn to open your eyes. How to do it?

1. **Open your eyes.**

   Be alert. Start looking out . . . EVERYWHERE . . . for "little" design-related things that irritate you. Things that turn you on.

2. **Read.**

   Read design magazines. Start with *I.D.* (*International Design*). Buy design books. Start with Donald Norman's *The Design of Everyday Things*; Christopher Lorenz's *The Design Dimension*; and Thomas Hine's *The Total Package: The Evolution and Secret Meaning of Boxes, Bottles, Cans and Tubes.* I.e.: Educate yourself.

3. **Tear out and save great ads, great illustrations, great junk mail, etc.**

   When you come across a great ad . . . or a great tagline in an ad . . . tear it out. (Also consider subscribing to *Advertising Age*. I do.) Same thing with a (rare) sparkling piece of junk mail.

4. **Be on the lookout for good forms . . . good letters . . . good business cards . . . etc.**

   Some forms are engaging, easy to use. (FedEx.) Some forms irritate the hell out of you! Become a "forms fanatic." Judge them . . . mercilessly. That is . . . again . . . pay attention!

5. **Analyze instructions and signage.**

You've ordered that barbecue grill. It arrives. You're thrilled. You lay out the parts, go to the directions, and get pissed. Pay attention to instructions . . . good, bad, indifferent. Pay attention to signage. I recently stayed at the Opryland Hotel in Nashville: 2,900 rooms. A vast facility. The signage may well be . . . the worst in the world. Can't find a damn thing! (Neither could anyone I talked with.) Signage is important.

6. **Create two file folders: "neat" and "crappy."**

Take notes! Become a string saver! Whenever you come across any-thing that smacks of/deals with good design . . . SAVE IT. Whenever you come across something that smacks of/deals with lousy design . . . SAVE IT. Build up your library. (And fine-tune your design antennae.)

7. **Go on a less-than-$10 buying spree.**

Look for "neat stuff" (well-designed stuff) that costs pennies. Post-it Notes . . . Bic pens . . . a Lady Sensor razor . . . a postcard . . . a paper clip . . . a candybar. The point: Sensitize yourself to the idea that sterling design can come in 59-cent packages . . . as well as for $59,000.

8. **Start a notebook from both ends: "neat" and "crappy."**

I started a few years ago with a plain old notebook. On one cover I

wrote "neat." On the other cover "crappy." (All right, all right, I wrote "shitty.") And then I started taking notes when I came across "design stuff" that turned me on (a great shopping bag from a little store in Gualala, California) . . . or off (an elevator control panel where "1" was the basement). In short order, I had dozens of entries. The idea (redux): DESIGN SENSITIZATION.

9. Translate!!

The idea of all this is not to ruin your day by making you sensitive to lousy signage. The idea is . . . obviously . . . TRANSLATION. That is, when you see lousy signage . . . or inept directions . . . or a crappy form . . . always ask yourself: To what extent does my organization do more or less the same thing to its customers? (BE HONEST!) Perhaps get everybody going with the design notebook idea. Or the file-folder routine. And then work together on translation: How about a quarterly Design Day? That is, an all-day meeting devoted . . . solely . . . to "little" design issues? Or: A half-day design field trip . . . to a shopping mall? I.e.: G-E-T S-T-A-R-T-E-D! N-O-W!

B-I-G IDEA:

Innovation = Design Is It!

big idea: THERE ARE WEE, PRACTICAL STEPS YOU CAN TAKE . . . NOW . . . TO BEGIN YOUR TREK TOWARD DESIGN SENSITIZATION/ DESIGN MINDFULNESS.

Design
is advantage!

"The old weapons for achieving real differentiation have become inadequate. No longer can comparative advantage be sustained for long through lower costs, or higher technologies . . . . The design dimension is no longer an optional part of marketing and corporate strategy, but should be at their very core."

—Christopher Lorenz,
The Design Dimension

This book is about pursuit . . . the desperate pursuit . . . of new avenues of advantage in a competitive battle turned white-hot . . . and getting hotter.

"What if everything worked?" An unthinkable question 20 years ago (at least unthinkable outside Japan and Germany). Well . . . just about everything works. So cars that start at -15°F in Vermont won't take us the next step up.

What will?

This chapter started with Bob Hayes . . . and ends with the late Christopher Lorenz, former management editor of the *Financial Times* and a leading U.K. design guru. Hayes' and Lorenz's messages: DESIGN IS THE BEST "NEXT BIG THING" IMAGINABLE.

I think they have a (DAMN GOOD) point.

B-I-G IDEA:

Innovation = Design Is It!

big idea: ANOTHER OPPORTUNITY NO. 1.

(THE HELL WITH THE LOGICAL FALLACY.)

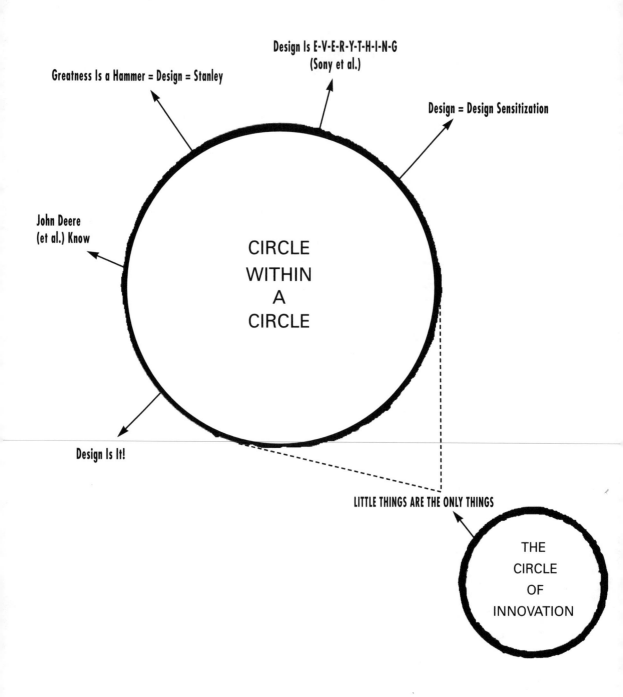

Design Is E-V-E-R-Y-T-H-I-N-G
(Sony et al.)

Greatness Is a Hammer = Design = Stanley

Design = Design Sensitization

John Deere
(et al.) Know

CIRCLE
WITHIN
A
CIRCLE

Design Is It!

LITTLE THINGS ARE THE ONLY THINGS

THE
CIRCLE
OF
INNOVATION

SEMANTICS ALERT No. 13

Design = John Deere (& Sony)

Design = Great hammers @ Stanley

Design Mindfulness

LITTLE (things) = BIG (things)

OPEN YOUR EYES!

OPPORTUNITY NO. 1 (Redux)

Yikes! Decommoditization/differentiation tactic number four. Another unsung Opportunity No. 1 (okay . . . call it OPPORTUNITY No. 1a). Namely: Design.

Design is wildly underappreciated as strategic opportunity . . . in manufacturing companies . . . and especially in service firms . . . and even for de facto/de jure independent contractors on or off someone else's payroll.

Love All, Serve All.

G-R-E-A-T service is the G-R-E-A-T-E-S-T innovation.

So why don't more companies OBSESS on service?*

*Beats the hell out of me!

Who's shopping now?

(Almost) nobody.

You need something else to worry about, don't you? Well . . . it's all yours: In just the last year, the time the average consumer spends shopping has dropped a whopping 1.3 hours per month . . . from 4.3 to 3.0. What's more, some 51 percent of consumers leave stores empty-handed, even though 68 percent of them know what they want when they walk through the doors. And a large share of shoppers (37 percent of women/61 percent of men) actually "dread" shopping.

The answer?

Elsa Klensch, CNN's style editor, gets it exactly right: "Stores must remember that no one needs anything anymore. Service, service, service is the key."

The Age of the Harried Shopper has arrived with a vengeance. Response? Obvious! A new Age of Service. Problem? All too few companies "get it."

Don't believe me? Try this: Say "great quality" and a dozen (or two dozen . . . or three dozen) companies readily come to mind, right? Say "great service" and who pops into your head? FedEx? Disney? Nordstrom? Caterpillar? Charles Schwab? The Ritz-Carlton? USAA? Saturn? But not many more.

Truth is . . . and for the life of me I can't figure out why . . . V-E-R-Y F-E-W companies have established an advantage (read . . . sustainable competitive advantage) based on service per se.

B-I-G IDEA:

Great Service Is The Greatest Innovation!

big idea: AWESOME SERVICE IS STILL A "BEST-KEPT SECRET" NOMINEE!

Who's loyal now?

(Almost) nobody.

Loyalty in the automobile industry is astonishingly low, especially when you consider the extraordinary sums spent on promotion and marketing. More than half of all consumers express little or no allegiance to auto manufacturers (Ford, General Motors, etc.) or their brands (Mercury, Chevrolet, etc.) and only the tiniest fraction pledge their loyalty to individual car dealers (Joe's Toyota, Bob's Jeep, etc.).

What's a carmaker (or a car dealer) to do?

Competing on quality (alone) isn't the answer. Sure, there will continue to be quality improvements. Overall, though, it's probably fair to say that automakers rate about an 8 on a scale of 10 (where 10 is perceived perfection). Moreover, the odds of any major car company being caught taking a quality nap . . . the way the Big Three were found Rip van Winkling by the Japanese 20 years ago . . . are low. Thus, the ability to "make a big difference" on the basis of improved quality is probably very low (say 3 out of 10); and the ability to sustain a significant new difference based on quality is lower still (about 2 on a scale of 10).

Competing on style (alone) also isn't the answer. The rating for style/raw excitement is below the quality rating. Call it a 5 or 6 out of a perfect 10. To be sure, the ability to make a big difference on the basis of an exciting image does still exist (Chrysler's flashy Neon is all the rage in Japan . . . despite some quality problems). On the other hand, a zippy image quickly begins to age . . . and the "other guy" normally catches up rapidly. So the sustainability of excitement is fairly low, no more than 2 or 3 on that scale of 10.

Why, I ask, don't car companies seek the huge, sustainable strategic difference that could surely come from . . . great customer service? All I can figure is that carmakers don't see service as an avenue to a huge . . . *and sustainable* . . . difference. That is, the Big Three can readily imagine advantage coming from R&D or marketing, but not from service per se. The reality is the reverse. Witness . . . S-A-T-U-R-N.

B-I-G IDEA:

Great Service Is The Greatest Innovation!

big idea: IT SEEMS THAT YOU CAN KNOCK OFF EVERYTHING . . . EXCEPT AWESOME SERVICE.

Who's winning now?

Saturn!

"We knew from the beginning that if Saturn was to succeed, we'd have to do more than just sell a good car. We'd also have to change the way cars are sold, the way the people who sell them are perceived, and the way customers feel about the experience of shopping for a car."

—Stuart Lasser, Saturn dealer

Saturn is a *quality car*... no question. But quality isn't what makes it stand out. Saturn is an *attractive car*, somewhat zippy. But its appearance isn't what separates it from the herd.

So where does Saturn stand out? As the mass-produced automobile marks its 100th birthday, Saturn is remarkable for totally reinventing the way automobiles are sold.

The Saturn story is... POSITIVELY BREATHTAKING.

Market research suggests that, among the 125-plus models sold in the United States, Saturn is the second most valuable... behind Lexus (a s-l-i-g-h-t-l-y... more expensive car). In fact, 95 percent of Saturn buyers (that's a higher percentage than Mercedes purchasers) urge others to join their club.

The reason? Joel Mandy, a Saturn regional manager, sums it up: About 25 percent of the car's appeal is the quality and excitement of the vehicle (many—meaning me— would say it's a smaller percentage than that). About 25 percent is ingenious marketing (e.g., the constant emphasis on the Spring Hill, Tennessee, Saturn "family" that produces the car). And 50 percent... as in Holy Toledo, Batman... comes from the "buying and after purchase experience." Read: C-U-S-T-O-M-E-R S-E-R-V-I-C-E!

The even B-I-G-G-E-R Holy Toledo is Saturn's explicit strategy of... CATERING TO WOMEN. It is the... UNABASHED CENTERPIECE... of the company's (phenomenal) (service) success!

B-I-G IDEA:

Great Service Is The Greatest Innovation!

big idea: IF YOU CAN MAKE IT IN THE SMALL-CAR MARKET THROUGH RAW SERVICE EXCELLENCE, YOU CAN MAKE IT ANYWHERE!

Who's winning now?

Ritz-Carlton!

A while back, I stayed in two different hotels on two consecutive nights . . . and I decided to observe both of them c-a-r-e-f-u-l-l-y.

My first stop was the Ritz-Carlton at Peachtree Center in Atlanta. In the course of my stay, I encountered 25 or 30 hotel employees. Some were housekeepers . . . some were waiters . . . some were maintenance people . . . some were accountants on their way to meetings with sheaths of paper under their arms.

Every one of them (including the accountants!) performed what I call The Ritz Pause. That is, they took a couple of seconds, stopped, looked me in the eye, and asked, "How's everything going? Is there anything I can do for you?" (I was tempted to ask the accountant to balance my checkbook, and I got the feeling he would have if I'd asked him.)

My second stop was at what I'll call a "good hotel." I had no customer service problems (no surly staff members, no unkempt room, etc.). On the other hand, of the 25 or so employees I came into contact with at this hotel, not one . . . NO ONE . . . performed anything like TRP/The Ritz Pause. The accountant scurrying to a meeting kept doing just that . . . scurrying. So, too, the maintenance person . . . and the housekeeper. I wasn't an overt annoyance to these people. I just didn't exist.

So let's examine The Ritz Pause: IS IT A LITTLE THING? In some sense, I suppose it is, since it takes just a few seconds. But to me . . . and I know I'm not alone (I've told this story to thousands now) . . . it is, in fact, a H-U-G-E  thing. It is, to a significant degree, the signature of the Ritz-Carlton hotels. It counts, in my book, for more than a lobby glittering with marble and brass do-dads.

IS IT COPY-ABLE? You could duplicate all that brass and marble, duplicate the award-winning architect's design . . . and, with a friendly banker or two, duplicate the great location. But copy The Ritz Pause? Damn near impossible!

Perhaps the competition doesn't take such practices seriously. Perhaps the issue is that such a "mechanical" act turns out to be anything but mechanical—that is, it stems from the deepest cultural wellsprings of the company. But practices like The Ritz Pause can be the basis for extraordinary . . . and sustainable . . . difference . . . IF ONLY YOU/I/WE WOULD TAKE THEM S-E-R-I-O-U-S-L-Y!

B-I-G IDEA:

Great Service Is The Greatest Innovation!

big idea: "LITTLE" (THINGS) = STRATEGIC ADVANTAGE

(AND THAT'S A V-E-R-Y HARD-TO-SELL IDEA).

Service obsession 1.0/

Who's winning now?

Disney!

In February of 1997 I stayed at Disney's Contemporary Resort at Disney World. I was giving a presentation to 900 senior executives. Also in my room was a projector that I could use to preview my 35mm slides. A little thing? I don't think so.

For example, I also found an instruction sheet for using the projector that was clearly the easiest instruction sheet . . . for anything . . . I've ever read. A little thing? I don't think so.

Then, on my second day there, I noticed the projector's power cord was taped down, so I wouldn't trip over it. A little thing? Again: I don't think so.

I could recount another dozen (or so) "little" things I encountered during my three-day stay. The point: It got me thinking. About things gone wrong (TGW) . . . and the opposite, things gone right (TGR). Disney is a Master of TGR.

It's also a Master of Magical Moments (what I call MMs). Disney Guests (and don't forget to capitalize that "G"!) get to take part in a l-o-n-g parade of unexpectedly nifty Magical Moments. I love that term . . . MAGICAL MOMENTS! The recruiting scheme, the training scheme, the reward and promotion scheme . . . all are hard-boiled systems at Disney . . . and all are aimed specifically at maximizing . . . MAGICAL MOMENTS.

Do you think the service you provide . . . at the bagel shop or auto-body shop or title-insurance shop . . . is made up of MAGICAL MOMENTS? Do you recruit Magical Moments producers? Train for Magical Moments? Reward MMs? Talk up MMs? Make MMs an explicit matter of culture . . . as Disney explicitly does? First step: Taking terms like Magical Moments seriously . . . VERY SERIOUSLY.

I'm inclined to turn pedantic. And order you . . . in a 4th-grade school marm's scratchy voice . . . to say (or write on the blackboard 100 times): I AM IN THE MAGICAL-MOMENTS BUSINESS! MY DEPARTMENT IS A MAGICAL-MOMENTS FACTORY!

B-I-G IDEA:

Great Service Is The Greatest Innovation!

big idea: TGRs/MMs . . . AND THE OVERT USE OF SUCH LANGUAGE IN YOUR (ACCOUNTING) DEPARTMENT.

Service obsession 1.0/

Who's winning now?

Carl

Hal

Herb

Katherine

Service Hall of Fame

Obsession for customers starts AT THE TOP! I'd like you to meet the (my) tops of the top: Carl. Hal. Herb. Katherine.

- Auto dealer CARL SEWELL (Sewell Village Cadillac dealership in Dallas, Texas . . . and many others) runs a half-billion-dollar empire these days. The secret of its success? Himself. He lives, sleeps, eats, and breathes . . . his philosophy . . . of CUSTOMERS-FOR-LIFE!

- Hal Rosenbluth . . . has revolutionized the travel-services industry. Giant Rosenbluth International uses the latest in information technology. Yet it's Hal's personal commitment to (obsession with!) service excellence (he serves High Tea to new employees brought in to the Philadelphia headquarters) that makes the difference.

- And Herb. Oh, yes . . . HERB! That is, Herb Kelleher, the crown/clown prince of Southwest Airlines. He's not distracted by outside activities (e.g., he serves on no other boards). He lives for Southwest's p-e-o-p-l-e . . . and the flying public. (Me!)

- Katherine Barchetti runs a couple of haberdashery stores in Pittsburgh. K. Barchetti Shops was declared the best at retail service by one renowned consultant who's visited similar shops . . . in 800 or so cities. (Not bad!) Everything Katherine Barchetti does is unmistakably aimed at . . . OVERWHELMING THE CUSTOMER. The Gospel According to Barchetti: "Make a customer, not a sale."

When it comes to customer service, it's the front line that counts. No doubt about it! (Never has been any doubt . . . to me.) But what sparks the front line is the obvious (even if your vision is 20/200) obsession for doing it right, making it right for the customer. All those at the top of the Hall of Fame Service Companies—all the Carls, Hals, Herbs, and Katherines—live for that opportunity.

B-I-G IDEA:

Great Service Is The Greatest Innovation!

big idea: WALK-THE-TALK. HOW ABOUT: RUN-THE-TALK?

THAT'S THE ESSENCE OF CARL-ISM, KATHERINE-ISM, ETC.

Service obsession 1.0/

How to win with service.

Forget customer service. Embrace the ownership experience.

Here's an idea I've swiped from Saturn: de-emphasize customer service. Emphasize instead the ownership experience (meaning the cradle-to-grave experience of owning a car).

Years ago, I fell instantly in love with Carl Sewell's Dallas dealership. The reason: The first time I visited, I saw no cars in the showroom, just great floral displays. Carl was selling "Sewellism" . . . or an ownership experience . . . not an HOH/hunk of hardware.

That's a nice story . . . but I want to keep this part of the discussion cool and calculated. That is, if you buy the potency of focusing on . . . LIFETIME CUSTOMERS/LOYALTY/OWNERSHIP EXPERIENCE . . . how about an org chart like this?

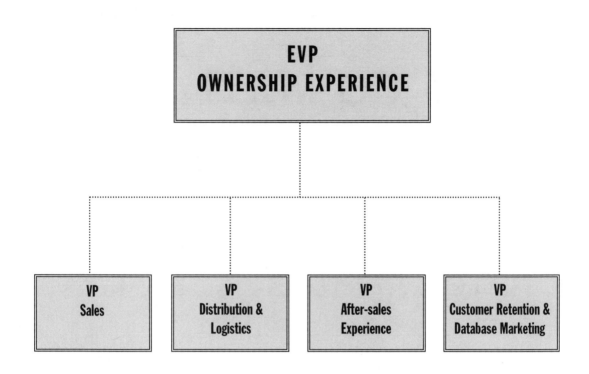

```
                    ┌─────────────────────────┐
                    │          EVP            │
                    │  OWNERSHIP EXPERIENCE   │
                    └─────────────────────────┘
```

| VP Sales | VP Distribution & Logistics | VP After-sales Experience | VP Customer Retention & Database Marketing |

B-I-G IDEA:

Great Service Is The Greatest Innovation!

big idea: CUSTOMER SERVICE IS A (V-E-R-Y)

LIMITED CONCEPT!

Service obsession 1.0/

How to win with service.

Hire, reward, and promote convivial, customer-obsessed folks!

Southwest Airlines has the best baggage-handling record around. The best safety record. The best on-time record. The fewest customer complaints. And it seems to pull it off year after year, invariably ranking at the top of the Department of Transportation's lists of the best.

A buttoned-down, tidy place. I have no doubt. On the other hand, what allows Southwest to keep this extraordinarily tidy company going . . . and add spunk to flying for customers . . . is the extraordinarily spirited gang of over 20,000 who staff the airline—from flight attendants and pilots to accountants and mechanics.

While doing some interviewing for a PBS show, *Service with Soul,* we asked Executive Vice President for Customers (Nice title, eh? Have you got one like it!?) Colleen Barrett what Southwest's employment criteria were. Her ready answer: "We look for . . . listening, caring, smiling, saying 'thank you,' and being warm."

I LOVE THAT!

Somebody said to me during a seminar, "Are those really the criteria you want when hiring a mechanic?" My answer: "Damn straight!"

I've got no problem with smart mechanics . . . who are good at the technical stuff. But let me tell you who I don't want maintaining the plane I fly in: the two guys I observed outside National Airport in Washington, D.C. a couple of years ago . . . sour pusses if ever there were ones, or so it appeared, with chips on their shoulders the size of Mt. McKinley. They're the ones I don't want within a country mile of my plane! I like surgeons with a good attitude. Pilots with a good attitude. Accountants with a good attitude. Mechanics with a good attitude.

There's a wonderful story told at Southwest about a pilot-applicant. Upon walking into the Dallas headquarters, he was not as friendly as he might have been to the receptionist . . . not realizing that the receptionist had a potentially decisive role in his subsequent hiring. When the company chose not to offer him a job, CEO Herb Kelleher commented, "There are a lot of people who can fly airplanes, not so many with great attitudes."

Amen! Is the story apocryphal? I know Southwest. Intimately. And I don't think so. But if it is . . . I'll bet you my Vermont farm that there's an even better story from Southwest . . . that's true to the last dollop.

So . . . how about topping your *formal* recruitment requirements list with Ms. Barrett's five magical phrases—listening/caring/smiling/saying "thank you"/being warm.

P-L-E-A-S-E!

B-I-G IDEA:

Great Service Is The Greatest Innovation!

big idea: HIRE SMILES. HIRE "THANK YOU." TAKE SUCH STUFF (V-E-R-Y) SERIOUSLY.

Service obsession 1.0/
How to win with service.

¡əsıɹdɹns

Just what is service excellence, anyway? Is it a particularly high return on investment? Something that stands out as "neat"?

Service excellence is about consistency. The invariably clean toilets at McDonald's of 25 years ago. (Back then, McDonald's did stand for consistency: Q, S, C, V . . . or Quality/Service/Cleanliness/Value.) But consistency isn't enough . . . or at least it isn't these days . . . when a clean toilet doesn't stand out the way it used to.

That's not to say I don't buy the consistency part of the equation. Consider Disney's peerless underpark, the clockwork mechanism that is the engine of those Magical Moments enjoyed by millions of customers up above. Nonetheless . . . and Disney is a good example again . . . the underpark/the perfectly calibrated mechanism is far from the whole story. A perfect underpark doth not a great (over)park make. It merely (one damn big merely!) paves the way for those MMs . . . Magical Moments.

The nature of a Magical Moment for the customer? Even though she/he knew what they were going to get at Disney . . . it's the little twists and turns . . . THE SURPRISES . . . that make their day.

An Excellence Machine has one hell of an Underpark. NO DOUBT OF IT. But even more, excellence is about surprise:

Excellence machine = Surprise machine

Surprise?

Surprise = Grace. Surprise = Excitement. Surprise = Bending the rules and going the extra mile. (The antithesis of a cookie-cutter response . . . even from a mass marketer.) Key point: I contend that *surprise* is not a soft word. Disney doesn't leave its Magical Moments to chance. Neither does the Ritz-Carlton hotel chain. Nor Southwest Airlines. They are all . . . UNABASHEDLY . . . in the surprise business. "Surprises, Inc.," you might say. They work like hell to induce their employees, among other things, to be themselves, to give of their (creative) personalities . . . at all times. Sure there are rules at Southwest, Disney, and the Ritz-Carlton. And without those rules they'd all three be in (very) deep yogurt. But what makes them special is—clearly, continually, and consistently—behaving in an unexpected fashion . . . that is . . . providing SURPRISE!

Think surprise!

Work on surprise!

Can you imagine a "surprise machine" at your auto dealership? Floral shop? Seven-person training department? Yes, the idea applies as much to training departments . . . and accounting departments . . . as to amusement parks.

> ## B-I-G IDEA:
> ## Great Service Is The Greatest Innovation!
> ### big idea: PURSUE INCONSISTENCY . . . A.K.A. SURPRISE.

Service obsession 1.0/
How to win with service.

"Love all, serve all."

—Credo, Hard Rock Cafe

SOUNDS LIKE GOOD B-U-S-I-N-E-S-S STRATEGY TO ME.

NO, MAKE THAT A "GREAT" PUBLIC/PRIVATE/INDEPENDENT-SECTOR STRATEGY!

B-I-G IDEA:

Great Service Is The Greatest Innovation!

big idea: L-O-V-E A-L-L. S-E-R-V-E A-L-L.

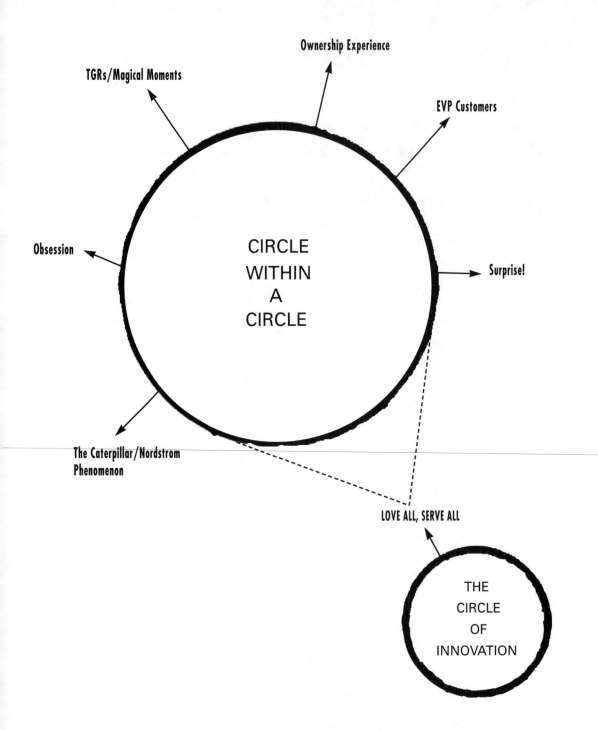

Ownership Experience

TGRs/Magical Moments

EVP Customers

Obsession

CIRCLE
WITHIN
A
CIRCLE

Surprise!

The Caterpillar/Nordstrom
Phenomenon

LOVE ALL, SERVE ALL

THE
CIRCLE
OF
INNOVATION

SEMANTICS ALERT No. 14

S-A-T-U-R-N-I-Z-I-N-G

TGRs/Things Gone Right

MMs/Magical Moments

Ownership Experience

Excellence = Surprise/Surprises, Inc.

Love All, Serve All

The fifth and last of the "decommoditization tactics" (Chapters 10 through 14) takes no back seat to the first four: Service (as-sustainable-strategic-advantage) seems to be a (very) deep (very) dark secret. Why?

God alone knows!

But the opportunity is . . . AGAIN . . . enormous . . . and is . . . AGAIN . . . underappreciated. And . . . AGAIN . . . the achievement of a true service edge requires wholesale restructuring.

****

These six chapters (Chapters 9 through 14) constitute enormous hurdles on the track to enormous opportunities. But given the competitive heat . . . WHAT'S THE ALTERNATIVE?

We're Here to Live Life Out Loud.

Passion demands passion!

It's missing at Harvard Business School (mostly).

And along corporate hallways (mostly). M-i-s-t-a-k-e!

Passion demands...
obsession!

Become A Charter Member of the
Lunatic Fringe!

General Electric chairman and CEO Jack Welch doesn't do things half way. He glommed on to quality . . . and he made it his latest initiative. And he's gone after it . . . Jack-like . . . i.e., like a prize-winning retriever goes after a duck. "You can't behave in a calm, rational manner," he says of his new-found (1997) commitment. "You've got to be out there on the lunatic fringe." GE execs are suddenly finding that almost half of their bonus program is directly tied to success with the new quality initiative.

Will Welch pull it off? I bet he does. Whether it's blowing the joint up ("Neutron Jack" of the early 1980s) or preaching empowerment ("Work-out Jack" of the early 1990s) . . . the bloke doesn't understand halfway measures.

Jack Welch: Charter Member of the Lunatic Fringe.

HOORAY!

B-I-G IDEA:

Innovation Demands Passion!

big idea: WINNING "STRATEGY" = PROFESSED LUNACY.

Passion demands...
enthusiasm!

"I have no pride. I'll do anything that's necessary to get people involved. I am a dispenser of enthusiasm."

—Benjamin Zander,
conductor, Boston Philharmonic

DISPENSER OF ENTHUSIASM!

Love that!

Ben Zander is an extraordinary conductor (and has become a much sought after speaker/management guru in his own right). Think "symphony" . . . and you are likely to think about command and control, authoritarianism, uniformity and order. All that's true . . . to some extent.

But what makes for a great symphony, Zander reminds us, is each member of the orchestra soaring to unimaginable heights. And that means . . . engagement and involvement (passion!) . . . not just memorizing one's part in Beethoven's Ninth.

And what does it take to get members from here to there?

How about . . . CHIEF-DISPENSER-OF-ENTHUSIASM: How do you stack up on the Dispenser-of-Enthusiasm Scale? Today? (In the last 30 *minutes*?) (Specifically?)

B-I-G IDEA:

Innovation Demands Passion!

big idea: CHIEF (OF ANYTHING)-AS-UNABASHED-DISPENSER-OF-ENTHUSIASM.

Passion demands...
fixation.

"I used to have a rule for myself that

at any point in time I wanted to

have in mind—and as it so happens,

also in writing, on a little card I

carried around with me, the three big

things I was trying to get done.

Three. Not two. Not four. Not five.

Not ten. Three."

—Richard Haass,
author, *The Power to Persuade*

Richard Haass was an effective Department of Defense official during the Bush Administration. He wrote a superb book about his experience ... *The Power to Persuade*.

Truth is, I disagree with Haass. My magic number ... TWO. No matter. Whether it's two ... or three ... I surely agree with "not four ... not ten."

Any idiot can leap out of bed at 6 a.m., rush to the computer, and tap out a "to do list" with 17 ... or 97 ... items on it. Genius is ... PURPOSEFUL RUDENESS ... disregarding all but two ... or three ... of those items ... and fixating on them.

Make that (long) list. Scratch ... scratch ... scratch. Leave no more than three items. (Or two!) Put it in your pocket. Tattoo it on your hand. Refer to it ... E-V-E-R-Y H-O-U-R.

B-I-G IDEA:

Innovation Demands Passion!

big idea: FORGET THE STUPID "TO-DO" LIST. DO TWO/THREE THING(S) V-E-R-Y MEMORABLY IN YOUR 4-YEAR STINT IN CHARGE OF PURCHASING (ETC.).

Passion demands

People stuff is real stuff.

p-e-o-p-l-e.

People stuff is the only stuff.

I have a good friend who loves sports . . . and sporting gear. He achieved his life's dream a while back by opening a sporting goods store with two partners. The two partners shared the same love. As the store grew to 35 or so employees, my friend also learned that he had a knack for dealing with "people stuff." (Or, more accurately, his two partners didn't have such a knack.)

But there was a problem . . . that I helped him suffer through. (I'm not sure I really did him much good.) He'd drag home at the end of a long day and invariably say, "I didn't do anything today. I was tied up with people issues." In my (quite lengthy) consulting experience, this is a (very) common complaint. People who focus on the "it" (sporting goods, hardware, books, children's clothing) feel vaguely—or not so vaguely—dispirited as they end up spending more and more time on "human resource" issues.

Some are good at "people stuff." Some are bad at people stuff. But as a firm grows, it becomes increasingly clear that . . . PEOPLE STUFF IS THE ONLY STUFF. And . . . to put it mildly . . . people stuff is (V-E-R-Y) R-E-A-L STUFF.

Which is another way of saying, to young managers in particular, if at the end of the day you feel as though you haven't "done anything" . . . except arbitrate this social issue or that . . . welcome to the real world! And if you get good at it . . . you have an awesome career in front of you! Top CEOs, though they may be so-called "visionaries," typically report that three-quarters (or more!) of their time is spent on "people stuff." (I.e., nurturing top talent.) Welcome to the club. Don't fight it! Join it! Study it! Obsess on it!

Passion demands...
truth.

Tell

the

truth!

"In trying to bring about fundamental change, what's the single most important thing a leader can do?"

That question came from a seminar participant recently. It stumped me. (It shouldn't have.) And then I heard myself blurt out: "Tell the truth!"

Organizations undergoing change bulge with rumors. Sometimes bosses—junior to senior—try to shade the truth. Often, it's because they don't know the truth . . . are confused themselves. Nonetheless . . . the best way (only sure way!) to make allies of people who are scared to death (all people confronted with significant change) is to tell the truth . . . AS BEST YOU KNOW IT . . . AT THE MOMENT . . . INCOMPLETE THOUGH IT IS . . . AND DIFFERENT THOUGH IT MAY BE TOMORROW.

The late Mike Walsh was the most effective change agent I ever met. He made a revolution, almost overnight, at the calcified Union Pacific Railroad. Mike was smart. He was "political." (I.e., astute.) But, mostly, he told the truth. He shot v-e-r-y straight.

A few years ago, I profiled (for PBS) a dramatic turnaround at an old General Motors parts plants in Bay City, Michigan. The turnaround artist was Pat Carrigan, who in a former incarnation was the first woman to run a GM assembly plant. I clearly remember talking to Jack Whyte, the local union chief, about Carrigan's approach. "Pat Carrigan ain't got a phony bone in her body," he said to me (and . . . thank God . . . the television camera).

Secret No. 1 to implementation success . . . particularly when an organization is awash in stress: She/he (wise leader at any level) ain't got a phony bone in her/his body. Secret No 2? As I said . . . there ain't none!

B-I-G IDEA:

Innovation Demands Passion!

big idea: CRAZY TIMES = PREMIUM ON TRUTH-TELLING.

Passion demands Loud!

"If you ask me what I have come to do in this world . . . I will reply: I'm here to live my life out loud."

—Émile Zola

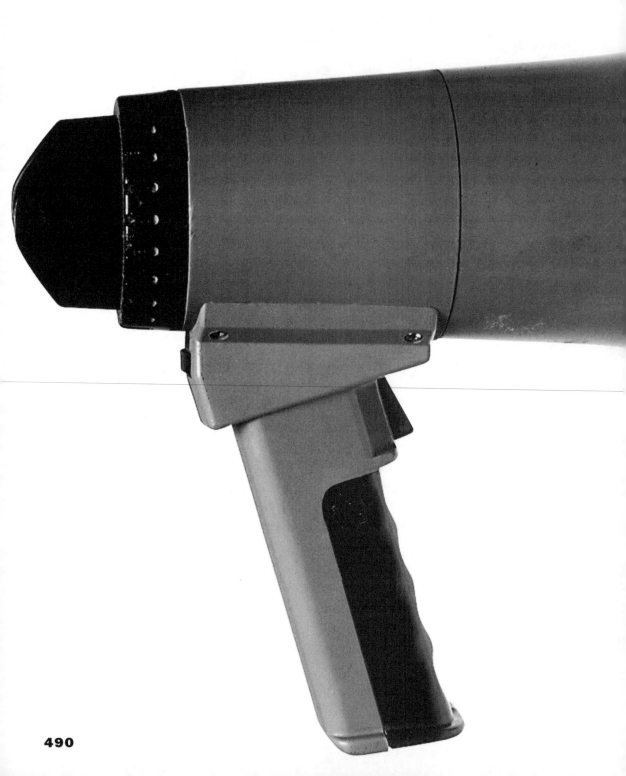

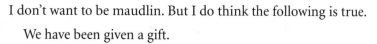

I don't want to be maudlin. But I do think the following is true. We have been given a gift.

In my Dad's time the message was, "Hunker down, keep your nose clean, don't make waves." (The Big Three.) It was the right message that he passed on to me, as a 15-year-old . . . in 1957. It's exactly the wrong message now . . . 40 years later.

By sheer accident, you and I are in positions of responsibility when the biggest change . . . in 250 years (or much more) . . . in the way the world's work gets done has come jouncing along. And the question is: Will we live up to the (insane) times? That is: Will you/me/we use the gift we've been given . . . or squander it? That's pretty blunt. But I think it's about right:

Will we use the gift?

Will we squander the gift?

Will we have the guts, the nerve, the persistence, the PAS-SION to live our life as loudly as these very loud times demand?

For your and my careers, for our units, for our organizations, for our families, for our communities, for our nation . . . it's the $64-trillion question. So . . . . . ??

LIVE LOUD!

Passion demands

outta control!

"If things seem under control,
you're just not going fast enough."
—Mario Andretti, race-car driver

Lucky ❖ HELL ❖ CANNON
DRIVERS

And on that (relevant) note...
goodbye...and good luck...
and thank you for your time
and attention.

Tom Peters
Palo Alto, California
September 1997

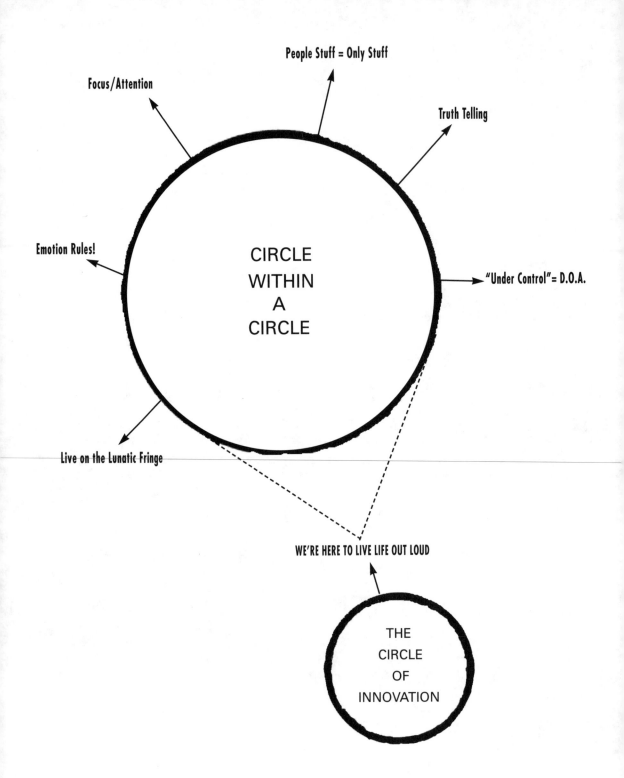

Focus/Attention

People Stuff = Only Stuff

Truth Telling

Emotion Rules!

CIRCLE
WITHIN
A
CIRCLE

"Under Control"= D.O.A.

Live on the Lunatic Fringe

WE'RE HERE TO LIVE LIFE OUT LOUD

THE
CIRCLE
OF
INNOVATION

SEMANTICS ALERT No. 15

Join the . . . lunatic fringe

Life (leadership) = Emotion

Dispenser of Enthusiasm!

Success = (Two) (Three) Big Things

People Stuff = The "only" stuff

(Leadership) success = Truth-telling

Success = Life out loud

In control = Accepting out-of-control

Leadership has been implicit in every page of this book. Now we get explicit: a deep and sustaining commitment to innovation means leader-as-dispenser-of-enthusiasm. I.e.: It's passion, stupid! These are unbalanced times . . . and they call for . . . yes . . . unbalanced leaders. Yo . . . Ted Turner! Yo . . . Martha Stewart!

To-Do's: A Baker's Dozen

Frustrated, the seminar participant almost begged, "But what, among this mass of ideas, should my priorities be?" I can't really answer . . . but . . . loudmouth that I am . . . I couldn't resist trying:

1. Create a draft, formal Renewal Investment Plan. (Next 30 days. Review with pals in subsequent 30 days. Then "sign up" . . . or at least make a pledge to yourself.)

2. Reformulate your principal current task into a full-fledged Project . . . criteria per P.C. 1.0, page 221. (Next 10 working days.)

3. If you are a staff unit boss, call a meeting to discuss launching the PSF 1.0/Professional Service Firm Conversion Kit process . . . per Chapter 6. (Kick-off discussions in next 15 working days. Formal program launch in 60 days??)

4. Begin a "decommoditization" conversation: Talk about "unexpressed wishes and needs"/"dreams . . . not furniture"/"only ones who do what we do"/Lust Hierarchy/etc. (Start informal discussion in next 5 working days; expand to action plan in next 30-60 days.)

5. Start work on a departmental Kill It/Forget It strategy. E.g., consider launching a 1-person, 3-month Skunkworks to explore weird stuff . . . page 101. (Next 20 working days.)

6. Develop a strategic Talent-Recruitment Plan . . . featuring odd inputs/sources, new hiring criteria: E.g., "demonstrated appetite for adventure" . . . Chapter 11. (Next 30-60 days.)

7. Review/revamp evaluation and promotion process to emphasize "architect of human possibilities"/"day job that matters"/etc. . . . . page 153. (Draft in 30 days. Formalize in 60 days.)

8. Conduct a preliminary Personal Brand Equity Evaluation. (ASAP . . . next 5-10 working days for draft . . . discuss with best pals subsequent 10-15 working days.)

9. Launch a unit/departmental Branding Initiative. (Draft a concise "What We Stand For" statement in 30 days; follow-up action plan in subsequent 60 days.)

10. Consider a Beautiful Systems Initiative. (Review one key process/document and apply the Beauty/Grace Test . . . page 285 . . . every 15-20 working days.)

11. Begin a (BIG DEAL) Strategic Disintermediation Study . . . and an E(c)/Empowerment (Customers) examination. (Set study parameters in next 30-45 days; conduct study in subsequent 3-5 months.)

12. Undertake a Women's Market Assessment . . . (Scope and launch the assessment within 45 days; conduct 1st phase in subsequent 90 days; establish a Permanent Revolution Plan in subsequent 60 days.)

13. Consider a major Design Initiative. (Set parameters in next 30-60 days; undertake initial design sensitization training . . . page 445 . . . in subsequent 60-120 days.)

Good Luck!

ACKNOWLEDGMENTS

First . . . those to whom the book is dedicated. *Susan Sargent* . . . Best pal. Supporter. Artist. Entrepreneur. Community leader. Role model. De-bunker of Tom's (occasional) pretentiousness . . . and spouse. *Donna Carpenter* . . . Pal. Supporter. Wordsmith and idea fount and editor. Entrepreneur and CEO of Wordworks. De-fuser of Tom's (more than occasional) wretched excess. *Ken Silvia* . . . Pal. Supporter. Designer. Conceiver of wholes. Muse. De facto father of Bailey, who helped cut (eat) the manuscript when it had gotten too long.

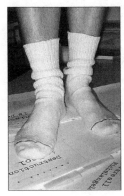

 Sonny Mehta . . . Pal. Supporter. Publishing Genius. Renaissance Man. (Mostly) patient . . . even understanding . . . at delayed . . . and delayed . . . ms. arrival. *Herb Kelleher* . . . Pal. Supporter. Founder, CEO, Business Guru and Chief Inspirer at profitable, on-time, kinky Texas-based airline . . . a.k.a. Southwest/LUV. Most creative . . . and sound . . . and funny . . . executive I've met. *Larry Holman* . . . Pal. Supporter. Entrepreneur. Maniac. Visionary. Co-boss (sorta) along with Bunny Holman . . . of WYNCOM, which sponsors the seminars which are the backdrop for this book. *Ian Thomson* . . . Pal. Supporter. Business partner. Renaissance Man. Prodigious reader . . . except for my books. Sole source of sanity in my insane world.

 And . . . at Wordworks (Donna's place) . . . Erik Hansen . . . project manager . . . worrier about all things large and (particularly) small . . . paranoid about tiny errors . . . and cause of ms. delay because of a full day that Ken and Tom had to spend with him searching for wool sweat socks with the perfect rib pattern. Maurice Coyle . . . co-editor with Donna . . . marvelous blend of ultra professionalism and bizarre sense of humor. Christina Braun . . . Ms. Fact Check . . . knows everything . . .

royal pain (hooray). Also at Wordworks: Ellen Mary Carr, Surrena Goldsmith, Chantal Laurie, Martha Lawler, Cindy Sammons, Katie Schofield, Pat Wright. And . . . at Ken Silvia Design Group . . . Nancy Cutter . . . who knows more about the manuscript than any of the rest of us.

At . . . The Tom Peters Companies . . . Leane Reelfs . . . creator of the slides that form the backbone of the book. And . . . Michelle Rotzin and Pat Reardon . . . who make my life work . . . while taking no shit whatsoever from me. And: Susan Bright Winn at Bright Typing, who transcribed the first, messy drafts of this ms. At . . . ICM . . . Esther Newberg . . . agent extraordinaire . . . supporter . . . conceiver of the series of books of which this is part.

And . . . Dean LeBaron . . . financial entrepreneur . . . ideasmith . . . Captain of Curiosity . . . who kindly (and supportively!) crafted the foreword to this book. Special thanks, re: "Women's Stuff" . . . to . . . Heather Shea . . . and the gang at Disney Institute.

And . . . at Alfred Knopf . . . the indomitable super-woman . . . Jane Friedman! And: Alberto Vitale, Jon Segal, Paul Bogaards, Katherine Hourigan, Ida Giragossian, Pat Johnson, Quinn O'Neill, Mel Rosenthal, Bill Loverd, and Marlene London of Professional Indexing Services. And . . . Cover Queen . . . Carol Carson.

***

A special tribute: Turnaround boss. Raiser-of-enormous-companies-from-the-near-dead. And utterer of "You can't shrink your way to greatness" . . . Arthur Martinez, he of Sears.

Thank you all!

N O T E S

INTRODUCTION

"Whatever made you...in the future": John H. Sheridan, "Lew Platt: Creating a Culture for Innovation," *Industry Week*, December 19, 1994, p. 26.

"It's the end...we know it": Peter Georgescu, "Looking at the Future of Marketing," *Advertising Age*, April 14, 1997, p. 30.

"News item: In...Ho-Hum? Or Ho-ly": Jim Rohwer, *Asia Rising* (New York: Simon & Schuster, 1995), pp. 42-44.

CHAPTER 1

3-4   "Carrying a call...Indonesia, and Taiwan": "The Death of Distance," *The Economist*, September 30, 1995, pp. 15, 27.

7   "Bill Gates, richest man in the world": AP(Associated Press), "Gates Three-peats as World's Richest," *San Jose Mercury News*, July 14, 1997, p. A4.

9   "Videogames are perfect...and computer simulations": J.C. Herz, *Joystick Nation: How Videogames Ate Our Quarters, Won Our Hearts, and Rewired Our Minds* (Boston: Little, Brown and Company, 1997), p. 2.

11   "Younger people are...with a person": Hal Kahn, "Shoppers Haltingly Embrace Machines Replacing Clerks," *The Denver Post*, April 19, 1997, p. A22.

11   "Xerox's legendary PARC...came up with!": Elizabeth Weil, *Fast Company*, April:May, 1997, p. 100.

13   "It was a...25 years ago": See Oren Harari, "Let Computers be the Bureaucrats," *Management Review*, September, 1996, p. 57.

14   "Stock market value...Caterpillar + Kellogg": John R. Dorfman, "Microsoft, Intel Take Over As the New Kings of Stocks," *Wall Street Journal*, March 21, 1997, p. C1.

16   "Consider these statistics...stock-market value": William C. Symonds, Brian Bremmer, Stewart Toy, and Karen Lowry Miller, "The Globetrotters Take Over," *Business Week*, July 8, 1996, p. 46.

19   "Boosting profits through...heat from layoffs": Fred R. Bleakley, "Going for Growth," *Wall Street Journal*, July 5, 1996, p. A1.

19   "You can't shrink...way to greatness": Quoted in John Greenwald, "Reinventing Sears: The Big Store, Once Close to Closeout, Has Become the Merriest Retailer under CEO Arthur Martinez. How Long Can He Keep it Going?" *Time*, December 23, 1996, p. 52.

20   "In the final...costs and grow": Quoted in Seth Lubove, "A Long, Long Last Mile," *Forbes*, October 10, 1994, p. 66.

20   "No business can...way to success": Bill Dahlberg, Speech, Marketing Meeting, The Southern Company, January, 1997.

21   "Wall Street won't...stretch for growth": Fred R. Bleakley, "Going for Growth," *Wall Street Journal*, July 5, 1996, p. A1.

22   "For the past...the top line": Peter Georgescu, "Looking at the Future of Marketing," *Advertising Age*, April 14, 1997, p. 30.

26   "Incrementalism is innovation's worst enemy": Nicholas Negroponte, "The Balance of Trade of Ideas," *Wired*, April, 1995, p. 188.

28-29   "The only sustainable...out-innovating the competition": James F. Morse, "Predators and Prey: A New Ecology of Competition," *Harvard Business Review*, May/June, 1993, p. 75.

29   "Wealth in the...seizing the unknown": Kevin Kelly, "New Rules for the New Economy," *Wired,* September, 1997, p. 140.

31   "Think revolution, not evolution": Tom Peters, "Column No. 500 Reviews Some Bedrock Beliefs," *Star Tribune,* August 30. 1994, p. 2D, citing Richard Sullivan, SVP of Advertising, Home Depot.

CHAPTER 2

44-45   "Low Tolerance [for variety]...always have roses": Joe Flower, "Of Communities and Hired Hands," *Healthcare Forum Journal,* May/June, 1997, p. 55.

46   "Selection processes can...on available diversity": Mike Hannan and John Freeman, *Organizational Ecology,* (Cambridge, MA: Harvard University Press, 1989), p. 21.

48   "The complexity of...react more quickly": Thomas H. Naylor, Rolf Osterberg, and William H. Willimon, "Work Without Meaning," *Chicago Tribune,* November 27, 1996, p. 25.

49   "Roger Enrico's conundrum:...fixing a conglomerate?": Patricia Sellers, "How Coke is Kicking Pepsi's Can," *Fortune,* October 28, 1996, p. 70.

52   "How Viacom's Deal...and Cultures Clashed": Eben Shapiro, *Wall Street Journal,* February 21, 1997, p. A1.

52   "I don't understand the name of synergy": Andrew Pollack, "Sony Embraces the Digital Age," *International Herald Tribune,* May 23, 1997.

54   "None of this...Disney and ABC": Leslie Eaton, "Market Place; Corporate Spinoffs are Getting a New Spin," *New York Times,* January 30, 1997, p. D1.

55   "Acquisitions are about...is a difference": John R. Hayes, "Acquisition is Fine, But Organic Growth is Better," *Forbes,* December 30, 1996, p. 52.

55   "A client agrees...(no) 'grand strategy'": Katharine Campbell, "People: Presiding Over 'Creative Chaos'-A Love of Travel Led the Young Peter Job of Reuters," *Financial Times,* October 10, 1994, p. 16.

56   "When asked recently...draw a blank": Mark L. Sirower, *The Synergy Trap: How Companies Lose the Acquisition Game* (New York: The Free Press, 1997), p. 4.

57   "Today's mergers are tomorrow's spin-offs": Leslie Eaton, "Spinoffs Become the Trendy Thing to Do," *New York Times,* January 30, 1997, p. D1.

57   "Acquiring firms destroy...a plain fact": Mark L. Sirower, *The Synergy Trap,* p. 18.

59   "Equity carve-outs...for the center": Patricia Anslinger, Dennis Carey, Kristin Fink, and Chris Gagnon, "Equity Carve-Outs: A New Spin on the Corporate Structure," *The McKinsey Quarterly,* 1997, Number 1, pp. 165-172.

60   "*Business Week* tells...entrepreneurial manager-leaders": Phillip L. Zweig, "Why Divorce Is Paying Off On The Street," *Business Week,* December 5, 1994, p. 84.

60   "Thermo-Electron has...game for years": Patricia Anslinger, Dennis Carey, Kristin Fink, and Chris Gagnon, "Equity Carve-Outs: A New Spin on the Corporate Structure," *The McKinsey Quarterly,* 1997, Number 1, pp. 165-172.

62-63   "Microsoft gets it...several times over": Kathy Rebello, "Bill's Quiet Shopping Spree," *Business Week,* January 13, 1997, p. 34.

66   "I believe in...important in creativity": *Newsweek,* January 15, 1996, p. 17.

67   "Mess is not...and creative fermentation": George Will, "Shadow World," *Newsweek,* May 4, 1992, p. 82.

CHAPTER 3

76   "The problem is...old ones out": M. Mitchell Waldrop, "The Trillion-Dollar Vision of Dee Hock," *Fast Company*, October:November, 1996, p. 79.

77   "Cybernetics founder Gregory...without an eraser": Tom Peters, "To Forget is Sublime" *Forbes ASAP*, April 11, 1994, p. 128.

78   "The greatest difficulty...about old ones": John Maynard Keynes, *General Theory of Employment, Interest and Money* (Harcourt Brace: 1989).

78   "A pattern emphasized...of impending death": James M. Utterback, *Mastering the Dynamics of Innovation: How Companies Can Seize Opportunities in the Face of Technological Change* (Boston: Harvard Business School Press, 1994), p. xxvii.

80   "We run like...we change direction": Alison L. Sprout, "Can it Become the Communication Company of the Next Century?" *Fortune*, October 2, 1995, p. 110.

80   "They're bloody fast": Catherine Arnst, "MCI is Swarming over the Horizon," *Business Week*, February 19, 1996, p. 68.

81   "We're quick to...to pull back": Catherine Arnst, "MCI is Swarming over the Horizon," *Business Week*, February 19, 1996, p. 68.

82   "I can't think...decisive, quick, breathtaking": Kathy Rebello, with Amy Cortese and Rob Hof, "Inside Microsoft," *Business Week*, July 15, 1996, p. 56.

83   "The company went...by 18 percent": Teena Hammond, "Banana Republic Eyes New Formats and Revived Catalog," *Womens' Wear Daily*, April 21, 1997, p. 1.

84   "Cannibalizing existing products...remain the leader": John H. Sheridan, "Lew Platt: Creating a Culture for Innovation," *Industry Week*, December 19, 1994, p. 30.

85-87   "Obsolete ourselves or...much of one": John Mickelthwaite, "Vital Intangibles," *The Economist*, March 29, 1997, p. 7. © 1997 The Economist Newspaper Group, Inc. Reprinted with permission.

86   "Failure is Silicon Valley's No.1 strength": Michael S. Malone, "Silicon Valley Primer," *San Jose Mercury News*, June 27, 1993, p. C4.

91   "You miss 100 percent...you don't take": Warren Bennis and Patricia Ward Biederman, *Organizing Genius: The Secrets of Creative Collaboration* (Reading, MA: Addison-Wesley), 1997, p. 21.

94   "I would suggest...the business. Experiment!": Scott Kirsner, "7 Seers," *Webmaster*, July, 1997, p. 48.

95   "It's impossible to...become so important": Scott Kirsner, "7 Seers," p. 47.

96   "Effective prototyping may...hope to have": Michael Schrage, "The Culture(s) of Prototyping," *Design Management Journal*, Winter, 1993, p. 65.

100   "*Inc.* magazine, one...less than $100,000": Martha E. Mangelsdorf, "Behind the Scenes," *Inc.*, October, 1992, p. 72.

103   "In this company...not making mistakes": Debora Vrana, "New Centurion; MTV Creator goes Boldly into Century 21," *Los Angeles Times*, August 27, 1995, p. D3.

103   "If you are...for you. Dead": "Failure," *Forbes ASAP*, June 2, 1997, p. 47.

108   "All great truths begin as blasphemies": George Bernard Shaw, *Annajanska*, 1919, according to *Bartlett's Familiar Quotations*, 16th ed. (Boston: Little, Brown, 1992), p. 571.

108   "If people did...ever get done": Jonathan Romney, *New Statesmen and Society*, March 26, 1993, p. 32.

114   "If you have...need duplication for": Richard Hoffer, "Sitting Bull; Phil Jackson May Invoke Sioux Lore and Zen Mysticism In Coaching Michael Jordan & Co., But the Real Message Is: Play Smart Basketball," *Sports Illustrated,* May 27, 1996, p. 76.

119   "There is always...the same time": Ingrid Sischy, "The man from Boss; Interview with Hugo Boss AG Head Peter Littmann," *Interview Magazine,* November, 1996, p. 26.

CHAPTER 4

124   "Ultimately our strategy...ultimate accountability strategy": Alan M. Webber, "XBS Learns to Grow," *Fast Company,* October:November, 1996, p. 115.

128   "Lakeland, in effect...requirements for patients": Julia Flynn Siler, "Hospital, Heal Thyself," *Business Week,* August 27, 1990. p. 66.

132   "Bill Charland, a...and hardware systems": William A. Charland, *Career Shifting: Starting Over in a Changing Economy* (Massachusetts: Bob Adams, Inc., 1993), p. 21.

133   Chart adapted from William A. Charland, *Career Shifting,* p. 21.

134   "Ours is the...lease on life": "They Dared to Dream," *BeautyInc.,* July/August, 1997, p. 32.

138   "Reason for switching...quality—49 percent": Richard C. Whiteley, *The Customer Driven Company: Moving from Talk to Action* (Reading, MA: Addison-Wesley, 1991), pp. 9-10.

138   "70 and 90...the service relationship": Barry Gibbons, *This Indecision is Final: 32 Management Secrets of Albert Einstein, Billy Holiday, and a Bunch of Other People Who Never Worked 9 to 5* (Chicago: Irwin Professional Publishing, 1996), p. 4.

138   "Its researchers examined...'poor in quality'": Richard C. Whiteley, *The Customer Driven Company: Moving from Talk to Action* (Reading, MA: Addison-Wesley, 1991), pp. 9, 10.

140   "What brings people...matters": Charles Trueheart, "Welcome to the Next Church," *Atlantic Monthly,* August, 1996, p. 56.

141   "What creates trust...for the followers": James O'Toole, *Leading Change: Overcoming the Ideology of Comfort and the Tyranny of Custom* (San Francisco: Jossey-Bass Publishers, 1995), p. 9.

142   "In essence, the...that is trust": James O'Toole, p. xiii.

144   "I set as...of human beings": David Williams, "Zander: Contribution to Business," *Encouraging Excellence,* Winter, 1995.

145   "The best thing...their own greatness": Warren Bennis and Patricia Ward Biederman, *Organizing Genius,* p. 27.

146   "In the digital...enriching the whole": Stanley Crouch, "Swingin' to the Digital Times," *Forbes ASAP,* December 2, 1996, p. 252.

CHAPTER 5

159   "Reengineering-pioneer Michael Hammer...systems/information technology manager": Michael Hammer, "Reengineering Work: Don't Automate, Obliterate," *Harvard Business Review,* July/August, 1990, p. 104.

161   "Add the 2000...of every 60": Andrew Brown, "Top of the Bosses," *International Management,* April, 1994, p. 26.

162   "If you can't...place, you're out": Brian Dumaine, "The New Non-Manager," *Fortune,* February 22, 1993, p. 80.

164   "If you're not...on someone else's": Marjorie Blanchard, Presentation, May, 1997.

167   "We must spread...at every step": Quoted in Philip K. Howard, "Overregulation yields 'culture of resistance', excess of laws, litigation turns good intentions to farce," *Rocky Mountain News,* June 20, 1995, p. A22.

167   "The word upon...word was CHOICE": Tom Robbins, *Still Life with Woodpecker* (New York: Bantam Doubleday Dell Pub., 1994), p. 190.

168   "In 1900, 50...to 7 percent": David Lamb, "'Lone Eagles' Flying From Cities to New Job Horizons," *Los Angeles Times,* August 18, 1993, p A1.

171   "The thing women...just take it": Stephen H. Dunphy, "The Newsletter," *Seattle Times,* June 27, 1997, p. D1.

175   "While reading a...'Leading Without Authority'": Ronald Heifitz, *Leadership Without Easy Answers* (Cambridge, MA: The Belknap Press of Harvard University Press, 1994).

177-178   "If I don't...important moral idea": Nathaniel Branden, *Taking Responsibility: Self-Reliance and the Accountable Life* (New York: Simon & Schuster, 1996), p. 110, 122.

180-181   "*Driver.* 'So why...Sir Ranulph Fiennes": Ffyona Campbell, *On Foot Through Africa* (Great Britain: Orion Publishers, 1994).

191   "Rick Kaminski understands...the slanting stands": Ellis E. Conklin, "Rick Kaminski: Peanut Vendor," *Seattle Post,* May 7, 1997, p. D1.

194   "Life is either...or nothing": Gary Wescott, *Russian Life,* March, 1997, p. 12.

195   "There is a vitality...keep the channel open": George Carlin, *Brain Droppings* (New York: Hyperion: 1997), p. ix.

CHAPTER 6

201   "All growth will...in-World standard": James Brian Quinn, Speech, February, 1997.

208   "Gary Withers, chief...of his organization": Conversation with author.

215   "First Gus Pagonis...Sears": Patricia Sellers, "How Coke is Kicking Pepsi's Can," *Fortune,* October 28, 1996, p. 70.

224   "Clerks trained to...savvy service companies": Walter Russell Mead, "A History of the Future," *Worth,* June, 1997, p. 35.

CHAPTER 7

230   "The intermediary is...is already clear": Patrick McGovern, "Circling Back to the Small and Simple," *Forbes ASAP,* December 2, 1996, p. 197.

230   "Free: Landmark Tower...As Is": Timothy Aeppel, "The Property Report: Free: Landmark Tower, 31 Stories, As Is," *Wall Street Journal,* December 20, 1996, p. 1.

231   "'Disintermediation'...It's all...the ticket itself": Graeme Kennedy, "Airlines' new buzzword cuts out tickets—and high costs," *The National Business Review,* July 5, 1996, p. 24.

232   "More Law Firms...with LL.D.S": Paul M. Barrett, "Legal Beat: More Law Firms turn to Temps with LL.D.S," *Wall Street Journal,* May 19, 1997, p. 1.

234   "A customer bypasses...bank's general ledger": Arno Penzias, *Harmony: Business, Technology and Life after Paperwork* (New York: HarperBusiness, 1995), p. 4.

236   "Campbell Soup recently...things to come": "Functional Foods growth requires industry decision," *Milling and Baking News,* December 17, 1996, p. 7.

238   "You'll find the...outlets by 1998": Linda Himelstein, "Wells Fargo Bets Big on Minibanks," *Business Week,* November 18, 1996, p. 160.

239   "Organizations will be...organizers, not employers": Conversation with author.

244   "CBIS pulled in...and Time Warner": Linda Haugsted, "MSOs Will Test Payment Card Option," *Multichannel*

News, December 23, 1996, p. 7.

244   "And if you...call them POWERHOUSE": Conversation with author.

251   "Interfirm links are broad, deep, and unique": Jordan D. Lewis, *The Connected Corporation* (New York: The Free Press, 1995), p. 8.

255   "Anything that tightens...from that customer": Heath Row, "The Electric Handshake," *CIO,* December 15/January 1, 1997, p. 50.

256   "The web allows...on the Net": Scott Kirsner, "7 Seers," p. 50.

257   "Changes in business...conducting it themselves": Raymond Lane, "The Information Age is Not Yet Here," *New Perspectives Quarterly,* March, 1997, p. 19.

CHAPTER 8

273   "The 'ord' in 'chaordic'": M. Mitchell Waldrop, "The Trillion-Dollar Vision of Dee Hock," *Fast Company,* October:November, 1996, p. 78.

275   "Reengineering guru Mike...bureaucratic system": Michael Hammer, "Reengineering Work: Don't Automate, Obliterate," *Harvard Business Review,* July/August, 1990, p. 104.

275   "Dr. C. West Churchman...an aesthetic sense": John R. O'Neil, *Paradox of Success: When Winning At Work Means Losing At Life: A Book of Renewal for Leaders,* (New York: G.P. Putnam's Sons, 1993), p. 48.

278   "21,000 people totally...25 million passengers": Ken Kaye, "Air of Anticipation," *Fort Lauderdale Sun Sentinel,* January 21, 1996, p. F1.

280   "The company's market...Does it work?": Roger Dow and Susan Cook, *Turned On: Eight Vital Insights to Energize Your People, Customers, and Profits,* (New York: HarperBusiness, 1996), pp. 22-23.

281   "Richard Sharp, boss...a lunch hour'": John Greenwald, "Buying a Car Without the Old Hassles," *Time,* March 18, 1996, p. 74.

284   "Raise awareness by...To anybody. P-E-R-I-O-D": Barry Gibbons, *This Indecision is Final,* p. 12.

286   "All depends on...of the conversations": Alan M. Webber, "What's so New About the New Economy," *Harvard Business Review,* January/February, 1993, p. 24.

286   "The indispensable complementary...the Boeing 747": Thomas A. Stewart, "Managing in a Wired Company," *Fortune,* July 11, 1994, p. 44.

286-288   "The Institute for...on-line sites": Etienne Wenger, "Communities of Practice: Where Learning Happens," *Benchmark,* Fall, 1991, p. 8.

289   "Research done at...human/social skills": David Stamps, "Are We Smart Enough For Our Jobs?" *Training,* April, 1996, p. 44.

290   "CEO Hatim Tyabji...urgency and sharing": William C. Taylor, "At VeriFone It's a Dog's Life (And They Love It!)," *Fast Company,* Premier Issue, p. 117.

CHAPTER 9

296   "There's an absolute...fashion-forward products": Conversation with author.

296   "The Sameness of...increasingly the same": Paul Goldberger, "The Sameness of Things," *New York Times Magazine, April 6, 1997,* pp. 56, 58.

297   "Quality as defined...a competitive advantage": J.D. Power and Associates Report, September 11, 1996, p. 1.

299   "The mainstream is...with special effects": Samuel Autman, "Sitting on Top of the Independent Heap; The Sundance Film Festival Showcases 127 Cutting-Edge Movies," *St. Louis Post-Dispatch,* January 26, 1997, p. 3C.

301   "I'd rather have...they've changed that": Bill Richards, "Sharper Image is Dropping Spa Line, Focusing on Home-Furnishings Catalog," *Wall Street Journal,* March 7, 1997, p. B9A.

302   "Curb the flavors...Genuine technological advantage": Jack Neff and Pat Sloan, "Procter & Gamble out to Simplify its Product Lines," *Advertising Age,* September 30, 1996, p. 21, 24.

303   "When we did...still pretty ordinary": Barry Gibbons, *This Indecision is Final,* p. 26.

305   "Quality is conformance...requirements, not goodness": Tim Stevens, "Quality is Free Because it's Built-In," *New Straits Times,* March 26, 1996, p. 11.

307   "With ISO 9000...defects. That's absurd": Ronald Henkoff and reporter Ricardo Sookdeo, "The Hot New Seal of Quality," *Fortune,* June 28, 1993, p. 116.

310   "The Ritz-Carlton...of our guests": The Ritz-Carlton credo.

312   "We didn't want...at 25,000 feet": "Secrets of the Empire Builders," *Success,* September, 1996, p. 30.

312   "We define a...amuse, surprise, entertain": Tom Peters, "On Excellence: Airlines' Soul Survivor," *The Independent,* October 2, 1994, p. 16.

314   "We do not...We sell dreams": Conversation with author.

316   "We need to...for our products": Alan Goldstein, "Inside Intel; How a Chipmaker Becomes a 'Benevolent Monopoly,'" *Dallas Morning News,* August 11, 1996, p. H1.

317   "You do not...what you do": Warren Bennis and Patricia Ward Biederman, *Organizing Genius,* p. 19.

323   "In 1994 and...Rubbermaid": Rahul Jacob, "Corporate Reputations; The Winners Chart A Course of Constant Renewal And To Sustain Culture That Produce the Very Best Products and People," *Fortune,* March 6, 1995, p. 54.

326   "The customer is...to the future": Conversation with author.

326   "*Newsweek* says he...reinvented the kitchen": Tara Weingarten and John Leland, *Newsweek,* June 9, 1997, p. 60.

326   "I just bought...what I like": Caroline E. Mayer, "Prophet Among the Pots and Pans," *Washington Post,* May 19, 1993, p. E1.

329   "Most companies don't...a better product": Rance Crain, "Callaway Stalking Tiger? Ely Hints He's on the Prowl," *Advertising Age,* May 26, 1997, p. 20.

CHAPTER 10

334   "The increasing difficulty...of the brand": Gillian Law and Nick Grant, "The Changing Face of the Marketplace 2001," *Management,* June, 1996, p. 64.

337   "Take Electronic Data Systems...in the first year": Bradley Johnson, "EDS May Pour $80 Million Into First Global Campaign; Spending Soars To Reflect Growing Businesses," *Advertising Age,* September 30, 1997, p. 4.

340   "Brand power...touch for promotion": Charlie Vestner, "What Does it Take to Stay Hot in the World's Most Fickle Business, *Individual Investor,* February, 1997, p. 40.

341   "Quite a lot...spread the word": "Secrets of the Empire Builders. The 25 Best Business Schools," *Success,* September, 1996, p. 30.

342   "I want to...invisible visible": Bill Burgess, Speech, Atlanta, January, 1997.

342   "Soon, you'll buy...the corn flake": Richard C. Greene, *Forbes* print ad.

344   "When you think...think about anybody!": Bill Dahlberg, Speech, Atlanta, January, 1997.

346   "We coined the...product, or service": Bernd H. Schmitt and Alexander Simonson, *Marketing Aesthetics: The Strategic Management of Brands, Identity, and Image* (New York: Free Press, 1997) p. 18.

CHAPTER 11

354   "Expose yourself to...you are doing": Steve Lohr, "Creating Jobs," *New York Times,* January 12, 1997, p. 14.

355   "For his product-development...Apple operating system": Jonathan Weber, "Cult. Company. Chaos." *Los Angeles Times,* December 10, 1995, p. 24.

357   "You say you...be rather limited": Patricia Pitcher, *The Drama of Leadership* (New York: John Wiley & Sons, Inc., 1997), p. 139.

359-360   "Our most beloved...out of step": Jack Mingo, *How the Cadillac Got Its Fins* (New York: HarperBusiness, 1995).

361   "Experience is out...fact of life": Alan Webber, "If anything, experience counts against you," *USA Today,* January 28, 1997, p. A11.

364   "I'm not interested...very, very talented": Quoted in Martha Duffy, "The Pope of Fashion," *Time,* April 21, 1997, p. 112.

365   "I love running...it's wonderful!": Jean Lipman-Blumen, *The Connective Edge: Leading in an Interdependent World* (San Francisco: Jossey-Bass Publishers, 1996), p. 308.

367   "He was respected...a reality change": Quoted in Richard Hoffer, "Mystical Methods; Phil Jackson Has Become a Kind of Spiritual Force for the Bulls, and However Quirky his Style, It Works," *Sports Illustrated,* June 19, 1996, p. 88.

367   "It's all so...of the world": James Clavell, *Shogun: A Novel of Japan* (New York: McClelland and Stewart Ltd., 1975).

368   "Hire for attitude...who don't apply": Peter Carbonara, "Hire for Attitude, Train for Skill," *Fast Company,* August:September, 1996, p. 73.

369   "Cheryl Womack runs...passion/flexibility/excitement": Charles Burck, "Succeeding with Tough Love," *Fortune,* November 29, 1993, p. 188.

369   "Gary Withers...appetite for adventure": Conversation with author.

371   "Harvard professor of...in point: Freud": Adapted from Thomas Armstrong, *7 Kinds of Smart: Identifying and Developing Your Many Intelligences* (New York: Plume, 1993), pp. 9-11. See also Howard Gardner, *Frames of Mind: The Theory of Multiple Intelligences* (New York: Basic Books, 1993); *Multiple Intelligences: The Theory in Practice* (New York: Basic Books, 1992).

372   "The leaders of...Connoisseur of talent": Warren Bennis and Patricia Ward Biederman, *Organizing Genius,* pp. 5, 12.

373   "One Great Group...in their eyes": Warren Bennis and Patricia Ward Biederman, *Organizing Genius,* p. 10.

376   "That's simple...cultures and disciplines": John Gerstner, "Cyber-Architect Nicholas Negroponte," *Communication World,* January/February, 1996, pp. 14-17.

377   "There's always a...personalities and backgrounds": Jean Lipman-Blumen, *The Connective Edge,* p. 307.

390   "Our circuits are...capacity to daydream": Jim Coyle, "Like swords? Funny hats and capes? Apply to Queen's Park," *Ottawa Citizen,* November 20, 1996, p. A15.

CHAPTER 12

| 396 | "10.2 million women...than their husbands": Don Longo, "The Top 500," *National Home Center News,* May 26, 1997, p. 29. |

396   "10.2 million women...than their husbands": Don Longo, "The Top 500," *National Home Center News,* May 26, 1997, p. 29.

396-398 "Consumer spending by...spent by women": Phyllis A. Katz and Margaret Katz, *The Feminist Dollar: The Wise Woman's Buying Guide* (Plenum Press, 1997).

398   "Women buy more...on sports shoes": "Out of the Box," *Brandweek,* December 2, 1997.

399   "Estimated size of...$4-6 billion/year": "Cool Companies," *Fortune,* July 7, 1997, p. 104.

400   "Just a few...women-owned businesses": National Foundation for Women Business Owners Brochure, September, 1996.

401   "65 percent of...influenced by women": Jean Halliday, "Ford Upping Magazine Spending In The Fourth Quarter," *Advertising Age,* July 7, 1997, p. 2.

401   "But only 7...salesmen are WOMEN": Linda Prochazka-Dahl, "They Really Are Different; Selling Cars to Women,", *Wards Dealer Business,* February, 1997, p. 31.

401   "The jock strap...42 million units": Erin Kuniholm, "Truth in Numbers," *Women's Sports + Fitness,* January/February, 1997, p. 27.

404   "American women are...54 percent female": Laurie Larwood and Marion M. Wood, "Training Women for Management: Changing Priorities," *Journal of Management Development,* 1995, p. 54.

404   "Some of the...standards,' and 'decisiveness'": Elaine McShulskis, "Update," *HRMagazine,* December, 1996, p. 14.

405   "Men and women...creating a relationship!": Faith Popcorn and Lys Marigold, *Clicking* (New York: HarperCollins, 1996), p. 160.

406   "Men focus on...care and protection": Adapted from Carol Gilligan, *In a Different Voice* (Cambridge, MA: Harvard University Press, 1993), pp. 22, 38, 40, 41.

407   "Men will sit...a rooting interest": Lani Guinier, Michelle Fine, and Jane Balin, *Becoming Gentlemen: Women, Law School and Institutional Change* (Boston: Beacon Press, 1997).

409   "The search for...percent of women": (BrainWaves study).

412   "One late Sunday...their own pleasure": Conversation with author.

414   "We had a...big 'ah-ha!' discovery": John Greenwald, "Reinventing Sears." *Time,* December 23, 1996, p. 54.

416   "As 1997 began...ads at women": Jean Halliday, "Ford Upping Magazine Spending In The Fourth Quarter," *Advertising Age,* July 7, 1997, p. 2.

417   "Westin Hotels &...of the century": Bill Brocato, "Women Travelers Get Their Due," *Successful Meetings,* July, 1996, p. 13.

423   "You Just Don't Understand," Deborah Tannen, *You Just Don't Understand* (New York: Ballantine Books, 1991).

CHAPTER 13

429   "Fifteen years ago...Tomorrow it's design": Larry Reynolds, "Is Your Product Design Really Protected?" *Management Review,* August, 1991, p. 36.

430   "Arguably he and...the product itself": Robert H. Hayes and William J. Abernathy, "Managing Our Way to Economic Decline," *Harvard Business Review,* July/August 1980.

440   "We should do...already doing it": Gale Eisenstodt, "Crazy is Praise For Us" *Forbes,* November 7, 1994, p. 174.

441   "Our job is...dreamed he wanted": Author's conversation with David Kelley, IDEO.

442   "Over the years...for a change": Donald Norman, *The Design of Everyday Things* (New York: Basic Books, 1988), p. xi.

448   "The old weapons...their very core": Christopher Lorenz, *The Design Dimension* (Blackwell, 1990).

CHAPTER 14

455   "You need something...is the key": Mickey H. Gramig, "Retailers Given a Stern Lecture," *Atlanta Journal and Constitution,* January 15, 1997, p. D1.

457   "Chrysler's flashy Neon...some quality problems": Edith Hill Updike, "Will Neon Be The Little Car That Could?" *Business Week,* June 10, 1996, p. 56.

458-459   "We knew from...(phenomenal) (service) success!": David Aaker, *Building Strong Brands* (New York: Free Press, 1996), pp. 37, 38-40.

468   "Southwest Airlines has...of the best": Research on Southwest Airlines was conducted by Peter Karl, Char Woods, and Tom Peters, Summer 1994. Additional information was derived from Kenneth Labich, "Is Herb Kelleher America's Best CEO?" *Fortune,* May 2, 1994, pp. 46-50.

468   "While doing some...and being warm": PBS show *Service with Soul.*

473   "Love all, serve all," credo of the Hard Rock Café.

CHAPTER 15

469   "You can't behave...the lunatic fringe": William M. Carley, "To Keep GE's Profits Rising, Welch Pushes Quality-Control Plan," *Wall Street Journal,* January 13, 1997, p. 1.

480   "I have no...dispenser of enthusiasm": David Williams, "Zander: Contribution to Business," *Encouraging Excellence,* Winter, 1995.

482   "I used to...Not ten. Three": Quoted in Richard N. Haass, *The Power to Persuade* (Boston, Houghton Mifflin Company, 1994), pp. 29-30.

489   "If you ask...life out loud": Salli Rasberry and Padi Selwyn, *Living Your Life Out Loud* (Pocket Books, 1995).

Hitler, Adolph, 371
Hock, Dee, 76-7, 149, 151
Holman, Bunny, 248
Holman, Larry, 248
Home Depot, Inc., 31
Honda Motor Co., Ltd., 212
Honeywell, Inc., 435
Hopper, Max, 215
horizontal linkage, 262-3
How the Cadillac Got Its Fins, 359-60
Hsieh, Tony, 362-3
HSM, 247-8
Hugo Boss Company, 119
Huizenga, Wayne, 106
human relationships, 250-1, 404-5
human resources. *See* businesspeople; talent

Iacocca, Lee, 433
IBM (International Business Machines Corporation), 60, 89, 244, 337
Ibsen, Henrik Johan, 148-50
ICI (Imperial Chemical Industries), 58
Idei, Nobuyuki, 51-2
IDEO, 200
imagination, 146-7, 206, 355, 357. *See also* creativity
Imagination (marketing services firm), 208, 212, 369
improvement, 25-7
In a Different Voice, 406
incentives, 211-12, 420, 463, 468
Inc. 500 list, 100, 248
incrementalism, 25-7
inefficiency, 66-7
In Search of Excellence, 37, 50, 206, 260
Institute For Research On Learning, 286-7
Intel Corporation
    brand at, 191, 336-7, 351; change at, 86-7; lust at, 316, 320; value of, 14-16
intelligence, 370-1, 402-4
interaction, 262-5
intermediaries, 229-69, 262-3
International Data Group, Inc., 230
International Design, 445
Internet, 9, 259, 286, 289
    Bill Gates and, 82; Netscape and, 259, 318; power of, 256-7; speed of, 87
investment clubs, 400
ITT Corporation, 58, 60
J. D. Power & Associates, 297, 417
J. P. Morgan & Co., 14
Jackson, Phil, 115, 367
Job, Peter, 55
jobs. *See also* businessing; spinoffs
    loyalty to, 168-9; performed by women, 400; as projects, 222-3
Jobs, Steve, 354-5
John Deere, 427, 431, 434
John F. Kennedy School of Government, 175
Johnson & Johnson, 81, 212
Jordan, Michael, 65, 318, 371

Joystick Nation, 10

K. Barchetti Shops, 465
kaizen, 25-7
Kaminski, Rick, 191
Karan, Donna, 106
Katzenberg, Jeffrey, 82
Kay, Alan, 373
Kellams, Cynthia, 162-3, 214, 220
Kelleher, Herb, 279, 312-13, 349, 464-5, 470
Keller, Helen, 194
Kellogg Company, 14, 342
Kelly, Kevin, 29, 68-9
Key, Joe, 172-3
Keynes, John Maynard, 78
King, Martin Luther, Jr., 175-6
Kiss Me, Guido, 300
Klensch, Elsa, 455
Knight, Phil, 433-4
knowledge, 254. *See also* education; learning development, 211, 217; transfer, 209, 216, 219, 289-91
Kodak, 14, 58, 60
KPMG Peat Marwick, 200
Krause, Jerry, 114-15

Lakeland Regional Medical Center, 128, 130-2, 139
Lane, Raymond, 257
Lange, Jessica, 214
Lasdon, Dewys, 441
Lasser, Stuart, 458
Law, Gillian, 334-5
Lawler, Ed, 4
Lawrence A. Pfaff and Associates, 404
Leaders, 104
leadership, 495
    authority and, 174-6; skills, 141-53; Warren Bennis on, 104; women and, 420
Leadership Without Easy Answers, 175
Leading Change, 141-2
learning, 75, 287, 380. *See also* education; knowledge
Levi Strauss Associates, Inc., 194, 323, 346-7
Lewis, Jordan, 250-1
Lexmark International Group, Inc., 60
Lexus, 459
Liberman, Alexander, 66
Limited, The, 59, 60-1
LinkExchange, 363
Littmann, Peter, 119
Lopez, José Ignacio (Inaki), 215, 241
Lorenz, Christopher, 445, 448-9
loyalty, 85-8, 179, 456, 466
Lucent Technologies, 60
Luker, Jeffrey P., 11
lunacy, 479
lust, 295-331, 335
LVMH Moet Hennessy Louis Vuitton, 364

Macintosh, 355, 441. *See also* Apple Computer, Inc.
Madan, Sanjay, 362-3

PICTURE CREDITS

About the Author

Tom Peters is the co-author of *In Search of Excellence* (with Robert H. Waterman, Jr.) and *A Passion for Excellence* (with Nancy Austin), and the author of *Thriving on Chaos, Liberation Management, The Tom Peters Seminar,* and *The Pursuit of Wow!* He is the founder of the Tom Peters Group in Palo Alto, California, and lives mostly on American Airlines, or with his family on a farm in Vermont or an island off the Massachusetts coast, thanks to the information technology revolution
(he can be reached at tompeters @businessedge.net).